Mexico Unveiled

CRITICAL MEXICAN STUDIES

Critical Mexican Studies
Series editor: Ignacio M. Sánchez Prado

Critical Mexican Studies is the first English-language, humanities-based, theoretically focused academic series devoted to the study of Mexico. The series is a space for innovative works in the humanities that focus on theoretical analysis, transdisciplinary interventions, and original conceptual framing.

Other titles in the series:

The Restless Dead: Necrowriting and Disappropriation, by Cristina Rivera Garza

History and Modern Media: A Personal Journey, by John Mraz

Toxic Loves, Impossible Futures: Feminist Living as Resistance, by Irmgard Emmelhainz

Drug Cartels Do Not Exist: Narcotrafficking in US and Mexican Culture, by Oswaldo Zavala

Unlawful Violence: Mexican Law and Cultural Production, by Rebecca Janzen

The Mexican Transpacific: Nikkei Writing, Visual Arts, and Performance, by Ignacio López-Calvo

Monstrous Politics: Geography, Rights, and the Urban Revolution in Mexico City, by Ben Gerlofs

Robo Sacer: Necroliberalism and Cyborg Resistance in Mexican and Chicanx Dystopias by David Dalton

Mexico, Interrupted: Labor, Idleness, and the Economic Imaginary of Independence by Sergio Gutiérrez Negrón

Serial Mexico: Storytelling across Media, from Nationhood to Now by Amy E. Wright

Sonic Strategies: Performing Mexico's War on Drugs, Mourning, and Feminicide by Christina Baker

Subjunctive Aesthetics: Mexican Cultural Production in the Era of Climate Change by Carolyn Fornoff

Fatefully, Faithfully Feminist: A Critical History of Women, Patriarchy and Mexican National Discourse by Carlos Monsiváis, translated and edited by Norma Klahn and Ilana Luna

Biocosmism: Vitality and the Utopian Imagination in Postrevolutionary Mexico by Jorge Quintana Navarrete

"We, the Barbarians": Three Mexican Writers in the Twenty-First Century by Mabel Moraña

Amplifications of Black Sound from Colonial Mexico: Vocality and Beyond by Sarah Finley

Mexico Unveiled
Resisting Colonial Vices and Other Complaints

Carlos Pereda
Translated by Noell Birondo
with Andres Bonilla

Vanderbilt University Press
Nashville, Tennessee

English-language translation copyright by Noell Birondo and Andres Bonilla 2025
Published by Vanderbilt University Press 2025
All rights reserved

Originally published in Spanish, *Pensar a México: Entre otros reclamos*, by
© Editorial Gedisa, S.A., 2021, Mexico City, Mexico

Library of Congress Cataloging-in-Publication Data

Names: Pereda, Carlos, 1944- author
Title: Mexico unveiled : resisting colonial vices and other complaints / Carlos Pereda ; translated by Noell Birondo with Andres Bonilla.
Other titles: Pensar a México English
Description: Nashville, Tennessee : Vanderbilt University Press, 2025. | Series: Critical Mexican studies | "Originally published in Spanish by © Editorial Gedisa, S.A., 2021, Mexico City, México"--Title page verso. | Includes bibliographical references and index.
Identifiers: LCCN 2025003872 (print) | LCCN 2025003873 (ebook) | ISBN 9780826507990 hardcover | ISBN 9780826507983 paperback | ISBN 9780826508003 epub | ISBN 9780826508010 pdf
Subjects: LCSH: National characteristics, Mexican | Postcolonialism--Mexico | Philosophy, Mexican | Mexico--Intellectual life
Classification: LCC F1210 .P39513 2025 (print) | LCC F1210 (ebook)
LC record available at https://lccn.loc.gov/2025003872
LC ebook record available at https://lccn.loc.gov/2025003873

TRANSLATOR'S INSCRIPTION

In loving memory of Karl Ameriks (1947-2025), Doktorvater

Contents

Translator's Acknowledgments   ix

Carlos Pereda's Porous Reason: A Critical Introduction
   Noell Birondo   1

	Preface: Indications of the Road Ahead	25
1	Colonial Vices: Outlines of a General Perspective	31
2	Fragments of Mexican Philosophy, For Example	57
3	Inconvenient Mexican Thinkers, and Irreverent Claims	79

Notes   113
Bibliography   141
Index   153

Translator's Acknowledgments

I would like to thank Carlos Pereda for approaching me about this project, which at first I was happy only to facilitate, since the binational region of El Paso–Juárez is rich with bilingual philosophers. But eventually—due mainly to the richness, complexity, and subtlety of Pereda's thought—the project of rendering the book into English slowly and somewhat surprisingly became my own. I hope the resulting translation will echo some of the tempo and playfulness of Pereda's writing and that it will in any case do justice to his provocative thinking on Mexican philosophy and the politics of identity. I would also like to express my deep gratitude both to Carlos Pereda and his wife, the composer Marcela Rodríguez, for their very gracious hospitality over several years now, during my frequent stays in Mexico City. It was on a recent visit there that we decided on the English title of this edition over lunch.

Ana Gabriela Sánchez and Andres Bonilla, both philosophy graduate students at the University of Texas at El Paso (UTEP), provided very helpful assistance at different stages and in different ways. Andres did preliminary work on a partial translation of the text, which helped prepare the ground for a more precise full translation. Ana's contributions were of a different order. Her keen editorial eye, earnest professionalism, and insightful suggestions on many aspects of the translation, drawing on a deep familiarity with Mexican literature and culture, have improved the text in countless ways. It was she who made me realize that a literal version of Pereda's original Spanish title (*Pensar a México: Entre otros reclamos*) was not going to work in English, and she who suggested (among other possibilities) "Mexico Unveiled" and "Resisting Colonial Vices." Ana's work as a developmental editor on this project has been invaluable. Her contributions to the production of this volume have been nothing short of heroic. For assistance with proofreading in the final stages of the project, I am grateful to Enrique Pineda Sanchez, Ana Gabriela Sánchez, and Ángel Rafael Sosa Muñiz.

The short passage of poetry by Carmen Boullosa in Chapter 1 was translated by Mariana Riestra Ahumada, a graduate student in the bilingual creative writing program at UTEP. Thanks to Mariana for this translation and also to my colleagues Rosa Alcalá and Daniel Chacón for suggesting Mariana for the translation. For other works quoted by Pereda, I have mainly used existing English translations known to me. In a few instances I have made minor alterations, but always toward greater literal fidelity. I have of course used the English originals if the quoted material in Pereda's Spanish text was originally published in English. The credits for existing English translations from the original Spanish and French are as follows: Emilio Uranga, *Emilio Uranga's Analysis of Mexican Being: A Translation and Critical Introduction*, translated by Carlos Alberto Sánchez (New York: Bloomsbury Academic, 2021); José Revueltas, "Possibilities and Limitations of the Mexican," translated by David W. Bird, in *Mexican Philosophy in the Twentieth Century: Essential Readings*, edited by Carlos Alberto Sánchez and Robert Eli Sanchez Jr. (New York: Oxford University Press, 2017); Jose Martí, *Our America: Writings on Latin America and the Struggle for Cuban Independence*, translated by Elinor Randall (New York: Monthly Review Press, 1977); David Toscana, *The Enlightened Army*, translated by David William Foster (Austin: University of Texas Press, 2019); Fernanda Melchor, *Hurricane Season*, translated by Sophie Hughes (New York: New Directions Books, 2020); and Montesquieu, *The Spirit of the Laws*, translated by Anne M. Cohler, Basia C. Miller, and Harold S. Stone (Cambridge: Cambridge University Press, 1989).

This project included some setbacks and significant course corrections, so I am especially grateful for the support of the following individuals. I would like to thank the friends who, on separate occasions, showed more understanding than I would have expected while I excused myself to work on this project during visits arranged to see them. For this I am grateful to Joey Pacis, my oldest childhood friend, and to David E. Soles and Deborah H. Soles, who also provided valuable suggestions from their own powers of philosophical expression, which helped me see my way out of a few blind alleys. Special thanks are due to Steven P. Rodriguez, my editor at

Vanderbilt University Press, for his guidance, patience, and very valuable encouragement. Most of all, I thank Lillian Dickerson for her many valuable suggestions as I worked on this project, and for her unfailing encouragement and quiet strength.

In this English edition of Carlos Pereda's book, I would especially like to acknowledge Mario López of Santa Monica, California, and before that, Puebla, Mexico, a great friend to me and my family for nearly my entire life, and my first teacher of Spanish.

—EL PASO, TEXAS, JUNE 2025

Carlos Pereda's Porous Reason
A Critical Introduction

Noell Birondo

Deconstructionist deniers may not always read books very well, but at least they may encourage people to read books, and to understand the history from which those books came. Science that takes on reductive ambitions does not encourage anyone to understand history at all. Like the more historically impoverished styles of philosophy, and, still more, in alliance with them, it stands in the way of our understanding who we are, what our concepts are, what we are up to, since there is no way of our understanding these things without a hold on our history.

Bernard Williams

While literature and imagination are deemed superfluous (especially) in satisfied societies, the first thing a dictatorship does is to censor writing, burn books, and exile, imprison, or murder writers.

Carlos Fuentes

The philosophical life can be a nomadic life, both in thought and practice. In the engaging and insightful work of the Mexican-Uruguayan philosopher Carlos Pereda, the more important of these is nomadic thought—a mode of thinking that moves and explores, that is not stationary or static, that is not stubbornly hidebound. This is a kind of nomadism that characterizes healthy or epistemically virtuous thinking in general, and that might indeed be indispensable to it. But a nomadism in practice—of migration, or exile, or cross-border transplantation—is certainly also central to Pereda's philosophical outlook. *Mexico Unveiled* brings together for an English-speaking audience some of Pereda's most recent reflections on the philosophical significance of these two different types of nomadism, with a special emphasis on nomadic thinking. That idea is the through-line for Pereda's thinking here. But the book also offers an idiosyncratic synthesis of twentieth-century

Mexican philosophy that considers the persistent influence of European colonialism on Mexican intellectual life, the politics of identity and inclusion, and the changing ideas of what it means to be Mexican.

I

Pereda's philosophical outlook has developed over more than four decades (his first book was published in 1980), and in the three essays collected here, this outlook is illuminated in many different ways. Pereda's project in the essays, as elsewhere in his many works on these topics, is situated between two major research programs that have, in more recent years, grown up around it. The first of these is the impressive work being done, in many different parts of the philosophical world, on epistemic virtues and vices, including the growing literature on "epistemologies of ignorance."[1] The second is the increasingly variegated work—in both form and content—being done on Latin American philosophy and Mexican philosophy. Pereda helpfully engages some of this contemporary work in the course of developing his own views and arguments. He specifically discusses the work of José-Antonio Orosco, Gregory Pappas, Carlos Alberto Sánchez, Robert Eli Sanchez, and Manuel Vargas.

Specialists in the two broad areas just mentioned will be attracted to *Mexico Unveiled* for multiple reasons. The book encapsulates a lifetime of reflection on twentieth-century Mexican philosophy and highlights its relevance for current social-political issues. Pereda's work is informed at a deep level by the fact that he was himself a participant in some of the most influential twentieth-century debates in Mexican philosophy—he recently celebrated his eightieth birthday. Thus, one of Pereda's central resources as a historian of twentieth-century Mexican philosophy is his own lived experience. For this and many other reasons, Pereda is certainly one of the greatest authorities we have today (if not the greatest authority we have today) on Mexican philosophy in the twentieth century, having critically documented some of its central debates in a landmark study published more than a decade ago.[2] But in addition to this historical perspective Pereda also develops an extended systematic discussion of "colonial vices" and "arrogant reason," patterns of thought and action that can hinder progress in all domains, whether philosophical, social-political, or personal, among others. Pereda's overarching philosophical interest is the theory of argumentation, and his focus here is on what he calls "nomadic thinking." His work therefore balances historical engagement with systematic development, in a broadly genealogical approach that aligns with some of the most rewarding philosophical work of our time.³ But Pereda's discussion also frequently moves beyond these two broad research programs, to make observations in other areas of philosophy or even outside philosophy, for instance on Mexican history, literature, and film. In general, Pereda's writing displays a deep historical understanding and a broad philosophical vision, and these virtues will ensure that *Mexico Unveiled* engages a wide audience including those interested in politics, nationalism, decolonial theory, argumentation theory, socially engaged epistemology, the complex histories of Mexico and Latin America, and the many ways in which our cultural histories shape our thoughts, habits, and customs.

II

One of the issues that is exceedingly important for me in relation to the topics discussed by Pereda—both as cause and effect of some of my central interests in Mexican philosophy and Latin American philosophy—is the notion of historical understanding. I currently live in El Paso, a city immediately adjacent to the US-Mexico border in far, far west Texas. El Paso is a great place to live and a really wonderful community (consistently rated one of the safest cities in the US for instance), but El Paso is also a place where the reality and the challenges, indeed the constant dehumanization, of the US-Mexico border are also ever present.

The importance of historical understanding even in non-philosophical contexts was driven home for me by a decal I saw on the back of a truck when I first arrived in El Paso. The decal was of a Texas flag overlayed with four words—words which I assume were making reference to the many recent discussions of school curricula in Texas and elsewhere around the US, especially discussions about the teaching of US history. The decal seemed inadvertently to advertise an awkward combination of lone-star sensibility, psychic fragility, and—insofar as it apparently mocks the Black Lives Matter movement—a willful permissiveness toward murder. The four words were: Guilt Free Lives Matter.⁴

In this context it might be helpful to consider the white supremacist beliefs reported by Pulitzer Prize–winning author Eli Saslow in his 2018 book *Rising Out of Hatred: The Awakening of a Former White Nationalist*.⁵ Saslow's book focuses on the transformational journey of a young Derek Black, the millennial heir to a distinguished white supremacist lineage. Derek Black's father was Don Black, a former Grand Wizard of the Ku Klux Klan, as well as the founder of Stormfront, the largest racist community on the internet and, according to the *New York Times*, the "leading edge" of the white nationalist movement. Derek Black's godfather was David Duke, the American vanguard in the effort to mainstream white supremacy in US political culture, and also himself a former Grand Wizard of the KKK. For nearly a decade, Derek Black used his popular radio show to reach a new audience, promoting the white supremacist beliefs he inherited from these two paternal figures. Such white supremacist beliefs constituted an outlook that Derek Black referred to as "white nationalism" or (rather less convincingly) "racial egalitarianism." More specifically, Black used his radio show to espouse the following beliefs:

A) White nationalists are only trying to save white people from "an inevitable genocide by mass immigration and forced assimilation."[6]

B) For white people, romantic race mixing is a traitorous act, since it risks polluting the gene pool and accelerating the ongoing white genocide.[7]

C) As a white person, Derek Black was himself "oppressed and victimized by a lifetime of anti-white discrimination."[8]

D) The word "racist" was invented in order to demonize well-meaning white people.[9]

E) The concept of *white privilege* resulted from a conspiracy to make white people feel guilty about their success.[10]

F) *Multiculturalism* is "an ideology based on hatred of us, of white people."[11]

These white supremacist beliefs display a truly astonishing caliber of ignorance—conspiratorial illusions, for instance, that drastically undermine the moral justifiability of these views. Pereda says that, "Over the years I have come to realize that perhaps arrogance is not simply a desire, a feeling or an emotion among others, but that there is something like an arrogant form of reason. It is a way of facing life and reasoning in which one is always walled in by false certainties."[12]

The white supremacist beliefs just mentioned do not *necessarily*, of course, form the basis of anyone's hatred toward anyone. But white supremacist beliefs such as these have often served quite effectively as the basis for racial hatred and racially motivated hate crimes. Recall some of the recent tragedies. In 2015 a white supremacist gunman killed nine Black people at worship in a Christian church in Charleston, South Carolina, the twenty-one-year-old gunman apparently intent on precipitating a "race war." In 2011 a white supremacist gunman massacred 77 people in Norway, most of whom were teenagers attending a summer camp. In 2019 a white supremacist gunman, also twenty-one-years old, killed 23 people and wounded 22 others at a Wal-Mart in El Paso, Texas, claiming to be defending white people against the pathological conspiracy of the anti-white "Great Replacement." The crime was thus racially motivated: He killed them *because* they were Mexican. The list of tragedies could go on and on.

III

Pereda's nomadic journey started a continent away in his native country of Uruguay. He completed his undergraduate degree there in 1968. One of his professors was a German refugee and a "direct disciple" of Hans-Georg Gadamer. With his professor's assistance, Pereda applied for and was awarded a DAAD scholarship from the German government to pursue graduate work in Germany. He began his time there in Heidelberg, where he sought out and obtained advice from Gadamer. The advice was that Pereda's German could be better; he might therefore study at the newer University of Konstanz, where—in something of a contrast to Gadamerian hermeneutics—Pereda was primarily trained in analytic philosophy. He completed his doctorate in philosophy and linguistics from the University of Konstanz in 1974. His doctoral dissertation was titled "The Theory of Practical Argumentation in Kant." As we are about to see, this Kantian background still influences Pereda's most recent reflections about arrogant reason and the politics of identity and inclusion in Mexico.

Not long after completing his doctorate, Pereda joined the Institute for Philosophical Research at the National Autonomous University of Mexico (UNAM) in Mexico City. The Institute for Philosophical Research is quite separate from the philosophy department at UNAM, being primarily focused on research; the Institute typically staffs, remarkably in comparison to US institutions, more than forty of its own full-time philosophers. Pereda has flourished in the Institute for more than four decades of his influential philosophical career. His work is especially influential in Mexico, of course, but also in other parts of Latin America. His work is also increasingly influential in the US, as evidenced by sustained engagement with his work by philosophers in the US, and by the steadily increasing number of his books and articles that have appeared (or are now appearing) in English.[13]

But without a doubt, Pereda's writing is highly idiosyncratic. Some of his sentences, for instance, can achieve such a length that they are able to incorporate a kind of hyperlink to themselves—a meta-observation on their own content or structure—or else they jut out of line to explore a nearby thought, to digress and then return—or not, as the case may be.[14] This tendency is one that Pereda seems to acknowledge without apology. His persistent use of very substantive endnotes is also worth mentioning, since they are often essential.

Pereda's philosophical argumentation can also be somewhat complex. It might therefore be useful to introduce, in schematic fashion, some of the central distinctions and tendencies deployed in his work. So here are eight "signposts" that I hope will be helpful to readers. These are my own understandings of some of the central strands in Pereda's systematic (as opposed to his historical) thinking:

A) The central theme of the essays, as indicated earlier, is the idea of nomadic thinking. *Nomadic* thinking contrasts with *static* thinking. I briefly characterized this distinction at the outset, but the main idea is unmistakable: static thinking is stubbornly inalterable or hidebound. For example, it might be ossified by traditional ways of thinking (about marriage, or sexual identity, or philosophy, and so on). Certain ideological outlooks, white supremacy for instance, incorporate static thinking as essential.

B) "Arrogant reason" is another central focus of the text. Pereda provides multiple characterizations and examples of arrogant reason, but this is a form of reason deployed in concert with attitudes of disdain, derision, condescension, or contempt. It constantly displays what it takes to be its prestigious affiliations ("In Tübingen it was done differently . . . ," and so on). Arrogant reason contrasts with a virtuous form of "porous" reason: a form of reason that features a radical openness to learning from others, including (perhaps especially) marginalized individuals whose perspectives might enrich our current ways of thinking and doing. Porous reason is antiexclusionary.[15] It is also important to note that Pereda characterizes these forms of reason as "abstract constructs" and "patterns of reasoning," analogous to the more familiar forms of "practical reason" and "instrumental reason." Thus, Pereda need not be committed—as some have apparently thought—to anything like a literal construal of the idea that there might be a "plurality of reason." Instead, a *single, unified* faculty of reason (this is surely one possibility) might manifest itself in different ways or in different patterns of activity.¹⁶

c) In general, a "fetish" as used by Pereda is some very bad pattern of thought. He distinguishes between "pure" and "impure" fetishes. The former should be eliminated, but the latter might provide "materials" that can be salvaged. For instance, unconstrained nationalism—or what Pereda calls *nationalist zeal*—is an impure fetish. We might be able to rescue enough materials from nationalist zeal for them to be refashioned into a healthy form of patriotism.¹⁷

d) "Headquarters of Power and Thought." This is an omnipresent placeholder in Pereda's thinking. The phrase can be used to signify any entity which is held in unusually high esteem by individuals or groups—and which is typically at something of a distance from the locus of thinking. Examples here might include "the World Bank," "Harvard," "Oxford University Press," "the United States of America" (usually referred to in this context as "America"—e.g., "In *America* it is done differently . . ."), and—one of Pereda's own favorite examples, used to indicate a traditional Mexican reverence for and subservience to all things French—"*Paris*." But he mainly uses the phrase as a placeholder to indicate some form of subservient thinking, e.g. "In the Headquarters of Power and Thought it is done differently . . ." This allows us to see that one *version* of "arrogant reason" is a potentially subservient instance of it, an instance of what Pereda calls "colonial reason," which trades on a claimed affiliation with some illustrious headquarters.

e) Pereda's work displays a great fondness for the use of *maxims* as a means of characterizing various ways of thinking—including both certain ways of thinking that he endorses, and other ways of thinking that he decries: for instance, he provides multiple examples of what he considers to be the *maxims* of arrogant reason. These maxims are sometimes very brief and seemingly precise, and so they might be thought to resemble Kantian maxims to a certain extent—those familiar principles of action—but other maxims articulated by Pereda seem rather clearly to depart from any previous paradigm. For instance, one maxim of porous reason, which is a virtuous form of reason that Pereda very much champions, is characterized as follows: "*Do not confuse patriotism with vainly or desperately embracing what is yours—your skin, your home, your region, your country, your language—, rather: let yourself be questioned. Also, let yourself be challenged in unexpected directions or even directions you dislike.*" To be sure, this does not very much resemble a textbook Kantian maxim.[18]

F) The maxims of arrogant reason might already constitute a certain kind of *colonial vice* (ch. 1, §II). But in addition to that, Pereda discusses three specific colonial vices that he considers to be prominent in Mexico and Latin America generally. These are the colonial vices of *subaltern fervor, craving for novelty*, and *nationalist zeal*. I will discuss subaltern fervor in the next section; nationalist zeal was mentioned in (c) earlier, and it is anyway the most extensively discussed by Pereda of the three. As for the *craving for novelty*, what Pereda has in mind is a subservient enthusiasm for "the latest" to be proposed by some Headquarters of Power and Thought (whether in policy, philosophy, law, or other area). For instance, the craving for novelty is what accounts for a sudden local enthusiasm, and a potentially significant change of course in the way local matters are conducted, simply on the basis of new developments that have just been reported from some illustrious foreign headquarters: "*European* experts now propose . . . , so we must change course," or "*American* philosophers now engage in XYZ . . . , so we must also engage in XYZ."

G) Pereda also introduces several *argumentative strategies* that he advocates in the deployment of philosophical argumentation. One example is what he calls the *strategy of transitions*. This is a form of argumentation that moves either from the more abstract (e.g., a principle or law) to alleged instances of it (a real-life case or a specific data set), or else it moves in the opposite direction, from particular instances to the articulation or consideration of something more abstract (e.g., a political policy or a conception of "Mexican being"). The first is called a "descending" transition, and the second is called an "ascending" transition. Needless to say, one might think the best implementation of this strategy is to move continually from one to the other, and Pereda says as much.[19] Several other argumentative strategies are introduced.

H) The three essays are divided into multiple sections. As a subheading to many sections is a specific claim that Pereda will address or support in that section. For instance, in Chapter 3, §V the subheading is: "*First claim of political prudence: since people and societies are to come extent modifiable . . .* ," and in Chapter 3, §VI the subheading is: "*Second claim of political prudence, or not ignoring that . . .*" The word for *claim* in these and other subheadings is the Spanish word *reclamo*, which can certainly be a claim, but might also be something stronger, such as a demand or a complaint. Hence the subtitle of this English edition of Pereda's book: "Resisting Colonial Vices and Other Complaints." (Obviously it is not very exciting to be told that one's book is about resisting colonial vices—and also other claims.) For the most part, "*reclamo*" has been translated as "claim," but it also appears as "demand" and "complaint."

In addition to those brief signposts, an overview of the three chapters might also be helpful. Chapter 1 introduces the idea of "nomadic" thinking in relation to the politics of identity and inclusion—or at least, as Pereda says, "nonexclusion." The discussion focuses on Mexican identity or the identity of "*the* Mexican." This phrase gestures at the twentieth-century project in Mexico known as "*la filosofía de lo mexicano*"—the philosophy of "Mexicanness." This project is a persistent theme of the essays, in part because the project has recently gotten uptake as a philosophical area of research in the US. The chapter also initiates Pereda's scrutiny of "arrogant reason" and "colonial reason." Colonial reason structures the three colonial vices in Mexico and Latin America that I mentioned earlier in (f). In his discussion of these three vices, Pereda offers an elegant overview of Mexican philosophy in the twentieth century.

The aim of Chapter 2 is to dissolve the false opposition between abstract universalism and cultural particularism in the methodology of Mexican philosophy and Latin American philosophy. Pereda examines the "radical republicanism" of two influential historical thinkers and their different appeals to cultural particularism: the nineteenth-century Mexican writer Ignacio Ramírez (known as "*El Nigromante*," the Necromancer) and the twentieth-century Mexican philosopher Luis Villoro. Chapter 3 offers insightful reflections on the mid-twentieth-century project of the Hyperion group (*el grupo Hiperión*). The project of the Hyperion group was *la filosofía de lo mexicano*. Pereda focuses on two central philosophers here. He discusses the philosophical project of Emilio Uranga in his book

Análisis del ser del mexicano (*Analysis of Mexican Being*), as well as Uranga's subsequent involvement in several controversial aspects of Mexican politics. Pereda also discusses the criticisms that José Revueltas deployed against this project and his peers in the Hyperion group. In the course of his discussion in this chapter, Pereda offers many illuminating observations about Mexican history and culture, from the writings of Bartolomé de Las Casas to contemporary anticolonial struggles and the haunting novels of Juan Rulfo and Fernanda Melchor.

IV

Why should English-speaking philosophers read Pereda? It depends on who they are. The answer would need to be addressed to two different constituencies of English speakers: those who have antecedent interests in Latin American philosophy or Mexican philosophy, and those who do not have such antecedent interests, but who are nevertheless open to a nomadic form of thinking—that is, they are open to learning from a tradition other than their own.[20] Individuals in the latter group might also simply, and more directly, be interested in "understanding who we are, what our concepts are, what we are up to"—to repeat Bernard Williams's humanistic formulation from the outset, who rightly emphasizes that there is no way of our understanding these things "without a hold on our history." I believe Pereda's work can contribute to our getting a hold on our history—even for those of us in the English-speaking world. But Pereda's work might also help philosophers engaged in Latin American philosophy or Mexican philosophy specifically, to reflect upon its strategies of engagement with the English-speaking philosophical community.[21] One question we might ask is: Has Mexican philosophy as practiced in the US fallen victim to the colonial vice of *subaltern fervor*?

Subaltern fervor is "the anxiety of exhibiting an identity affiliation with some Headquarters of Power and Thought." Subaltern fervor therefore "seeks to promote offshoots of those beliefs, theories, activities, public, private, or intimate, that someone favors—in most cases, which they favored when they were young" (ch. 1, §V). Pereda also claims that subaltern fervor is an *impure fetish*—which means that it is a corrupted pattern of thought from which we might salvage valuable materials. What does uncorrupted or virtuous thinking look like here? Pereda's idea is that in the case of subaltern fervor, the "virtue of *consistency* has become a vice, as barriers are erected against nomadic thinking and new experiences." Because of these erected barriers, "any learning that could be done along the way is blocked in advance" (ch. 1, §V, my emphasis). So subaltern fervor is a kind of stalwart subservience (in beliefs, theories, activities) to the authority of some Headquarters of Power and Thought.

A recent book on the importance of Mexican philosophy for the twenty-first century reflects on Mexican philosophy's marginalization within mainline Anglo American philosophy. The book addresses what it refers to as the "struggle for legitimacy," where legitimization is equated with whether Mexican philosophy "is written about in English."[22] Addressing the motivation for this legitimizing goal, the author writes that "I am motivated by an assumption that seems quite obvious" to people who work in these areas, namely "that Mexican philosophy *is not currently counted* among the many philosophical traditions we currently count."[23] But who is the "we" being referred to here? This "we" presumably does *not* comprise the members of the Society for Mexican American Philosophy (SMAP); it presumably does *not* comprise the editorial board of (or the contributors to) the *Journal of Mexican Philosophy* or *APA Studies on Hispanic/Latino Issues*, two premiere venues for the publication of Mexican philosophy, and where Mexican philosophy certainly is already being written about in English. But if that is right then what motivates projects in Mexican philosophy such as the one under discussion is something like the following assumption: that Mexican philosophy is not currently counted among the many philosophical traditions that *Anglo American philosophers* currently count.

But why, one might ask, are the opinions of Anglo American philosophers (the total membership of the American Philosophical Association for instance) being granted such authority regarding the value or status of Mexican philosophy? Why grant such authority to this Headquarters of Power and Thought, only afterward to hanker for the approval vested in that authority? So it does seem to be a fair question: Has Mexican philosophy as practiced in the US fallen victim to the colonial vice of subaltern fervor? Is this hankering for "legitimization" an instance of the colonial vice that Pereda refers to as the "anxiety" of exhibiting an affiliation with some Headquarters of Power and Thought?[24] Alternatively, is Pereda perhaps mistaken to think that this subaltern anxiety constitutes a colonial vice?[25]

The overall value of Mexican philosophy and Latin American philosophy will only be amplified by asking and discussing these questions. But it matters what our motivations are, because it will affect the content and the value of our work. It is certainly important not to become like someone who demands to know why Anglo American philosophers do not consider Gloria Anzaldúa to be a philosopher, without the slightest attempt to demonstrate the value of Anzaldúa's work. As Pereda's discussion suggests, such a person seems merely to reflect an "anxiety" for affiliation with some illustrious headquarters, but without any attempt to illustrate, through the hard work of philosophical explication and argumentation, the philosophical value to be found in the work of Gloria Anzaldúa.

A better strategy is the one Pereda initiates here: *to argue* that Anzaldúa's views are superior along some dimension in comparison to the views of others. In this case, Pereda argues (even if very briefly) that Anzaldúa's conception of *nepantla*—of being in between, of being in an "*always-in-transition space lacking clear boundaries*"—is superior to the conception of *nepantla* employed by Emilio Uranga. Why? Pereda says that Anzaldúa's conception is superior because "in Uranga the word *nepantla* directly expresses an *ontological structure* of *the* being of the Mexican," whereas "Anzaldúa articulates, with immense acuity, a *historical condition* of women, men, and children obliged, often illegally, to cross the border" (ch. 3, §II). Thus, Pereda's idea seems to be that a desire for genuine historical understanding, adverting to real-world historical conditions, is superior to a philosopher's development of an "ontological structure," the development of an all-too-abstruse "analysis of Mexican being" (which only gestures, Pereda seems to suggest, at genuine historical understanding). Thus a more advantageous strategy here—especially since we are philosophers—would be to demonstrate through argumentation the value of Mexican philosophy, by bringing its value to bear on those philosophical conversations to which we want to contribute—not merely to complain and cajole, insisting that here is Mexican philosophy, and it demands to be counted.[26]

V

How did I—a Los Angeles native with no familial connections to Mexico or even Latin America—come to be engaged with Pereda's world and work in Mexico? My first experience at UNAM was almost twenty years ago, as a job candidate. I do not know whether Pereda attended the talk I gave on that occasion, and I could not accept the offer from the Institute at that time, but I made myself an agreement that if I continued to work in the US, I could travel in Mexico as much as I wanted for the rest of my life.[27] In the following decade I traveled in Mexico for a month or two every year, often putting the entire content of my apartment in storage for the summer so that I could avoid paying rent. This nomadism from the US to Mexico and within Mexico still continues today, although I have greater responsibilities in the US.

But I am not myself Mexican or Mexican American—or even "Latinx." It is true, however, that my paternal grandfather was, at one point in his early life, one of the Filipino migrant workers who, along with many Mexican and Mexican American migrant workers, among others, traveled the California Central Valley to find work that depended upon the seasonal rotation of agricultural harvests—this was *after* being a police officer in the US territory of Hawai'i (the birthplace of my grandmother). For Mexicans, Filipinos, and the "darker races" more generally, such manual work, coupled with the intentionally limited educational and career opportunities that forced them into such work, was thought to be appropriate given their race, and the intellectual limitations imposed upon them by "nature." In such cases, a scientistic conception of the normativity of nature eclipses the possibility of what I consider to be the supreme virtue in cases of intercultural understanding: a radical hermeneutical charity, or what would be in Pereda's outlook a virtuous deployment of porous reason.

It was Alejandro Santana, the inaugural president of SMAP, who on a rooftop pulque and mezcal bar in Oaxaca even before the pandemic, first drew my attention to the fact that among the initial organizers of the earliest California farm workers unions were Filipino leaders (most notably Larry Itliong, co-founder of the United Farm Workers union, and Philip Vera Cruz, the UFW vice president and highest-ranking Filipino officer) who worked together with Cesar Chavez and Dolores Huerta, the Mexican leaders who are much better known today. But there are other strong overlaps in the histories of Mexican and Filipino peoples: Spanish colonization, devout Marian Catholicism, and the "Manila galleons" carrying Chinese porcelain and other precious cargo to Mexico—including enslaved Filipinos (known also as *indios*) who were destined for the silver mines of Zacatecas or Guanajuato.[28] So maybe it is no mystery that I would be attracted to the many resources and insights to be found in Mexican, Mexican American, and Latin American philosophy—having focused mainly on Western moral philosophy and the history of ethics for the past thirty years. A solid training in the Western philosophical tradition allows us to appreciate (or *can* do so) the need for historical understanding, in order to understand ourselves and what we are up to, and to begin to move further along in a struggle against the aggressive exclusions purportedly justified by arrogant reason and static thinking (for instance, by a scientific conception of nature). Pereda's work provides engaging reminders of the importance of historical understanding for reflecting on the many ways our histories shape our thoughts, habits, and customs.

Earlier I discussed the white supremacist beliefs of Derek Black, who eventually—this is the subject of the book written about him—renounces his white supremacist upbringing. But Black might just as easily not have done so. He might have retained the beliefs he inherited from his father, Don Black, and his godfather, David Duke—both former Grand Wizards of the KKK—and gone on to become a white supremacist military or police officer, or white supremacist paramedic or national politician. In such cases we see dominantly situated individuals who—in addition to the entitlements afforded by their everyday, "plain-clothes" social identities—have also been entrusted, in their professional roles, with powers intended to serve the common good. In these cases the combination of ignorance and white supremacist exclusion is not only unjustifiable, and contemptible, but ultimately lethal, reflected in policies affecting—or even targeting—the most desperate and the most vulnerable among us.

The original title of Pereda's book is *Pensar a México: Entre otros reclamos*. That title works better in Spanish than in English ("Think of Mexico"). The title *Mexico Unveiled* was chosen for this edition in discussion with Carlos Pereda. The title hints at Pereda's discussions of arrogant reason and subaltern fervor. The idea is to peel back the colonial accoutrements signaling affiliation with, and subservience to, distant centers of power, and to begin to investigate what this reveals. Pereda laments the lack of resources for answering this question in the authors he explores, suggesting that it can leave us unable to see our own faces, unable to find our own ways of expressing ourselves. "Unfortunately," he says, "criticisms of colonialism are often so general that they never touch on points like this: the loss of one's own voice."[29]

NOTES

Epigraph. Bernard Williams, "Why Philosophy Needs History," in *Essays and Reviews 1959–2002* (Princeton: Princeton University Press, 2014), 412. The "deconstructionist deniers" are those "who claim that the concept of truth does nothing for us in our inquiries or in our conceptions of freedom and other values" (410–11); Williams mentions that he has Richard Rorty in mind. On the importance of historical understanding consider also the highly sensible observation of Pereda's colleague at UNAM, Mauricio Beuchot, made in reference to Mexican philosophy: "If it is true that we live within a tradition, how can we advance in it or even oppose it if we do not have at least a minimum knowledge of it?" See Beuchot's "The Study of Philosophy's History in Mexico as a Foundation for Doing Mexican Philosophy," in *The Role of History in Latin American Philosophy: Contemporary Perspectives*, ed. Arleen Salles and Elizabeth Millán-Zaibert (Albany: State University of New York Press, 2005), 114. I draw on this and other thoughts from Beuchot in an earlier discussion of imperialism and intercultural understanding: see Noell Birondo, "The Virtues of Mestizaje: Lessons from Las Casas on Aztec Human Sacrifice," *APA Studies on Hispanic/Latino Issues in Philosophy* 19, no. 2 (2020): 2–8, winner of the APA Essay Prize in Latin American Thought. (Pereda briefly engages this article here in ch. 3, §VI.)

Epigraph. Carlos Fuentes, foreword to *The Underdogs: A Novel of the Mexican Revolution*, by Mariano Azuela, trans. Sergio Waisman (New York: Penguin Books, 2008), ix. Fuentes's observation is quite general; for a textured discussion of political oppression in contemporary Mexico, see Oswaldo Zavala, *Drug Cartels Do Not Exist: Narco-Trafficking and Culture in the US and Mexico*, translated by William Savinar (Nashville, TN: Vanderbilt University Press, 2022).

1. Here I will mention especially (among many other valuable works in this expanding area of research) Quassim Cassam's *Vices of the Mind: From the Intellectual to the Political* (Oxford: Oxford University Press, 2019) and Linda Martín Alcoff's very potent article, "Philosophy and Philosophical Practice: Eurocentrism as an Epistemology of Ignorance," in *The Routledge Handbook of Epistemic Injustice*, ed. Ian James Kidd, José Medina, and Gaile Pohlhaus Jr., 397–408 (New York: Routledge, 2017). For a more rounded picture of the work being done in this area, see the works cited by Alcoff and Cassam, which have a smaller overlap than some might expect, as well as the articles in the Routledge Handbook just cited, and the highly valuable work of its three editors. It is noteworthy that in a recent talk, José Medina argues for a notion of epistemic "border-crossing" that might helpfully be brought into dialogue with Pereda's understanding of nomadic thinking. See Medina's "Epistemic Border-Crossing: Polyphonic Decolonial Resistance and Collective Epistemic Self-Empowerment," International Conference on Epistemic Oppression and Decolonization, May 29–31, 2024, Université du Québec à Montréal.

2. See Carlos Pereda, *La filosofía en México en el siglo XX: Apuntes de un participante* [Philosophy in Mexico in the twentieth century: Notes from a participant] (Mexico City: Conaculta, 2013). Pereda's UNAM colleague Guillermo Hurtado should certainly also be mentioned here as a leading authority in twentieth-century Mexican philosophy, whose two most recent books have both been reviewed in the premiere English-language journal *Notre Dame Philosophical Reviews*. The two books are: Guillermo Hurtado, *Biografía de la verdad* [A biography of truth] (Mexico City: Siglo Veintiuno, 2024); and Luis Villoro, *La razón disruptiva: Antología compilada por Guillermo Hurtado* [Disruptive reason: An anthology compiled by Guillermo Hurtado] (Mexico City: Penguin Random House, 2023). In what follows I discuss the work of Carlos Alberto Sánchez, one of the most prominent writers on Mexican philosophy in the US today: see §IV.

3. In the works collected here, Pereda does not generally engage with philosophers whose work does not directly address his central concerns—especially Mexican philosophy and culture, or more broadly Latin America—although he does mention explicitly (in addition to unavoidably influential philosophers such as Quine, Rawls, Strawson) the work of Bernard Williams and Robert

Brandom, and this provides a clue to Pereda's own methodological orientation. In this connection I would also myself mention Charles Taylor and Alasdair MacIntyre, as well as several Mexican philosophers in the twentieth century discussed by Pereda here, especially (in my view) Leopoldo Zea and Luis Villoro. For an earlier discussion of methodological issues, see Pereda's "Explanatory and 'Argumentative' History of Philosophy," in Salles and Millán-Zaibert, *The Role of History*, 43–56.

4. It is not implausible to think that at least some of the severe allergic reactions from mainline Anglo American philosophers to any version of a historical understanding of their own discipline might be traceable to a more or less explicit version of a thought residing somewhere in this neighborhood—on the assumption that philosophers are people too, and that we therefore exhibit human vices.

5. Eli Saslow, *Rising Out of Hatred: The Awakening of a Former White Nationalist* (New York: Anchor Books: 2018). I presented the following examples at UNAM as part of a larger discussion of hatred and ignorance for a conference in honor of Carlos Pereda in 2024. My interests in hate and ignorance grew out of my work on *The Moral Psychology of Hate*, ed. Noell Birondo (Lanham, MD: Rowman & Littlefield, 2022); for viewpoints on hatred that intersect with some of Pereda's concerns, see especially the chapters by Grant J. Silva and Richard Paul Hamilton in that volume.

6. Saslow, *Rising Out of Hatred*, 13.

7. Saslow, *Rising Out of Hatred*, 35.

8. Saslow, *Rising Out of Hatred*, 65.

9. Saslow, *Rising Out of Hatred*, 54.

10. Saslow, *Rising Out of Hatred*, 89.

11. Saslow, *Rising Out of Hatred*, 21.

12. See Martínez González, Victor Hugo, Sergio Ortiz Leroux, and Álvaro Aragón Rivera, eds., *La imaginación ilustrada: El ensayo filosófico, político y cultural de Carlos Pereda* (Mexico City: Gedisa Editorial, 2024), 143. It has been suggested to me that racial prejudice in Mexico, for instance against Mexicans who are indigenous or Black, differs from racial prejudice in the US because racial prejudice in Mexico seems to lack the element of racial hatred that I highlight in these remarks. This very helpful suggestion was from the director Nicolás Pereda, Carlos Pereda's son.

13. English translations of two other books by Pereda (in addition to many articles) have already been published: *Practical Holism and Nomadic Thought*, trans. Sean Manning (Lanham, MD: Lexington Books, 2023), and *Lessons in Exile*, trans. Sean Manning (Leiden: Brill-Rodopi, 2018). Carlos Alberto Sánchez (e.g.) recently engages Pereda's thinking in the following works: *Mexican Philosophy for the Twenty-First Century: Relajo, Zozobra, and Other Frameworks for Understanding Our World* (London: Bloomsbury Academic, 2023), and *Contingency and Commitment: Mexican Existentialism and the Place of Philosophy*

(Albany: State University of New York Press, 2016). I discuss Sánchez's work in what follows in §IV.

14. I would immediately add that Pereda's training in analytic philosophy is evident in his acute article, "Assertion, Truth, and Argumentation," in *Perspectives on Habermas*, ed. Lewis Edwin Hall, 51–70 (LaSalle, IL: Open Court, 2020). In the translation I have tempered the tendency about sentence length in cases where not doing so would render the text inaccessible to English-speaking readers, who are perhaps less accustomed to this tendency.

15. See also my "Virtue and Prejudice: Giving and Taking Reasons," in *Virtue's Reasons: New Essays on Virtue, Character, and Reasons*, ed. Noell Birondo and S. Stuart Braun, 189–202 (New York: Routledge, 2017), where I describe the boundaries between alternative moral outlooks and schemes of living as being—in productive hermeneutical encounters—"helpfully porous" (200).

16. Carlos Alberto Sánchez has written that Luis Villoro (anticipating Pereda) "proposes that we can overcome the arrogance of our reason if we accept that there is more than one way to experience and make sense of the world; if we accept that there is a plurality of reason (what Pereda calls 'porous reason')." However, accepting that there is a "plurality of reason" is *not* what Pereda calls porous reason. This is because, as I indicated in the main text, porous reason (as such) has nothing to do with accepting that there is a "plurality of reason," any more than the existence of "instrumental reason" has to do with accepting that there is a "plurality of reason." Although it is not completely clear, the plurality claim seems to be meant literally: Villoro says that the worldly analogue here is that "one would have to accept a reality essentially plural." See Sánchez, *Mexican Philosophy*, 154–55. In contrast to a "plurality of reason," there can obviously be a plurality of *reasons*—multiple considerations on differing sides of an issue, for instance—and it is precisely *this* multiplicity that makes *conversation* the model of humanity for Pereda, and what makes deployments of "porous reason" virtuous.

17. See also my "Patriotism and Character: Some Aristotelian Observations," in *Handbook of Patriotism*, ed. Mitja Sardoč (Cham: Springer, 2020). In that chapter I distinguish a virtuous form of patriotism from what I now consider to be a form of anti-patriotism (often based in ignorance and arrogant reason). In a virtuous form of patriotism, one's patriotic enthusiasm is constrained by other virtues, and porous reason might indeed be among them.

18. In his Preface, Pereda mentions the following as a maxim of nomadic thinking: "*Strive to put aside arrogant reason, while at the same time trying to desire, think, and act according to the maxims of porous reason*." He says that this maxim is introduced "already in Chapter 1." But no maxim with this precise formulation occurs in Chapter 1, although there *are* maxims with partially overlapping content with this one. Thus Pereda's idea of "the same maxim" does not seem to rely on a very precise formulation of the content of the maxim; his maxims seem to have less precise identity conditions than a standard Kantian conception of maxims.

19. See Sánchez, *Contingency and Commitment*, 84–92, on the idea of "oscillation." Pereda suggests this back-and-forth way of deploying the strategy of transitions as a sober methodological approach in philosophy and elsewhere. It is not an oscillation based in any kind of *zozobra*.
20. This is still very much a growing constituency, and it notably includes members of the Society for Mexican American Philosophy (SMAP), a community of philosophers with which I have been fruitfully engaged for almost a decade. I am grateful to the members of SMAP for welcoming me, especially since I am not myself Mexican or Mexican American—or even "Latinx," in any straightforward sense of that intentionally inclusive term. By this I do not mean to suggest that there is any kind of racial identity requirement: the late Jamaican American philosopher Charles W. Mills, for instance, often attended SMAP sessions at American Philosophical Association meetings.
21. These considerations might also be applicable to other philosophical projects that contribute to a more inclusive philosophical environment in the English-speaking world.
22. Sánchez, *Mexican Philosophy*, 1, 195 n. 1.
23. Sánchez, *Mexican Philosophy*, 1 (emphasis original).
24. In a recent interview Pereda explains his ideas about subaltern fervor by reference to philosophical practice in Mexico today. He says that: "We are almost completely unaware of what our colleagues do. In general we are not interested in learning from their work. We are seduced by what I like to call 'subaltern fervor': commenting on what is thought in what we consider to be the central capitals of thought, that fiction of distance." González, *La imaginación ilustrada*, 133. One practical reason for Sánchez's desire to see Mexican philosophy "normalized" is that normalization means "that teaching it, writing about it, or promoting it in various ways will not be a risky practice; that one can still get tenure, promotion, and book contracts; moreover, that seeing it appear on conference programs or journal table of contents will not be cause for panic." Sánchez, *Mexican Philosophy*, 5. This pragmatic reason is one with which I have no quarrel; it is especially relevant to graduate students and junior faculty and reflects a conception of philosophy as constructively open minded or porous.
25. For Sánchez's criticisms of a narrower understanding of subaltern fervor (based on Pereda's earlier characterizations of it), see his *Contingency and Commitment*, 84–86. However, what Sánchez says there is insufficient to address the fuller understanding of subaltern fervor that I discuss here. In order to balance the tenor of these somewhat critical comments, I would add that Sánchez's *Contingency and Commitment* holds a very high importance for me in coming to think and work in some of these areas.
26. The healthier philosophical strategy—the one that involves dialectical incursions into current topics—is helpfully deployed by Manuel Vargas in "The Philosophy of Accidentality," *Journal of the American Philosophical Association* 6, no. 4 (2020): 391–409. It is also reflected in the general orientation of Sánchez's

more recent book, *Blooming in the Ruins: How Mexican Philosophy Can Guide Us toward the Good Life* (New York: Oxford University Press, 2024). In a very different way, the work of Santiago Castro-Gómez is relevant here in its emphasis on the porous nature of "Latin American" reason, which has historically been in constant dialogue with European and Anglo-American philosophy. See Santiago Castro-Gómez, *Critique of Latin American Reason*, translated by Andrew Ascherl (New York: Columbia University Press, 2019 [1996]). Castro-Gómez tempers his view somewhat in a later discussion, *Zero-Point Hubris: Science, Race, and Enlightenment in Eighteenth-Century Latin America*, translated by George Ciccariello-Maher and Don T. Deere (Lanham, MD: Rowman & Littlefield, 2021 [2005]); see especially Castro-Gómez's methodological discussion in chapter 1.
27. Now published as "Kantian Reasons for Reasons," *Ratio* 20, no. 3 (2007): 264–77.
28. This overlap in the cultural histories of Mexican and Filipino peoples has also recently been indicated by a Filipino American sociologist, Anthony Christian Ocampo, whose qualitative research in California communities, including in my own hometown in Los Angeles, was published in a book with this arresting title: *The Latinos of Asia: How Filipino Americans Break the Rules of Race* (Stanford, CA: Stanford University Press, 2016). On Zacatecas and Guanajuato as destinations for enslaved Filipino and indigenous workers, see Andrés Reséndez, *The Other Slavery: The Uncovered Story of Indian Enslavement in America* (Boston: Houghton Mifflin Harcourt, 2016).
29. González, *La imaginación ilustrada*, 157. I would like to thank Ana Gabriela Sánchez for research assistance in the preparation of this chapter. Some of the material was presented previously at 80 Años con Carlos Pereda, a conference held at the Institute for Philosophical Research, UNAM, in April 2024; some material was presented at the Society for Mexican American Philosophy group session at the American Philosophical Association, Pacific Division Meeting, San Francisco, 2023. I am grateful to Moisés Vaca and Aurelia Valero Pie for the invitation to present at the conference at UNAM, and to the discussants on each of these occasions for helpful feedback. Special thanks are due to Carlos Sánchez for feedback on an earlier version of this chapter and to Steven Rodriguez of Vanderbilt University Press and Carlos Pereda for their feedback and very valuable encouragement.

REFERENCES

Alcoff, Linda Martín. "Philosophy and Philosophical Practice: Eurocentrism as an Epistemology of Ignorance." In *The Routledge Handbook of Epistemic Injustice*, edited by Ian James Kidd, José Medina, and Gaile Pohlhaus Jr., 397–408. New York: Routledge, 2017.

Beuchot, Mauricio. "The Study of Philosophy's History in Mexico as a Foundation for Doing Mexican Philosophy." In *The Role of History in Latin America*, edited by Arleen Salles and Elizabeth Millán-Zaibert, 109–129. Albany: State University of New York Press, 2005.

Birondo, Noell. "Kantian Reasons for Reasons." Ratio 20, no. 3 (2007): 264–77.

———. "Virtue and Prejudice: Giving and Taking Reasons." In *Virtue's Reasons: New Essays on Virtue, Character, and Reasons*, edited by Noell Birondo and S. Stuart Braun, 189–202. New York: Routledge, 2017. Originally published in *The Monist* 99, no. 2 (2016): 212–23.

———. "Patriotism and Character: Some Aristotelian Observations." In *Handbook of Patriotism*, edited by Mitja Sardoč. Cham: Springer, 2020.

———. "The Virtues of Mestizaje: Lessons from Las Casas on Aztec Human Sacrifice." *APA Studies on Hispanic/Latino Issues in Philosophy* 19, no. 2 (2020): 2–8.

———, ed. *The Moral Psychology of Hate*. Lanham, MD: Rowman & Littlefield, 2022.

Cassam, Quassim. *Vices of the Mind: From the Intellectual to the Political*. Oxford: Oxford University Press, 2019.

Castro-Gómez, Santiago. *Critique of Latin American Reason*. Translated by Andrew Ascherl. New York: Columbia University Press, 2019 [1996].

———. *Zero-Point Hubris: Science, Race, and Enlightenment in Eighteenth-Century Latin America*. Translated by George Ciccariello-Maher and Don T. Deere. Lanham, MD: Rowman & Littlefield, 2021 [2005].

Fuentes, Carlos. Foreword to *The Underdogs: A Novel of the Mexican Revolution*, by Mariano Azuela, trans. Sergio Waisman. New York: Penguin Books, 2014, vii–x.

Hurtado, Guillermo. *Biografía de la verdad*. Mexico City: Siglo Veintiuno, 2024.

Martínez González, Victor Hugo, Sergio Ortiz Leroux, and Álvaro Aragón Rivera, eds. *La imaginación ilustrada: El ensayo filosófico, político y cultural de Carlos Pereda*. Mexico City: Gedisa Editorial, 2024.

Medina, José. "Epistemic Border-Crossing: Polyphonic Decolonial Resistance and Collective Epistemic Self-Empowerment." International Conference on Epistemic Oppression and Decolonization, May 29–31, 2024, Université du Québec à Montréal.

Ocampo, Anthony Christian. *The Latinos of Asia: How Filipino Americans Break the Rules of Race*. Stanford, CA: Stanford University Press, 2016.

Pereda, Carlos. "Explanatory and 'Argumentative' History of Philosophy." In *The Role of History in Latin America*, edited by Arleen Salles and Elizabeth Millán-Zaibert, 43–56. Albany: State University of New York Press, 2005.

———. *La filosofía en México en el siglo XX: Apuntes de un participante*. Mexico City: Conaculta, 2013.

———. *Lessons in Exile*. Translated by Sean Manning. Leiden: Brill-Rodopi, 2018.

———. "Assertion, Truth, and Argumentation." In *Perspectives on Habermas*, ed. Lewis Edwin Hall, 51–70. LaSalle, IL: Open Court, 2020.

———. *Pensar a México: Entre otros reclamos*. Mexico City: Universidad Nacional Autónoma de México, 2021.

———. *Practical Holism and Nomadic Thought*. Translated by Sean Manning. Lanham, MD: Lexington Books, 2023.

Reséndez, Andrés. *The Other Slavery: The Uncovered Story of Indian Enslavement in America*. Boston: Houghton Mifflin Harcourt, 2016.

Sánchez, Carlos Alberto. *Mexican Philosophy for the Twenty-First Century: Relajo, Zozobra, and Other Frameworks for Understanding Our World*. London: Bloomsbury Academic, 2023.

———. *Blooming in the Ruins: How Mexican Philosophy Can Guide Us toward the Good Life*. New York: Oxford, 2024.

Saslow, Eli. *Rising Out of Hatred: The Awakening of a Former White Nationalist*. New York: Anchor Books: 2018.

Vargas, Manuel. "The Philosophy of Accidentality." *Journal of the American Philosophical Association* 6, no. 4 (2020): 391–409. Now reprinted in *The Latinx Philosophy Reader*, edited by Lori Gallegos, Manuel Vargas, and Francisco Gallegos. New York: Routledge, 2025.

Villoro, Luis. *La razón disruptiva: Antología compilada por Guillermo Hurtado*. Mexico City: Penguin Random House, 2023.

Williams, Bernard. "Why Philosophy Needs History." In his *Essays and Reviews 1959–2002*, 405–12. Princeton, NJ: Princeton University Press, 2014.

Zavala, Oswaldo. *Drug Cartels Do Not Exist: Narco-Trafficking and Culture in the US and Mexico*. Translated by William Savinar. Nashville, TN: Vanderbilt University Press, 2022.

Mexico Unveiled

Preface

Indications of the Road Ahead

With the lively and somewhat pretentious expression "Mexico unveiled," I bring together three relatively modest works, organized as variations on recurrent themes in the politics of identity and inclusion, or at least of nonexclusion. I will not propose a continuous argument. These reflections were worked on at different times and with different purposes. But I believe the ideas complement each other, and the tireless repetitions might even clarify them.

One of these concerns is the examination of collective identities such as "Mexican identity" or "the identity of *the* Mexican" and some of their addictive consequences. Thus, with some fairly abstract reflections in the erratic and somewhat disorganized Chapter 1, "Colonial Vices: Outlines of a General Perspective," I discuss in a roundabout way the habits that in Latin America distort beliefs and desires, and also moods, emotions, and even economic programs. The vices here are opposed but at the same time feed off of each other, such as *subaltern fervor*, *craving for novelty*, and *nationalist zeal*, all typical of what I propose to describe as an arrogant perspective of looking at the world, or "arrogant reason."[1] In this way I suspect that what I describe, inspired by specifically Mexican circumstances, could be applied, with relevant differences and nuances, to analogous situations around "Chilean identity," "Colombian identity," "Argentine identity," or "Latin American identity." It is worth noting, then, that the vices of the politics of identity are ubiquitous and branch out, and that in several of these branches the meaning tends to evaporate.

On the other hand, when I discuss beliefs, thinkers, or events, I let myself be guided by the following hermeneutical maxim:

> In your discussions, gather data relevant to the matter you are dealing with and do not fail to investigate this data, because some of the data are not just mistaken but fetishes. But you should distinguish between pure fetishes that should be eliminated and impure fetishes from which you can rescue valuable materials.

Starting from this maxim of *data, fetishes, and materials*, the focus of each of the chapters is as follows. In the very general essay of Chapter 1, on colonial vices, the focus is on the collection of *data* and the criticism of those *fetishes* that make up colonial vices, although I pay particular attention to *nationalist zeal*. By contrast, the attention is more focused in the essays of Chapter 2, "Fragments of Mexican Philosophy, For Example," and Chapter 3, "Inconvenient Mexican Thinkers, and Irreverent Claims." An attempt is made to rescue *materials* that are specifically Mexican having to do with various events, thinkers, claims, and desires.

It is important to note, however, that in approaching these perplexities, I am concerned with something like a *meta-problem*, or if you like, a methodological problem: the need for *nomadic thinking*. This nomadism echoes, in theory and thought in general, a living nomadism that occurs in practice, both socially—the great voluntary and involuntary migrations—and personally. Such nomadism in various forms, some rather more painful than others, is common in the experiences of many inhabitants of Mexico, and Latin America in general, although not only there. On the other hand, the maxim just mentioned is one of the principles of nomadic thinking. This way of thinking strives to cross boundaries and borders, whether imposed explicitly or implicitly.[2] It is usefully contrasted with a static way of thinking: a way of thinking that clings, a bit anxiously, to traditional distinctions and categories, and even to currently established topics, and that's it.

I will not develop, systematically, what the nomadic way of thinking consists in across all cases, but as I have already begun to do, I will list several of the principles that articulate it. I hope that by introducing these principles in the midst of the discussion, they can in some way guide it while also gaining meaning and value. For instance, already in Chapter 1, I introduce other principles of nomadic thinking, for example:

> *Strive to put aside arrogant reason, while*
> *at the same time trying to desire, think, and act*
> *according to the maxims of porous reason.*

These principles are not entirely comprehensible at this point, although they will become somewhat clearer when they are taken up again to elaborate on this or that problem in the course of the discussions. I only want to emphasize here that one version of what I mean by arrogant reason—*one* version, among others, albeit a persistent one—consists of reasoning or pseudo-reasoning that colonizes people's desires, beliefs, emotions, and behaviors, and predictably, excludes other desires, beliefs, emotions. Indeed, arrogant reason, and therefore this instance of it, colonial reason, corrodes people's integrity and bolsters an aggressive politics of exclusion. Even now? Yes, even now. As indicated by the vices discussed in Chapter 1, colonized desires, beliefs, emotions, and behaviors abound, even if one does not live in a colony in any strict sense. After all, there can be colonialism without colonial legality, as often happens in several areas of public, private, and even intimate life in Latin America.

In the essay on Mexican philosophy in Chapter 2, the aim is to dissolve the false opposition between abstract universalism and cultural particularism. To this end, I outline fragments of a Mexican corridor of nomadic thought as an example of how to dissolve this opposition. Instead of saying "I outline a corridor of thought," perhaps one could appeal to an observation made by Emiliano Monge in his novel *No contar todo*: "But what I have barely outlined here is not what matters. These are only the events. And the events are never history. Not even the facts are history. History is the invisible current that moves everything in the background."[3] As two possible instances of this current in Mexico, which *moves everything in the background*, I consider in Chapter 2 the radical republicanism, in the better part of the nineteenth century, of Ignacio Ramírez (*"the Necromancer"*), and in the second half of the twentieth century and the beginning of the twenty-first century, that of Luis Villoro.

Later, in the turbulent essay of Chapter 3, I return to the perplexities around identity and nonexclusion. At the beginning of the chapter, the discussion starts with a reading of two complex characters, Emilio Uranga and José Revueltas. Both aroused frenzied passions in Mexico, for and against, in the second half of the twentieth century; and in the case of Uranga, *when* he is remembered at all, he still arouses them. However, by engaging in these readings I also strengthen the assumption that those who criticize the impure fetishes in their writings can extract useful materials from their works.

Nevertheless, when beginning such heterogeneous reflections, it is better not to rush. We need to attend patiently, and with a more or less broad perspective, to the two parts—the two points of interest—in the ambitious expressions "Mexico unveiled" and "colonial vices and other complaints." Ambitious expressions in what sense?

Let us consider the first part: "Mexico unveiled." When one reflects on a country, one usually turns to the vicissitudes of its history—perhaps political history in the broadest sense—which includes conquests, defeats, wars, revolutions, changes in laws and constitutional regimes, national and international peace treaties, transitions, popular movements, struggles between political parties, and biographies of heroines, heroes, and villains. In recent times, the history of the economic structures that sustain a country and its changes has not ceased to be questioned. At the same time, such histories no longer neglect the narratives of daily life and its breakdowns in sensitivity, the continuities and ruptures in the development of the arts, the customs with which sexualities and taboos are articulated.

Those troublesome histories barely make an appearance in the following claims. As one might expect in reading these indications of the road ahead, what is sought is rather to think of Mexico from an unconventional point of view. Even more than unconventional—perhaps this point of view is considered "secondary" and even "abandoned in recent times." It is a point of view that embraces intellectual history, and in particular, the history of philosophical ideas. Is it still worthwhile to engage in such an endeavor? I suspect that from this often-neglected angle, we may be forced to investigate events and figures that were and still are highly significant, although they were disregarded. Following their lead can frequently end up illuminating—this is my other suspicion—what has been overlooked in other, better-known, louder histories.

Let us now go to the second part: "colonial vices and other complaints," or rather, "many, many other complaints." Contrary to what one might expect, this second point of interest is more important than the first, and is often urgent. Thus, in many of the reflections in these chapters, I stray quite far from what the first part promises, "Mexico unveiled." With nomadic thinking and its companion, centrifugal imagination, I explore concrete practical and theoretical demands (*reclamos*), but also general problems. There should be no doubt: such demands can be infectious ways of thinking; they often multiply in unexpected directions, frequently introducing new vocabularies. One starts with one claim and then another one follows, and another, and soon the claims branch out into a very present future or past. Moreover, no future or past is immune to the claims and demands of the present; and obviously the past does not cease to make its claims on us, sometimes from as far away as the claims formulated by Aristotle or Tocqueville.

Nevertheless, at other times in these reflections, certain claims take on the urgency of a member decree; hence another principle of nomadic thought:

From time to time, focus on the place and time in which you live;
think about what you believe, what you feel, and what you desire.

As indicated, the politics of identity and nonexclusion are the main themes. What is of primary concern, then, is how we know and justify beliefs, desires, and emotions about ourselves and those around us, and at the same time, how we include or exclude others. However, the member decree just introduced also includes a mandate: from time to time, it is critical to think about these perplexities starting from the place and time in which you live. In particular, this thinking will be difficult and painful if it concerns one of the despised places classified by arrogant reason as not belonging to the Headquarters of Power and Thought.

I have indicated that these reflections constitute demands or complaints (*reclamos*). To summarize here, I claim: many things will be protested, narrated and interrogated, requested or demanded; testimonials will be offered; appeals will be made and interpreted. So don't expect rigorous empirical investigations or exhaustive conceptual treatments. I will only work with a set of observations, debates, reasoning, readings—too excessive?—, repetitions, many questions, and far too many footnotes. The purpose is to get intertwined with some of the difficulties presented by the politics of identity and aggressive exclusion in Latin America, especially in Mexico, and to rethink them. The difficulties are intersecting, recurring, and, often, discouraging.

CHAPTER 1

Colonial Vices

Outlines of a General Perspective

What do I mean by colonial vices? How do such vices shape desires and beliefs? Moreover, how do they operate to implement aggressive policies of exclusion among us in Latin America or in any of its regions, in Mexico among others? Before dealing specifically with the Mexican situation, I will start, in a very roundabout way, from a quite general perspective.

For now, an elementary point: colonial vices do not occur alone. They are organized and reinforced in corridors of *static* thought, which sometimes produce that version of *arrogant reason* which is the colonial vision of the world, that efficient machine for producing aggressive exclusions and violence. Because "violence and colonization are inseparable and reinforce each other."[1] Thus, every colonial vision of the world contains a politics of the hostile. But what exactly does such a "vision" entail?

I

Once again it is useful to claim:

Be careful with words.

Listening to that claim, and in order to get a little closer to the set of distorting techniques—moral, legal, political, economic, and cultural techniques—as well as to the ways of believing, desiring, feeling, and acting that make up colonial vices, it is illustrative to recall a family of words which incorporate the adjective "colonial."

- Colony: territory under the military, social, political, economic, and/or cultural domain of another territory.

- Colonial: dominion—often fierce—exercised by a power over foreign territory and its inhabitants.

- Colonialism: the practice of a society or a state of extending its military, social, political, economic, and/or cultural domain over foreign territory and its inhabitants to take advantage of them.

- Colonialist: practitioner, or at least a sympathizer with colonialism.

- Colonized: someone who has been the victim of colonization.

- Colonizer: the oppressor—often ruthless—who exercises military, social, political, economic, and/or cultural dominance over foreign territories and their inhabitants.

Since ancient times the continuum of individual violence has been a constant in the relationships between people, social groups, and states. This violence includes everything from the focused exercises of dominance in the seemingly compassionate actions of a family that teaches about the "dangers" of freedom, to more or less open suppressions like forced extortions and kidnappings. Also familiar but more dangerous—much more dangerous—is the continuum of *institutional* and, above all, *structural* violence. These latter forms of violence systematically exclude; they create everything from subjugation disguised as benevolent paternalism in factories, to the terrible establishment of institutions which, precisely *because* they are colonial, become zombies or mercenaries. Why "terrible"? It is worth noting that under colonial domination it is mandatory to transfer the wealth of the dominated territories (whether material, cultural, etc.) to the metropoles, and in general, to disdain all of colonial life, subordinating it with violence—when necessary—to metropolitan interests.

Perhaps if one considers the first word listed ("colony") it will be objected that the dark age of colonial domination was finally left behind during the twentieth century. One has to answer immediately: Some forms of colonialism do not rely on territorial expansionism with direct political, economic, and military control over a territory, as with former colonial powers. Thus, if certain social phenomena can be classified under the description "deterritorialized colonial power," then it can be granted that the force of a specific instance of colonialism might be based not only on its ability to rule markets, but also desires, beliefs, moods, and emotions.

Perhaps this objection will continue as follows: More or less since the second half of the twentieth century, the economic strength of nation states is replaced by multinational companies. These changes—real or apparent—call for new historical differentiations to analyze economic asymmetries, and more generally, the asymmetries of power. From ancient times, for example, economic policies between states have not been consolidated, and it is difficult to imagine how they could have done so without individual, institutional, and structural violence. To make such violence effective, organized force was and is needed. This force, at least in the case of structural violence, cannot do without the presence, latent but vigilant, of an army ready to act if needed. At the same time, the consolidation of such forces cannot do without a powerful arms industry. Thus, the political and economic power of states and their instruments, such as military power and structural violence, are essential to continue supporting a large part of the "colonial" relations of "multinational" companies. It must be conceded, then, that in the twenty-first century the word "colonialism," in the strict sense of "colonialism with colonies," designates few if any social realities. On the other hand, it is undeniable that the rest of the terms of this family: "colonial," "colonialist," "colonized," and "colonizer," retain their use—for example, in Latin America, for example, in Mexico, although not exclusively there.[2]

This type of colonialism, apparently contradictory since it does not have colonies, is more dangerous since it is more difficult to detect: There are no subjugated territories, no rituals to any crown, no triumphal arches to the viceroys. . . . Thus, in the case of colonialism without colonies, for example in Latin America, we are facing, on the one hand, a colonialism that is *only* concerned with power and with economic, military, and political transactions, which can often only be deciphered with difficulty, through the explanatory histories of the social sciences. On the other hand, it is a form of colonialism so internal that it is difficult to perceive because it *only* has to do with vices of subjectivity: "a permanent aspiration to stop being what we are."[3] Consequently, from the perspective of colonialism without colonies, the concepts of "colonized" and "colonizer," and their associated vices, obtain a central weight: The various forms of colonial domination to some extent *depend* on the entrenchment of vices which construct deformed subjectivities: "the suicidal renunciation of what one has," or rather, of what one is.[4]

II

I will continue with substantial detours. I pointed out that colonial reason is a form of *arrogant reason*. But what is the purpose of this version of reason? One strategy of nomadic thinking is the strategy of transitions: when investigating, one lowers or raises the level of abstraction. I will first make an ascending transition. I will attempt a more or less approximate characterization of this abstract construct: arrogant reason. It is a mechanism for producing policies of exclusion, of which colonial reason is, as has already been noted, one instance. What do I mean?

Perhaps the most annoying thing about arrogance as a personal vice is not the excess of those who display it (often this is nothing more than ridiculous), but their disdain and open contempt for everything foreign. This pretension is often reduced to the mere gesture of *dramatizing* contempt. Or, in the worst case, it *licenses marginalization.* As it is sometimes said: The arrogant "look down on others, look down their noses, but without clarifying to what this sulky disdain is owed." Surely one will ask: How is it even possible, from this mere personal vice, to approach what I have called "arrogant reason"? Perhaps it will be doubted: Is there even such a thing as an arrogant *reason*?

For now, let us locate this abstract construct at a level analogous to that occupied by "practical reason" and "instrumental reason." These abstractions refer to patterns of reasoning, but also observing and analyzing, and they even set an agenda—or at least an outline—of problems. But first, what would the maxims be that constitute arrogant reason?

Those who succumb to arrogant reason care a lot—they care desperately—about ostentatiously exhibiting a prestigious belonging, however vague that might be. Regarding the form of arrogance which is colonial reason, the affiliations in question run the gamut from the ridiculous to the disastrous. For example, I am passing through Jojutla, and suddenly the temperature drops excessively. I approach a lady who sells clothes at the door of her house, and when I ask her about scarves she points to some poorly cut pieces of what might have been an old rug. She tells me: "They are scarves brought from Paris, they cost 40 pesos." (I buy the scarf—because of the cold that makes me shiver?, because of the ridiculously low price?, or maybe because of the magic of the word "*Paris*," which has produced so many elegant and not so elegant mistakes in Latin America?) It is dangerous, on the other hand, when reasons are sought for implementing public policies—to raise or lower the minimum wage, to promote or not promote privatization, to borrow money from abroad—and the only answer given expresses some kind of affiliation. It simply declares: "These are directives from the World Bank," "In 'the Headquarters of Power and Thought' they have been very successful," and other similar remarks. In both situations, however dissimilar they may be to each other, an affiliate identity is assumed, or rather, an imaginary affiliation, whether the glamor of Paris or the power and wisdom, or rather the supposed wisdom, of this centralized headquarters. That affiliate identity paralyzes; it eliminates the need to argue or even to offer tiresome justifications and counter-arguments. Hence, we can already establish a maxim of arrogant reason that mandates: *Act by exhibiting an affiliation, real or imaginary.*

Moreover, this desire for affiliation—frequently as fanciful as it is impossible to satisfy—receives as part of its support, in fact as its only support, the disdain or contempt, or the open repudiation of desires, beliefs, plans that oppose it or are indifferent to it, or that have interests that are irrelevant to the pattern of privileges to which the affiliation aspires. (For example, when national identities become paralyzing identities, the mechanisms of xenophobia are set in motion, producing not merely exclusion but persecution everywhere, without admitting the slightest counterargument.) Regarding arrogant reason, this is a maxim that mandates: *Act by justifying yourself with nothing more than disdain or contempt.*

On the other hand, to be able to justify or pseudo-justify oneself in this way, one has to convert one's premises into assumptions immunized beforehand from any critical questions—questions of understanding or truth or value—and thus from the *maxim of data, fetishes, and materials.* Whoever calls one of these assumptions into doubt, for instance in Mexico, will receive only rejections, irony, arrogant behavior, sarcasm in response—"You poor thing, how behind the times you are. Don't you travel? Do you only read your neighborhood culture news?" Sometimes, at the limit, if the situation warrants it, they resort to violence. Here, then, is a third maxim of arrogant reason: *Faced with difficulties about your affiliate identity, shield yourself.*

It seems clear that even though they are underdetermined in the extreme, these maxims—exhibiting an affiliation, leaning into disdain, and shielding oneself—in a way constitute colonial vices. In this way, arrogant reason—not just colonialism without colonies—becomes its own feedback loop. The colonial vices that construct these policies also contribute to supporting aggressive exclusions, and consolidating and strengthening them. This in turn consolidates and strengthens public vices, and so on. However, it is now time to address some very specific colonial vices. The vices involved here are simultaneously epistemic and practical vices, which with arrogant reasoning multiply left and right.

III

I will focus first on the vice of *subaltern fervor*. This vice is about the anxiety of exhibiting an identity affiliated with some Headquarters of Power and Thought. As a result, it seeks to promote offshoots of those beliefs, theories, activities, public, private, or intimate, that someone favors—in most cases, which they favored when they were young—in what they perceive to be the hopeless condition they currently experience. It is common for a certain current of thought from a distant country, for example, to dazzle someone in their youth, the years often remembered with an idealized nostalgia, when they went to university or studied abroad. But later, victim to imaginary losses, and frequently poisoned by life's failures, they no longer look in any other direction. What once liberated, now imprisons. So for the rest of their days they keep repeating formulas which, in political or intellectual or economic exchange, keep aging until they become obsolete. Examples here include neoliberalism, neoconstitutionalism, anarchism, multiculturalism, deconstructionism, speech act theory, possible worlds theory, or whatever. Sometimes the content of such formulas was already expired at its origin. For example, an old-fashioned form of Platonism, the Marxist positivism of Althusser, prevailed with *subaltern fervor* in many Latin American universities, and Mexico was no exception. That is how it works—as they say—with the false opposition between, on the one hand, theory (the supposed science of the laws of history!) and, on the other hand, ideology, or if you like, *doxa*. The term *ideology* was used to refer to anything related to intersubjective experiences, such as work, its precariousness, its harms, and also the bitterness and joys of life. It is no coincidence that when, little by little, this silly Platonism—which of course does not deserve the name of Platonism—began to disintegrate, certain youth ran away, frightened, in any direction opposed to such fraud, for example into politics.

As in many regions of the planet, for example in Latin America, the Headquarters of Power and Thought is thought to be elsewhere, and both collective and personal practices are reduced to fortifying themselves within the franchise to be defended—with an energy more appropriate to a better cause. At the same time, in order to support these franchises, other options are discounted, ones that are barely atoned for in competition. Thus, there is no risk of exploring with nomadic thinking. On the contrary, with both enormous insecurity and enormous arrogance (often two sides of the same coin), subjectivity is shielded. One settles comfortably into a position in government or private enterprise, or in an institute for "research"—or better: for repetitions—and, as often happens in Latin America, life is reduced to droning on with out-of-date phrases. We are therefore faced with a less painful form of servitude, although more monotonous, and consequently, more boring than others. The mindset—or cowardice—that operates in the vice of *subaltern fervor* can be represented by the saying: "Better the devil you know (in culture, in politics, in the economy . . .) than the devil you don't." But whoever has such a mindset certainly does not admit it, but disguises it as a prudent, all-too-prudent excuse: "Better the devil you know than to risk the unknown, which could be a disaster."

However, it should not be overlooked—and this warning should not be forgotten in Mexico—that this vice is an impure fetish. A virtue of consistency has become a vice, as barriers are erected against nomadic thinking and new experiences. Any learning that could be done along the way is blocked in advance.

IV

Let us examine another habit of bad coexistence. Sometimes, with the colonial vice of *craving for novelty* (foreign novelties, of course), someone pompously declares that what they are in fact reacting against is the vice of *subaltern fervor*. Instead of being encapsulated in beliefs that have already been shown to be false, we are instead very open, and it does not matter to what, or rather, it does not matter what comes next, as long as it is accompanied by verified affiliation with some Headquarters of Power and Thought. So one is adrift. In politics, for example, populism is accepted, or postmodernism, or racism, or fascism, or any neodespotism. More recently, "the latest" is accompanied by the *craving for novelty*, such as when I accepted the Parisian scarves in Jojutla, or when one tastes a disgusting dish because someone whispers that the restaurant is "very expensive" and has a foreign chef. It should be obvious that if we participate in public life while prey to such a vice, we tend to become effective opportunists. Consequently, what concerns us is no longer acting with greater responsibility and efficiency, but only that we can continue receiving "breaking news" (whether political, economic, cultural . . .). But be careful because we are again faced with an impure fetish: By destroying the vice of *craving for novelty*—for shiny new things, but also horrors disguised as shiny new things—the virtue of curiosity begins to appear, that genuine desire to understand more and know more. However, those who are legitimately curious consider everything they learn with arguments and counter-arguments: They do not accept it just because, but ask for evidence and investigate, something that does not happen if you are addicted to the *craving for novelty*. For example, if those who are prey to this vice are given objections, they do not consider them with arguments. They respond not with arguments but with gestures. (These gestures, good practices of arrogant reason, usually reduce to taunts expressing disdain.)[5]

V

Attitudes such as *subaltern fervor* and *craving for novelty* are vices that corrupt public, private, and even intimate efforts. Hence it is not surprising that against *subaltern fervor* and *craving for novelty*, those other corridors of thought are not only static but even servile in many regions of Latin America, such as Mexico; and in numerous areas which are similar in some economic, political, legal, or cultural aspect, a call goes up to liberate themselves. We are urged to stop looking outward so much, in order to appreciate, a little, our differences: What we have been and are, and what the circumstances that surround us have been and are. We have to spit out the subalternity that harasses, impregnates, and subdues. We have to decolonize. We have to recover the historical memory of countless catastrophes so we can begin again. It is too bad that these very reasonable reasons, which have been repeated over and over again, soon degenerate into a new colonial vice: *nationalist zeal*. But is that true? Is nationalist zeal, for example in Mexico, really a bad habit and an even worse custom? Surely some will react with alarm.

But even more, perhaps it will be objected that the vices I have enumerated—*subaltern fervor, craving for novelty, nationalist zeal*—are not only *colonial* vices, since some of them or combinations of them, are also found in prominent forms in the habits and customs of those who inhabit the great colonial powers of the past, such as Spain, Portugal, the Netherlands... This is certainly not a very strong objection. Indeed, it is not difficult to find that one or more aspects of these ancient powers, such as their economy or their cultural life, have also suffered recolonizations.

Maybe the last observation will make some angry. So we had better stop to address this alarm and this anger. But how?

In situations like these, genuine thought appeals to its nomadism to find support in scientific materials, in this case in social sciences such as history, anthropology, sociology, and economics. (This is why at many points in this civil pamphlet, I seek help from fragments of the intellectual history and sociology of Mexico.)

But it is also sometimes useful to use literary materials, with a nomadic aesthetic, as I will do in the next steps. So to reaffirm that *nationalist zeal* must be described as a vice, at least as dangerous as *subaltern fervor* and *craving for novelty* (and without going into further detail, as would be appropriate to such blinding passions), I will begin by collecting little bits of Mexican literature that count against *nationalist zeal*: one or two episodes from a novel by David Toscana and some verses by Carmen Boullosa. In each case I will try not to neglect this claim and warning:

> *Be careful with words, including the words*
> *you read and how you read them.*

VI

I will begin my rejection of *nationalist zeal* with a reading of the novel *El ejército iluminado* (*The Enlightened Army*) by David Toscana.[6] I will do so with a nomadic aesthetic—with *a reading that moves to the horizon of the reader, and questions them*, or a type of *itinerant, self-referential reading*.[7] With this type of reading I am interested in going over several of the events in the novel, because these events propose a first approximation of nationalist zeal. We play hide and seek with the hopeless, "I want but I cannot have." The game begins with an intimately painful but commonplace and ordinary event: Ignacio Matus is expelled from the school where he teaches history. Extravagance is soon introduced in the form of a parody: Ignacio Matus, furious about being fired, decides to undertake the enterprise that will redeem him. This is nothing less than going to war against the United States in order to recover the territories lost by Mexico, and therefore to restore national honor. Predictably, the enthusiastic Matus does not receive many volunteers to join him in besieging the Alamo. ("He's just deranged," says a police office who is watching him.[8]) But Matus recruits five mentally challenged individuals: Fatso Comodoro, Azucena, Ubaldo (to whom Matus, being the perverse evangelist that he is, at one point whispers that "you have to forget reality a bit"), Milagro, and Cerillo.[9] Don't the bizarre names seem to imply a nod to the stories of Voltaire, those parodies that champion Enlightenment and reason, and do so with sarcasm, or else by provoking a good laugh? Also recruited is Caralampio, "the crybaby with dirty underwear," but ultimately in vain.[10]

On the one hand, it should be noted that the number of combatants coincides, irreverently, with the number of the young cadets who defended Chapultepec against the North American invasion on September 13, 1847, and who are known in Mexico as the "Niños Héroes" (child heroes). At the same time, Caralampio does not ultimately go to war because Comodoro forgets him in the toilet. Another cruel parody: General Monteverde was also absent from the battle of Chapultepec because apparently, like Caralampio, he frequently had to use the toilet. Even for the most distracted reader of *El ejército iluminado*, here we find a first deficiency (*descalificación*) of the colonial vision that concerns us.

Nationalist zeal is a delusion, the product of impotence. I will now abandon, with some regret, the grotesque episodes of the novel and take a leap in the narrative because my interest is to pursue other deficiencies of nationalist zeal. In battle, or something that is perceived or imagined as such, Comodoro reflects on the need for heroes. (In other times the need for heroes has been thought of, somewhat more soberly, as a kind of nightmare.)[11] For Comodoro, heroes are urgently needed: "And that's why I'm here, the illustrious Comodoro, the survivor of the Rio Grande, the survivor of piranhas, the young master of Condestable, and the favorite one of the Immaculate Lady, I'm here to provide history with stories."[12]

Question: the phrase "provide history with stories," put in the mouth of a mentally challenged man who has fallen prey to the vice of *nationalist zeal*, seems to suggest that those "received" stories that enthusiastic nationalists count as "the true history" are nothing more than fetishes, which, like "little bits" of stories from history, divert attention away from what has happened and is happening to us. What do I mean?

Suddenly, as if in passing (although the information cuts like a knife that splits the reading in two), we learn that once they are captured by the Mexican military the combatants of this enlightened "army" were *not* charged with any crime. But even more, its members are immediately released. The novel takes place far from the capital; the events happen in the north of the country, almost on the border with the United States. Without a tremble in the voice of the novel, it slowly becomes clear why the army has released these madmen: "because with all that's going on in Mexico City, what we least want is for the army to continue to attract attention."[13]

"All that's going on in Mexico City." We are in 1968. But what is it that is evoked with this vague insinuation and at the same time remains hidden? To answer we have to stop reading and start remembering or investigating. We do not have to investigate too much. With a certain *nationalist zeal*—in this case, however, we are facing a very diminished and even controversial zeal among nationalists—it wants to hide the crime by not mentioning the massacre of Tlatelolco.[14] In this way, at the crossroads that is *El ejército iluminado*, we encounter a path running opposite to that of the parody, *the corridor of violence in which everything moves in the background*. If we take this into account, a second deficiency of *nationalist zeal* can be proposed, even scarier than the first:

Nationalist zeal is often a cover for crimes in lands that seek that zeal for cover. Consequently, *nationalist zeal* is nothing more than a generator of stories to cover up the horrors of one's own history, or more directly, to make them disappear. But it is not only about that. Anyone who reads this novel carefully, especially those in Mexico or with knowledge of the country, will likely be aware of a topic that is frequently discussed in the media, as well as in everyday conversations. I am referring to the issue of illegal Mexican migration to the United States. Thus, the reader will have a hard time ignoring the insulting parallelism between the delusions of glory fantasized by "the enlightened ones," and the terrible violence and misery experienced at each step by undocumented immigrants. (That parallelism becomes even more sinister if one considers that in much of US politics these defenseless people are classified as "invaders," and that it seeks to contain them—as in the Middle Ages—by building walls). In this way, and continuing with this personalized itinerant reading of *El ejército iluminado*, we discover another deficiency of the vice that concerns us:

Nationalist zeal is often a distraction from problems in the places that produce such zeal. Has the concern of *nationalist zeal* been clarified as a vice and *not* as an adequate response to the colonial vices of *subaltern fervor* and *craving for novelty*? Those who accept the observations made above will respond affirmatively. I will add, then, a fourth description, the fourth deficiency of this vice:

Nationalist zeal is a generator of traumas and resentments, or sickening uses of arrogant reason.[15] One of the most influential texts of modern Latin American thought, *Nuestra América* (Our America, 1891) by the Cuban author José Martí, can also be read as a report on some colonial vices and their remedies. *Nuestra América* begins with another deficiency of *nationalist zeal*:

> The conceited villager believes the entire world to be his village. Provided that he can be mayor, or humiliate the rival who stole his sweetheart, or add to the savings in his strong-box, he considers the universal order good, unaware of those giants with seven-league boots who can crush him underfoot, or of the strife in the heavens between comets that streak through the drowsy air-devouring worlds. What remains of the village in America must rouse itself. These are not the times for sleeping in a nightcap, but with weapons for a pillow, like the warriors of Juan de Castellanos—weapons of judgment, which conquer all others. Barricades of ideas are worth more than barricades of stone.[16]

It is now necessary, however, to attend to two types of distinctions that I consider useful in order not to distort, at least not too much, this and perhaps any debate about nationalism. Here are two conjectures:

- There is a *nationalist zeal* from above and another from below.

- There is a nationalism that is blind and delirious: the impure fetish of *nationalist zeal*, and a responsible nationalism that appears when that fetish is destroyed, patriotism.

If we consider these four deficiencies of *nationalist zeal* starting from below, we find attributes that consolidate the paralyzing politics of identity. It is strange, or not so much, that the very impotence that leads to raving about self-glorifying enterprises (the first deficiency of *nationalist zeal*) also seduces people into self-pity (the fourth deficiency of *nationalist zeal*). Because even if one is right, and one lives in a country or region that has suffered abuse and subjugation, it does not help to obsess over it. Resentment, rancor, and the desire for revenge only wear down one's own community and thus sabotage it. You cannot corral a hurricane.

In a contradictory way, then, as victims, we grope for the reverse: to find that we are not victims or not so much; that our impotence is not so all-embracing and feverish. Therefore, past crimes and present horrors are hidden (the second and third deficiencies of *nationalist zeal*), among other reasons, in order to weaken what is degrading in us, which however . . . At the same time, in the *nationalist zeal* from those below (those victims that we want and do not want to be), by blinding themselves and turning in on themselves, they are once again fighting to defend a paralyzing identity politics and its inevitable companion, the politics of aggressive exclusion. Because we have to repeat again: that the vice of *nationalist zeal*—which includes as prey both those from below and those from above—is also content with despising, or at least saying that it despises "everything that comes from abroad." (This is a fashion that also "comes from abroad.")

But we have already warned that *nationalist zeal* is an impure fetish. No Hegelian assumptions are needed in order to admit that changes in degree will mean changes in quality. Hence we face many complications with nationalism; changes in degree introduce changes in purpose. This change has announced a second distinction. Indeed, by destroying the impure fetish of *nationalist zeal*, we can extract the virtue of patriotism. I return to that member decree that is also a principle of nomadic thought:

> *From time to time, focus on the place and time*
> *in which you live; think about what you believe,*
> *what you feel, and what you desire.*

In general, the population of a certain territory, based on nationalism, and prey to *nationalist zeal*, are understood as being an "organic whole." Its constituents (institutions, people . . .) are subordinated to its purposes by belonging to that "whole." Thus, for example, moral restrictions are worthless, and legal restrictions even less so, if they seek to limit the interests of the "organic wholes" which are nations. However, is the concept and experience of belonging reduced to that subordination to the "whole"?

Let us continue with the *strategy of detours* of nomadic thought. Since we can remember (it is a property of many animals), human animals are not merely born and situated in a place, but develop a sense of belonging by inhabiting it. This belonging is reinforced each day by social influences, like stories about one's own history, songs, commemorative dates, monuments, distinguished names of public spaces . . ., which then become ways of believing, wanting, feeling. Thus, each human animal, when born in a place, inherits more than the material goods that allow it to survive. That is why it is not surprising that, as part of one's cultural heritage, one also inherits loyalties that motivate interaction with one's compatriots and with the institutions of the state, in a different way than one's interactions with other people and institutions. Hence it is also part of such feelings of belonging that the various inhabitants of the state are willing to sacrifice. This sacrifice includes paying taxes, and with this practice we contribute to building and controlling institutions, such as the government and its public policies. Among other things, this is about controlling economic or security policies, and so, although it is sometimes difficult to recognize, policies regarding the army and the police.

However, early in life the "I belong" of childhood breaks down into a growing plurality of belongings that often come into conflict. I am Mexican, but I am also from Michoacan, I am Latin American, I am a husband, I am a father, I am a small business owner, I have a father from Guerrero and an Italian mother, and I have friends from here and there with conflicting religious and political beliefs, I am a human animal of the male gender. The plurality of "belongings" therefore multiplies without limit. What to do about it?

Since antiquity, organizing the plurality of "belongings" of different, but not unequal, people is a task known as the passion of the patriots. So patriotism—this is at least its purpose—calls on certain practices to contribute to the integration of society itself. But we are not seeking to build an "organic whole." Republics of *differentiated* peers are required.

For this reason, when a Mexican poet like Carmen Boullosa turns her deep concern into a furious cry about the violence that harasses and tends to disintegrate that plurality of belongings in Mexico at the beginning of the twenty-first century and its surroundings, does she not write in *La patria insomne*, as if she were an anthropologist studying a distant society with foreign lenses?"[17] I quote a few verses which express the feeling concerned, that sense of torn belonging. They are verses that urgently need to be read with an itinerant reading:

> *Now I breathe pure ash, I inhale.*
> *My own blood abandoned me.*
> *My flesh closed like a stone.*
> *The smell of public blood drowns me.*
> *The blood of others rolls in the street.*
> *So, so much death.*
> *There is nothing else.*

Unfortunately, I will not go on to explore the political and moral virtues of patriotism, virtues that are revealed by destroying the impure fetish of *nationalist zeal*. I will continue with the detours about colonial vices (a bit like a migrant who, without a fixed goal, explores the surroundings he crosses), and I will use the *strategy of transitions* in another way. Perhaps at the beginning it seems that we are already in another reflection, exploring other problems, because in what follows I will examine much more theoretical claims that introduce distinctions and nuances. They are *claims of methodological prudence*.

VII

First claim of methodological prudence that leads to distinguishing the innocent, paralyzing, and strategic uses of expressions of identity.

We often run into implicit or explicit oppositions between expressions such as "culture in Argentina" and "Argentine culture," or "physics in Mexico" and "Mexican physics," or "philosophy in Mexico" and "Mexican philosophy." If I am not mistaken, these are occasions in which problems about the discourses of identity are discussed, for example national identity. For now there are those who condone the use of only one type of these expressions, say, "philosophy in Mexico."[18] However, that decision is also annoying.[19] Of course it is good that the distinctions which concern identity—of this or other types—open up discussions, although it matters more that they do not close them, and that they do not impose vices.

On the other hand, expressions that allude directly or indirectly to problems of identity begin by having two uses, one innocent and the other paralyzing and sometimes aggressive. There is no problem about the innocent use. In most of the situations in which the "Mexican economy" is mentioned, the economy introduced or developed in Mexico is being referred to, without pretending that this economy somehow has its own profile. By contrast, there is also a paralyzing use of expressions like "Mexican philosophy." This falsely essentialist use creates a kind of sect and exercises "centripetal imagination": the imagination that viciously does nothing but return us from ourselves to ourselves and opposes us to others. So occasionally the expression "Mexican philosophy," and even "Mexican politics," seems to suggest that there would be idiosyncratic characteristics—completely their own?—of those thoughts or public policy measures which, more than just distinguishing them, separate them from the philosophical (or economic, or historical, or sociological) work done in other latitudes. Once again we have surrendered to the vice of *nationalist zeal.* (As if Mexicans were a natural class, like lemons and rodents, rather than histories, multiple and unpredictable, which intertwine with other histories).

Continuing along this path, but no longer with an aggressive tone, but more subordinate, lowering one's head, perhaps the thought is that Mexican philosophy, or Mexican sociology, or Mexican anthropology, needs to focus exclusively on *the* Mexican (whatever that abstraction might be—which ignores times, places, classes, genders, and other peculiarities). Or perhaps the suggestion is (even worse) that expressions such as "Mexican philosophy" or "Mexican sociology" or "Mexican anthropology" indicate a division of labor: that philosophy or sociology or anthropology in Mexico—and in places similarly considered marginal—should concern themselves *solely* with Mexican issues, above all problems of "applied philosophy" or "empirical sociology" or "local anthropology," such as, for example, the much publicized "transition to . . . democracy," or the exclusion of women from certain jobs, or the policies on abortion and euthanasia in different states of the country. Consequently, we would need to leave the general problems, the persistent human concerns—freedom, social structures and changes, the meaning of life, the social impacts of science and technology, and even the methodological problems of philosophy, sociology, or anthropology—to more prepared people who think better: the directors and managers of the Headquarters of Power and Thought.

However, the entanglements of the politics of identity do not end here. Why not? As anticipated, and contrary to the paralyzing politics of identity, both aggressive and subordinate, a *first form of resistance* emerges—using identities as strategies. In what sense? The word "strategy" refers to a way of behaving; these are often carefully planned procedures to achieve a goal.

Strategic actions are therefore those means—some subtle, others brutal—that are used to achieve an end. As a result, it is *sometimes* appropriate, in contrast to the crippling uses of identity, to employ essentialist phrases such as "Mexican philosophy" or "Mexican politics," as a strategy to attain a goal. Which goal? In its nomadic moments, good thinking needs to support marginalized practices as well—or to strengthen areas of research and public policy which have been marginalized in the past and in the present. In this way we can strategically exaggerate in order to attend to social inheritances that are frequently overlooked.

These exaggerations often constitute the strategy of *interrupting* the vices, among others, of *subaltern fervor* and *craving for novelty*, while at the same time *interrupting* the dominant identity monologues of the Headquarters of Power and Thought. It is noteworthy that *interrupting* the dominant discourses—even to a minimal degree and for a short time—promotes good habits, that is, virtues in both ethics and politics.

There is no doubt: Whoever assumes their own place with strategies that *interrupt* colonial vices also assumes their own voice and even their own body—perhaps "of another color" or with other characteristics considered contemptible—and after gaining strength they feel capable of expressing their desires, beliefs, emotions, without apologizing for them. At the same time, those who are *interrupted* are given the opportunity to recognize the other, who until now had been left out of sight. In this way, they are invited to review the established costs of their convictions and to ask about their own way of wanting, believing, and feeling. With this strategic use of identities, not only do we air out the house by opening the windows, and even the door, but by doing so we *discover* materials that were hiding in plain sight: that any house has walls which, in order to learn, must be left behind.

VIII

Second claim of methodological prudence in which a contrast is made between explanation and argumentation, in particular, between explanatory history and argumentative history, and between explanatory reading and argumentative reading.[20]

With respect to a considerable part of the social sciences and humanities, "explanatory history" is understood—at least in Latin America—as those histories presented in textbooks. These tend to summarize the ideas of, for example, a social theory or thinker, with a somewhat distorted gloss of their central ideas. Thereafter, the explanations are usually limited to descriptions or chronologies: they link these ideas with those of their predecessors or contemporaries. Of course a history or an explanatory lecture can go deeper. It is possible to try to elucidate *how* some phenomena are described and reasoned, and even to try to explain *why* problems, solutions, and types of arguments are transformed or disappear. Sometimes carrying out these tasks rigorously means reintegrating fragments of these discourses with their contexts of production, for example, developments in science, religious and political conflicts, or the economic transformations of a society. One can also try to reconstruct the *why* of these artifacts, and to elucidate the function of a controversy in a certain place, at a certain time.[21]

Nevertheless, research in the humanities and social sciences, and other manifestations of culture, also has a more complex relationship with the past, because often their yesterdays are *present pasts*: pasts that have not ceased to pass. They are dazzling or terrible pasts that still confront, question, challenge, and, sometimes, like traumas, haunt. They are pasts that question. Consequently, someone who reads (for example) a Mexican thinker with an argumentative history encounters arguments that are not archaeological ruins to be observed, but reasons to be rejected or retained in order to solve their own problems. That is why the questions to be asked in a history or an argumentative reading are not those of a historian who only seeks to describe and explain, but rather those of someone who participates in a discussion. They are questions of *understanding*, of *truth*, and of *courage*. These questions aim to understand what the text says, to criticize it if it seems not to tell the truth or if one disagrees with it. Moreover, we will inevitably ask what we can learn for our own inquiries, appealing to the meta-rule of all argumentative reading, this principle of nomadic thinking: the maxim of *data, fetishes and materials*.

Thus, in the readings of argumentative history, one does not read in order to discover something hidden behind the text: neither political interventions or economic interests nor the motives of a biographer—two causes that can contribute understanding but also tempt us into the genetic fallacy—in order to help us continue thinking. Hence it is not only important to find out how to interpret the interventions of the thinker we read, but also whether they are true, and what value they have.

In his book *Contingency and Commitment: Mexican Existentialism and the Place of Philosophy*, Carlos Alberto Sánchez outlines, among other contributions, what we might reconstruct as a "theory of violent reading," which in its most radical aspects takes the form of an adventure.[22] If I am not mistaken, this way of reading can be categorized as an extreme type of argumentative reading. Why extreme? A violent reading does not establish a dialogue but rather, as an extreme argumentative reading, sets up harsh and even hostile confrontation between text and reader. The reader seeks to appropriate the text—from their own situation, from their own time and place—as one who appropriates a known land. So, on the one hand, as Sánchez points out, one reads "without losing what is truly one's own, namely, one's history and one's identity."[23] On the other hand, Sánchez clarifies that: "These are not passive readings that will leave the text unharmed (as with distanciation); they are done without any permission and legal right, and so free to be creative and enhancing, loving and violent."[24]

In this way such "violent readings" turn their backs on the guardians of explanatory readings (which are often pseudo-explanatory), readings packed with philology and historical ideas, readings which are allegedly unique, supposedly definitive readings (which are therefore appropriate as epitaphs?). By contrast, in the violent readings discussed by Sánchez, it is not so much fidelity to a text that matters, but above all, what the reader actively *does* with the text (which, I would add, must happen *to some extent* with all argumentative readings of assertive speech, and with all itinerant readings of a literary text). Further on, Sánchez specifies that: "The violence of reading lies in the fact that our encounter with a text is less an allowing-the-text-to-speak and more of a shakedown."[25] Engaging in the act of reading is not therefore a matter of calming oneself down and falling asleep, but of waking oneself up. In the happiest cases, paradoxically, it is a matter of waking from a dogmatic slumber, like Kant reading Hume, or perhaps Kierkegaard reading Hegel, and discovering that that was not the way for him, and occasionally, that that was not the way.[26]

In Latin America, to limit oneself to engaging with descriptive or even explanatory readings is a symptom, not only of laziness, but also of colonial vices, such as *subaltern fervor* or *craving for novelty*, with which one seeks to avoid the risks of the nomadic thinking to which we have been invited by those we read. Moreover, among us readers (although we fantasize otherwise), the abundance of readings that aspire to be explanatory readings, without actually being so—that barely gloss, if not simply lay out—is a symptom of this perversion. In these cases, by remaining in their *subaltern fervor* or their *craving for novelty*, these vices underline not only the reader's passivity but, even more seriously, his will to bind himself to an irresponsible subalternity. It is about the frivolous anxiety to keep re-reading what has been read so much and lost its meaning, or to learn about discussions that take place far, far away in the Headquarters of Power and Thought, but without daring to speak and to take part in that discussion. Therefore, one's own impotence is admitted in advance. Others are allowed to belittle us, and worse: we belittle ourselves, we retire from life. But we also retire those around us from life. Consequently, from such perversions the past and, at the same time, the present, is buried. We do this with a horrendous lack of respect: we are not taking those close to us seriously. We assume that nothing is to be learned from their friendship and commerce. For example, Mexican predecessors and colleagues become figures to be considered on holiday or in an obituary. But it is strongly encouraged not to waste too much time. Such figures should not be consulted about understanding, truth, and value—because it is impossible to have a serious discussion with ephemeral apparitions that are not even ghosts that haunt and cause problems nearby.

No doubt I have already abused the strategy of detours, in this case to elaborate on the distinctions between explanatory and argumentative history, and between explanatory and argumentative reading. However, in addition to the value of these distinctions in themselves, the contrast also helps to construct a second form of resistance against the paralyzing uses of identity and the politics of identity. How so?

This form of resistance consists in teaching us not to limit ourselves to the explanatory history of a certain identity's past and present, but to question, case by case, in what sense, by appealing to what truths and values, certain pretensions or demands can be supported by declarations of identity. Thus, when faced with a moral, or legal, or political, or economic, or cultural problem, one says: "I have been Mexican for three generations, and therefore . . . ," or "I am an adult male, and therefore . . . ," or "I speak Spanish, and therefore . . ." In each case we should ask about the meaning, the truth, and the value of this "therefore." In many situations, one's saying "I have been Mexican for three generations" or "I speak Spanish" or any other expression of identity may have nothing to do with the solution to the problem we are facing. Even worse, in some cases it is worth pointing out: "If we want to solve this problem, the best thing to do is to start by forgetting many—even all—of the identity statements that you or I may make, because at the moment those statements just get in the way."

However, be careful not to exaggerate in the wrong direction. The contrast between explanatory history and argumentative history, or between explanatory reading and argumentative reading, should not lead to a static form of thinking which separates them into fixed compartments, so that from the vantage of an argumentative reading, any form of explanatory history is simply dismissed.

IX

Third claim of methodological prudence that recalls the need to use the strategy of transitions in a descending direction as well. For example, here is an account outlining a basic explanatory history of philosophy in Mexico in the twentieth century.[27]

Before recounting that history, I will take a step back. Latin American philosophy is often divided into three stages: the founders, the forgers, and the technicians. However, in order to adapt this scheme to the truth, it would be convenient, among many other corrections, to replace first of all the word "founders," with the ugly word "forgetters" (*olvidadores*). The word "founders" seems to remove the rich Novohispanic philosophical past in many Latin American countries, and in almost all of them, the nineteenth-century republicanism (which sometimes held more interest than is supposed, as indicated in the reflections in Chapter 2). Of course in this scheme indigenous thought (nothing to see here!) is also spurned. That is why I allude with charity to "refounders." Secondly, the term "technicians" should often be replaced by people completely dominated by the vices of *subaltern fervor* and *craving for novelty*.

I return now to relate the history of philosophy in Mexico in the twentieth century. I simplify to the point of caricature. I divide this history into several phases:

A) *The generation of the "refounders"* irrupts in Mexico around 1910. It was led by Antonio Caso (1883–1946), and more publicly by José Vasconcelos (1882–1959). Both were trained in positivism, but reacted strongly against it in the Ateneo de la Juventud; this constituted the starting point of a renovation of Mexican culture. Among other aspects, the content of this renovation in philosophy was given through a call to unlearn the colonial vice of *subaltern fervor*, and to listen to the voices of universal philosophy without adhering to the currents of thought then in vogue (Spanish neoscholasticism, French positivism, the challenges of nineteenth-century liberalism). We also find in Caso and Vasconcelos a deep and persistent concern for the Mexican circumstance, without succumbing to the vice of *nationalist zeal*, as well as an interest in metaphysics and aesthetics, and their confidence in education as an instrument of social progress. Together with these thinkers, Samuel Ramos (1897–1959) can be considered the third member of this generation. Caso was his teacher and the one who got him interested in aesthetics. However, some negative considerations that Ramos advanced about Mexican culture were different than, and hostile to, the reflections of Caso and Vasconcelos. (This fact causes many to consider it questionable to group them together).

B) *The "transplants."* Due to the defeat of the second Spanish republic and the triumph of Francisco Franco's dictatorship, a contingent of philosophers arrived in Mexico who, as José Gaos wished, did not live as "exiles" (*desterrados*), but rather as "transplants" (*transterrados*). The most influential, both for his teaching and research—which, to remove any suspicion of *subaltern fervor* or *craving for novelty*, includes an immense and generous interest in the history of Mexican thought—was precisely José Gaos (1900–1969). The brief stay of María Zambrano (1904–1991) also left traces, diffuse but deep. For his part, the teaching of Eduardo Nicol (1907–1990) carried great weight in the Faculty of Philosophy and Literature at UNAM.

C) *The era of the "big blocs."* Directly or indirectly these various blocs were formed from the teachings of the Spanish *transterrados*. (Predictably, these teachings also frequently promoted colonial vices). The "big blocs" to which I refer were:

— *The "Mexicanism"* of the *Hiperión* group, with thinkers such as Jorge Portilla (1919–1963) and Emilio Uranga (1921–1988). Outside this group, we must take into account the more historiographic work of Carmen Rovira.

— *"Latin Americanism."* The best-known philosopher was Leopoldo Zea (1912–2004). At a later date this bloc could also include the more comprehensive theories—indebted to a certain teleology and to Marx—of Enrique Dussel, the best-known representative of Latin American liberation philosophy.

— *Marxism*, whose most influential philosophical figure, in his time, was Adolfo Sánchez Vázquez (1915–2011), with his reasoned and energetic proposal of a philosophy of *praxis*. But it is also important, extremely important, to take into account Bolívar Echevarría (1941–2010), with his revaluation of the baroque *ethos* as a way of thinking, and his attack on the "metaphysics of whiteness" as the generator of a certain modernity. Nor should we overlook fragments of the work of Carlos Pereyra (1940–1988), both that which is, to a certain extent, indebted to Althusserian Marxism, as well as the pages that testify to a progressive critical distancing from such a perspective.[28]

— *The metaphysical tradition*. Unlike the other blocs, in this case we are facing a "negative bloc," which could perhaps also be called "the heterodox bloc." Their members have little or nothing in common with each other, other than resisting the other blocs. In this respect it is worth mentioning the names of Antonio Gómez Robledo (1908–1994), fragments of Uranga's thought, and, of course, Ramón Xirau (1924–2017) and Juliana González. Belonging to a younger generation, but with work that has attracted attention, we can place in this group Mauricio Beuchot and his theory of analogical hermeneutics.

— *The analytical tradition*. Eduardo García Máynez (1908–1993), with his contributions to legal logic, introduced analytical philosophy among us very early on. On the other hand, after severe criticism of the phenomenological training they received from their teacher Gaos, Luis Villoro (1922–2014), Fernando Salmerón (1925–1997), and Alejandro Rossi (1932–2009) gave a great impetus to analytical philosophy, with the purpose of "professionalizing" and thus "normalizing" philosophy in Mexico. According to this proposal, philosophy should cease to be a "personal confession"—as Gaos once characterized it—or a set of social and political proclamations, and become instead a rigorous research discipline, like the other sciences. (It should be noted that this was only one of the many stages in Villoro's vast trajectory, which began and ended with a deep and meticulous, at once rebellious and generous, reflection—a pretty good mix—on the ancient greatness and the present misery of the indigenous world).

— *Feminism*. The theoretical contributions of the monumental writer Rosario Castellanos (1925–1974), and the pioneering academic work of Graciela Hierro (1928–2003), should not be overlooked in this regard.

D) *The "irruption of the archipelago."* Since the 1980s, with the fall of the Berlin Wall and the subsequent collapse of the Soviet Union, Marxism, to some extent, both in Mexico and in the rest of the Western world, lost its appeal or part of it. We need to remember that in Mexico, and in many regions of Latin America, what provoked the most widespread versions of Marxism, was the vice of *subaltern fervor*, such as the crazed desire to multiply franchises of Louis Althusser and his disciples in our universities and colleges. But also in Paris in recent years there has been a fierce criticism of Marxism, which we have also inherited, including attacks that display silly misunderstandings of Marx. (This much we know: One is harshest and most unjust toward beliefs once hastily and passionately embraced, but today no less hastily considered out of fashion). On the other hand, it is worth remembering that academic Marxism in Mexico was not just another bloc, but a "provocative bloc." So, by being torn to pieces, the militant resistance of others lost its meaning; hence the use of the metaphor of an archipelago.[29] One could also appeal, instead, to the metaphor of a shipwreck.[30] But Guillermo Hurtado does not allude only to a shipwreck, but to a "dialectic of the shipwreck," which, if we know how to take advantage of it, allows the shipwrecked people we have become—or, if you prefer, the archipelago dwellers we have become—to also risk engaging in "dialogue as an adventure," and in this way we can combat the colonial vices that afflict us.[31]

In this neat account of Mexican philosophical thought in the twentieth century, one could indicate the presence of colonial vices such as *subaltern fervor*, *craving for novelty*, and *nationalistic zeal*.[32] However, guided by the maxim of *data, fetishes, and materials*, I am more interested right now in rebuilding a corridor of nomadic thought, one that will allow anyone who destroys these impure fetishes to regain momentum and continue thinking.

Because if we start by using identity as a strategy and then destroy the vices mentioned, we can extract various materials from the *efforts* which typify these metaphors, the ones used in this account of the phases of philosophy in Mexico in the twentieth century.

Thus, the efforts of Caso and Vasconcelos *to refound (refundar)* contain characteristics of deep and rigorous thinking. Moreover, any form of thinking that takes itself seriously cannot fail to make a provisional "clean slate" from time to time, and thus to insist on re-examining problems as if no one had ever examined them before: to think from the beginning. (At the same time we know, of course, that such a liberating gesture is nothing more than an attitude of methodological hygiene, and also an act with which to regain strength and drive. Because no one is at the beginning, but always already *in the middle of.*)

No less significant was the *transplantation* effort carried out by the refugees of the second Spanish Republic, because all philosophy which is genuine philosophy is often built in concert with strange views, and people from abroad, often exiles, refugees fleeing in desperation, emigrants. We are, inevitably, heirs. The challenge lies in distinguishing between—a slippery contrast—the virtue of *transplantation* and the vice of *subaltern fervor*. It is worth emphasizing: We are heirs to many inheritances, some from kind strangers, others from faraway foreigners, and even—at first glance— from disagreeable or hostile peoples, even enemies. Such observations can lead us to another vice, the *craving for novelty*. However, let us not be confused: The act of *transplantation* differs from these vices because it is a way of continuing to think for oneself, and therefore to think not only in continuity but also in a break with foreign traditions, unlike the vices of passively consuming thoughts.

On the other hand, the establishment of large blocs of thought in conflict—at least when it does not blind—awakens us from our frequent dogmatic slumbers, and so challenges our discussions. As a result, it takes effort *to argue* in new and different ways, to reply to counter-arguments, and to question entrenched beliefs and interests. In this way, we have an opportunity to examine the viewpoints of others and also ourselves.

Let us finally address the metaphor of the archipelago. The sea not only separates the islands that compose an archipelago, in this case the diverse members of philosophy in Mexico; it also relates them in a fluid way— which returns us indirectly to one of the proposals making up the background of these reflections: the effort *to integrate*, the practice opposed to exclusion.

It is still worth noting: The practices of *refounding* and *transplanting* are forms of nomadic thought which *interrupt* distinctions, concepts, arguments, discussions . . . and even current preoccupations. This opens up possibilities for thinking and acting which were previously overlooked, or not even imagined. The practices of *arguing* and *linking* instead introduce and consolidate the need to acknowledge and recognize oneself in the *integrative interaction*. These practices therefore operate as therapies against bad coexistence.

X

Fourth claim of methodological prudence: in order to fight against colonial vices, it is necessary to strengthen porous reason.

In addition to perverting subjectivity, bad habits arrange *permissions for us to marginalize ourselves and to marginalize our societies*. It is therefore inadvisable to deal with colonial vices only as bad habits of character (which they are), but also to face up to them as customs to be resisted: social patterns to be worn out.[33] Therefore, if those habits and customs are weakened, and even some eliminated, we might be able to use the politics of identity as a strategy against paralyzing identities. Above all, we need not cease working with the materials that were rescued with argumentative reading from the account of twentieth-century Mexican philosophy: actions such as *refounding, transplanting, arguing,* and *integrating*. Suppose these actions take root in Latin America—or at least in Mexico. Thus one is capable of other encounters, of continuing the march of nomadic thinking. What happens in that case with arrogant reason and its vices, such as colonial vices? To answer, I will take another detour, or better, another leap. In this way, in this not very linear reflection on colonial vices, I will introduce maxims of the typical and equally abstract counterpoint to arrogant reason: *porous reason*.

With the use of porous reason we can predict: that we can weather the storms by taking into account (as our compass) not only multiple affiliations, but also our interrelationships with other perspectives of wishing, getting excited, imagining. These affiliations and interrelationships affect the present, as well as plans for the future. From these considerations, I formulate the first maxim of porous reason: *When confronted with doubts, ambiguities, and conflicts, act with multiple affiliations and interrelationships.*

It was pointed out that the colonial vice of *subaltern fervor*, as an impure fetish and an excess of consistency which closes in the face of new human relations, must also be rebuilt. Two things thus get confused: cultivating the integrity that gives a person increasing degrees of autonomy and refusing to continue learning. However, even unadventurous men and women, who have *not* succumbed to arrogant reason, try at least to peak at other possibilities. Even within one's own mind one appeals to the support of different points of view—to first- and second-person points of view, not to mention the reflective and scientific third-person point of view. I formulate as follows a second maxim of porous reason: *Act based on conversations in which you interlace processes of desiring, believing, feeling, imagining, and reasoning, without neglecting the possibility of frequently introducing explicit arguments into such conversations.*

It was also pointed out that the vice of *craving for novelty* forms an impure fetish: it invites us to welcome desires, beliefs, and, in general, other voices. However, this invitation often becomes an excuse for the anxiety of "being up to date," concerning what is at this moment making noise—no matter the reason—in one of the Headquarters of Power and Thought. Hence, instead of facing the problems of a changing world, and equally of its changing people, with strength and gratitude, those who have succumbed to such a vice replace the virtue of hospitality with that form of irresponsibility which consists in being terrified of "looking bad among one's chosen identity affiliation." Consequently, those who have become addicted to the *craving for novelty* do not correct their own errors, but continue intoxicating themselves with others'. (In these cases the maxim enforced is, *more of the same is always good*, even if more of the same is self-destructive). However, to assume numerous *links*, and at the same time to exercise the art of conversing and imagining, and (when it is pertinent and possible) *to argue* explicitly, are tasks that demand complicated efforts. On the one hand, those who try to be attentive to various friendships must train themselves not only to concentrate their attention on those friendships, but at the same time to pay attention to their surroundings. Thus we should not get carried away by the most familiar schemes of appreciation and the most familiar ways of advertising and announcing, without realizing how distorting the sabotaging characters can sometimes be. Therefore, the task of dealing with one's own circumstances and the urgent problems with which they confront us is radically misunderstood.

In this way (as we have not ceased repeating) one succumbs to another colonial vice: the impure fetish of *nationalist zeal*. Against such a fetish, no less dangerous for being common, we must act according to a third maxim of the porous reason: *Do not confuse patriotism with vainly or desperately embracing what is yours—your skin, your home, your region, your country, your language—rather: let yourself be questioned. Also, let yourself be challenged in unexpected directions or even directions you dislike.*

We already have, then, another weapon to fight against colonial vices if only we put *porous reason* into practice.

CHAPTER 2

Fragments of Mexican Philosophy, For Example

Discussions about Latin American philosophical thought, and about any of the philosophies of the region, Mexican philosophy, for example, often get tangled up in the opposition between abstract universalism and cultural particularism. With the use of nomadic thinking, I will seek to dissolve this opposition.

I

In order to approach this false opposition—as widespread as it is dangerous—I appeal once again to the strategy of detours. As a starting point, I will consider the question, "Does Mexican philosophy and its history have any importance?" It is often helpful to ask a question about bizarre contexts, among other reasons so that when we are surprised, we can rethink it: to make an effort to discover what genuinely matters when such a question is asked. That is why, on this occasion, I specified this concern in an unusual way. I want to ask, "What could be the point of studying Latin American philosophy, especially Mexican philosophy, outside of Mexico, for example in the United States?" Sometimes assuming a point of view outside our immediate situation illuminates it: It allows us to see it with different eyes.

Let us inquire, then, about the possible general interest in studying Mexican philosophy. The short answer is: studying that philosophy—or if one prefers, more broadly, the philosophy done in Latin America—is a way to expand the philosophical tradition and thus to enrich it with new voices and problems, perhaps with other theories, methodologies, arguments, and even warn in general about possible vices—epistemic, moral, political— that can be acquired by thought. When this short answer is given, doubts immediately arise: Why should these *other* voices, problems, and arguments be addressed? This question leads me to a medium-length response. However, like many problems that are usually qualified as philosophical—language reference, rigid designators, virtues and vices (practical and epistemic), freedom, etc.—as soon as answers to these concerns are proposed, they become starting points for further discussions that lead to long, very long answers. Since we have to start somewhere, I will concentrate on developing a medium-length answer to the question at hand.

Regarding the short answer, it was doubted why it should be of interest, for example, to analytic or "Continental" philosophy, or any other type of philosophy practiced in a philosophy department in the United States, to introduce into its canon or its traditions, voices, problems, methodologies, virtues and vices from Mexican philosophy. Predictably, the answer to this question will depend on what is meant by "Mexican philosophy." I will start again from a distant reference. In his paper, "The Philosophical Gift of Brown Folk: Mexican American Philosophy in the United States," José-Antonio Orosco presents a detailed map with various ways of understanding this philosophy.[1] I will rearrange that map somewhat in what follows.

The first way to understand Mexican philosophy is as *abstract universalism*. According to this position, there is nothing distinctive about the reference of expressions such as "Mexican philosophy" or "Latin American philosophy." Philosophy is a field of research like mathematics or the natural sciences. Therefore the truths of philosophy are *only* universal.

A second way is as *cultural particularism*. Under this denomination I subsume what Orosco calls "culturalism": philosophy as a discourse that articulates a worldview and its culture, or some of its fragments, as it is assumed that Samuel Ramos, Leopoldo Zea, or Jorge Portilla did with respect to Mexican philosophy.[2] I will also include as a variant of this position, Jorge Gracia's proposal to understand Latin American philosophy as an "ethnic philosophy."[3] By the philosophy of an *ethnos*—or what is perhaps somewhat similar, a tradition—Gracia renders historical the Wittgensteinian metaphor of the family: an extended group that has unity, or at least "family resemblances," given by certain historical contingencies, without all members of the group possessing the same properties.

Orosco also offers another way of understanding Latin American philosophy, which he calls "criticalism." As an example of criticalism, Orosco recalls statements by Augusto Salazar Bondy where he points out that since Latin America has lived under a "culture of domination," it has not had the possibility of developing an authentic philosophy. Still, it could do so, given different economic and political circumstances.[4] I do not consider this another way, much less a specific way, of doing Latin American or Mexican philosophy. Instead, it is one of the many constituent parts of any philosophy, insofar as philosophy has been, is, and must continue to be, if it is not to betray itself, critical thought.[5]

As a result, two positions remain on the map that seem to corner us into a discouraging alternative. It is the destructive false opposition, previously mentioned, that I am interested in dissolving. Because if current philosophy departments accept an abstract universalism, then it will surely be pointed out that the canon is already jam-packed. If, by chance, an exceptional figure or an unexpectedly novel problem appears in Mexican philosophy that until now no one had taken into account, it will be considered; however, to provide such attention, a course in "Latin American philosophy" or "Mexican philosophy" is not necessary. This is a way to respond gracefully, but in an arrogant way: "don't bother." (Or, if one is more critical: this is another chance to use *the license to marginalize*). If, by contrast, cultural particularism is accepted, the reaction will be roughly equivalent. Perhaps it will be said that some neopositivists have already taught us that worldviews are one thing and philosophy is another. Maybe history, anthropology, sociology, or literary theory might have the interest and the means for studying worldviews, but whoever insists on studying them in philosophy will be told the same thing again: "don't bother." (Consequently, the chance will once again be seized to use *the license to marginalize*). What can be said?

Here is a conjecture: perhaps we can understand this map of Latin American or Mexican philosophy from two perspectives. The first perspective consists of a form of understanding that follows a static epistemology. Consequently, with the positions of abstract universalism and cultural particularism, one operates with static concepts that lead to an opposition, one that is no less false for being habitual. This forces one to choose: either you work with abstractions and general problems, or you abandon philosophy and attend to more or less concrete problems, the product of "worldviews," or the specific circumstances of certain social groups, or even the experience of individuals. Nevertheless, it will be concluded regarding the latter—not without a certain arrogance—that it has already been done and is not a topic of philosophy.

However, it is also possible to understand this map according to a way of thinking already introduced: starting from a nomadic epistemology, and, in general, with nomadic thinking. In this second perspective, the positions of abstract universalism, and the particularisms of cultures, and even of social or personal singularities—those that concern the experiences and problems of a social group and even of an individual—will cease to be in opposition.

On the contrary, they will become the extremes of a *continuum* of nomadic thinking and its use of the strategies of detours and transitions. We will be faced with frequent comings and goings of knowledge and inquiries between what happens in one place and what happens in another, between the abstract and the concrete. What do I mean?

The more or less particular difficulties and problems—or apparently particular, or even unique—which arise from concrete experiences concerning the body, gender, skin color, language, or territory of origin, can also become starting points for formulating challenges to deep-rooted habits and customs. In this respect, it can be predicted that one can question not only an ethical or political theory, but also an epistemology, and from this, a metaphysics about the place of the body, gender, skin color, language, or territory of origin. Furthermore, one might also wish to generalize and specify the catalogue of questions and examine which problems are taken into account and privileged, or left aside, in various theorizations. Are such colonial vices as *subaltern fervor*, *craving for novelty*, and *nationalistic zeal*, as well as what resists them, problems of epistemology? Should the good and bad organizations of the territory and persistent concerns in the life of human animals, such as sexuality, desire, and violence, also be concerns of metaphysics? Or do we seek to think of "being" or "what there is," or, if you prefer, "reality"—such words!—without that somewhat annoying phenomenon: life? But why think "what there is," without animals, and therefore, without human animals, which are born in certain places in certain conditions, and sooner or later die? But be careful with the problems that are taken to be valid, because the concerns that get excluded cast light and shadow on what is included.

At the same time, a nomadic epistemology considers universal learning that must operate as restrictions on particular or peculiar customs that may have to be rejected. In this way, we must defend, among others, the so-called "human rights." In all regions of Latin America, for example in Mexico, we must resist the constant violations of the rights of women, of indigenous populations, of people in misery, or of what are considered "divergent sexualities," and the abuses that are often disguised as "protective attitudes." (They are also, more hypocritically, called "cultural traditions.") Or it becomes necessary to inquire how a condition as universal as truth places severe restrictions on the most diverse beliefs both explicit and implicit in practice. (For example, it is important to distinguish news from *fake news* or news fabricated to deceive).

In this sense, for a nomadic way of thinking, two very useful resources have already been noted from the reflections of Chapter 1. Horizontal nomadism, or the strategy of detours, allows us to address, as we have done, apparently extravagant ramifications. With this strategy, several more or less indirect paths are taken. This is done not only to illuminate experiences and actions along familiar pathways, but also to widen debates: to enrich them with problems, descriptions, stories, which sometimes irrupt unexpectedly. (For example, when discussing with nomadic thinking the moral, legal, and political problem of violence, detours should be taken to discuss its political and economic presuppositions. Or in the epistemology of belief, nomadic thinking will consider not only the virtuous but also the vicious uses of beliefs). It is, therefore, a strategy that operates like a window leading to other windows.

For its part, vertical nomadism, or the strategy of transitions, changes the level of abstraction. By moving from more abstract to more concrete levels of inquiry, or vice versa, this technique enables reciprocal illuminations. (For example, perhaps we are considering the way social corruption and violence in Latin America shape phenomena that, although local, generate thought: They have repercussions that are not usually suspected. Or when a nomadic epistemology is adopted, it may be of concern how biases and prejudices distort beliefs in Mexico or in certain social groups in Mexico, or perhaps in all of Latin America). Predictably, these transitions leading to other transitions also become windows leading to other windows.

In order to provide characteristic examples of nomadic thinking, I will linger a bit—though not long enough—on the claims of two Mexican thinkers.

II

In nineteenth-century Mexico the radical republican Ignacio Ramírez (1818–1879) knew the dangers of the colonial vices of *subaltern fervor* and the *craving for novelty*. His judgment was emphatic: "Servile imitation debilitates and degrades nations." The following story, which tended to perpetuate itself, is typical of the course of his hectic days. From prison "Ramírez manages to escape in disguise and heads toward Sinaloa, but is captured by forces of the conservative Tomás Mejía, who sends him to the prison in Querétaro, and after threatening to shoot him, the troops end up mocking him, paraded on the back of a donkey while the soldiers insult him and throw stones at him."[6] Experiences like these might have been what made him so extremely critical of his country.[7] To avoid the many dangers of his time, he used the strategy of detours by taking on the most diverse occupations: thinker, poet, politician, journalist, judge, professor, geographer, historian, philologist.

Moreover, regarding this diversity of interests, Ramírez did not fail to mix history and arguments with satire and caricature in his writings. As Liliana Weinberg points out: "his semi-comic style is far from being superficial or circumstantial, since it aims both at a disengaging criticism and a profound reform of society, and thus it constitutes the bridge that links the moralizing illustration of Lizardi and the criticisms of Fray Servando, with ideas coming from the French Revolution."[8] Ramírez also intermingled these proposals with challenges. Thus this atypical thinker, who sought to recover the clarity of the European Enlightenment, adopted in 1845 an obscure and hermetic pseudonym, *the Necromancer*.[9] His collaborations in favor of reason and experience were signed with this demonic pseudonym. Of course the choice of this pseudonym came at a price. As Carlos Monsiváis observes: "The pseudonym, or rather, the term that journalistically and popularly complements Ignacio Ramírez has little to do with his precise work, but it adequately describes the image of dread, the superstitious mood, the mixture of anger and fear with which Ramírez was regarded by the society (the only society) of his time."[10] At the same time, several uses of the *strategy of detours* in his writings are also instances of the *strategy of transitions*. For example, Ramírez seeks to *transplant* to the Mexican situation complex, more or less general traditions such as modern rationalism and empiricism, and the very diverse histories that precede them. Moreover, it is obvious that when we resist *licenses to marginalize*, every human animal, from time to time, can be seen as embodying all their heritage: as the entirety of history. In one of his last poems (1876), three years before his death, and dedicated to a friend in prison, Ramírez makes this present to us with verses that invite an itinerant reading, the kind of reading typical of a nomadic aesthetic:

> *The learned Greek and Hebrew antiquity*
> *teaches him the secrets of their languages*
> *and for the sake of his country, he employs them.*

These verses are another testimony to his nomadic thinking. It is important to clarify that this nomadism made him gather not only "the learned Greek and Hebrew antiquity," but also the indigenous past, and also, as a good, enlightened republican, as I mentioned, the rationalism and empiricism of the time. Evidence of this effort to naturalize thought is his *Ensayo sobre las sensaciones* (Essay on sensations). Regarding this text, Weinberg observes: "its first antecedent is, of course, Locke's *Essay Concerning Human Understanding* (1690)," but Ramírez "simultaneously enters into implicit dialogue with another group of empiricist and sensualist philosophers: Hume,

Condillac, Helvetius, La Mettrie, concerned with the role of sensations in the production of ideas."[11]

Thus Ramírez, going back and forth between the abstract universalism of tradition and the cultural particularism of his circumstance, produces what can be described as outlines of the morality, legality, and politics of integration. In this case it is a claim against the paralyzing identity politics that produce a triple exclusion:

- The exclusion of indigenous people
- The exclusion of women
- The exclusion of "day laborers": *campesinos* or workers

His attack consists of demands against a past still present. We need to put an end to all those stories where indigenous people, women, farmers, and workers do not appear as agents. They are not even ghosts that disturb the rest of society. They are nobody. But there is no freedom in these aggressive exclusions, maybe not even for those who exclude.[12] In this regard, let us review the old and persistent forms of exclusion that worried Ramírez and that should still concern us today.

THE POLITICAL CLAIM FOR THE SOCIAL EXCLUSION OF INDIGENOUS PEOPLE

Around 1810, Ramírez published a poem in the newspaper *El demócrata* in which he bluntly declares (to a society that did not want to hear such declarations):

> *In being an Indian my vanity is grounded.*

Likewise, in his long poem "La representación nacional" (National representation), we encounter tercets denouncing the oppression under which indigenous people scarcely manage to survive. The verses articulate comparisons that amount to fighting words:

> *You will find ten as rich as kings,*
> *subjecting a thousand leagues to their dominion,*
> *while a thousand Indians have ten magueys.*

Ramírez immediately adds verse resistance against arduous work and undeserved leisure:

> *The Indian, takes pulque and corn out of the mud;*
> *the rich man does not even touch the ground:*
> *that one enjoys nothing, and this one everything.*

Reading these verses with an itinerant reading is an initial propaedeutic to his article, "To the Indians," which caused a lot of scandal in his time.[13] Ramírez addresses them as "sons of generous and unfortunate races," and he agitates and encourages them: "To recover the joy and splendor that you enjoyed in the times of Nezahualcóyotl—without the traces of barbarism that marred the cradle of your society, and with all the resources in which the Enlightenment of the century abounds ... Consider not only that are you oppressed, but that your enemies are advancing to ensure that you do not belong to the human species."[14]

The passage is a good example of the use of the *maxim of data, fetishes, and materials*. Ramírez is sure to collect as data "the joy and splendor of the past." However, he is not blind: he does not dwell on the nostalgia of a time *also* marked by cruelty and barbarism. Ramírez does not succumb to any form of the vice of *nationalist zeal*. Rightly so: there is no need to continue being the worst of ourselves. As a critical citizen, and therefore as a participant concerned with his own past, Ramírez surely exaggerates in referring to indigenous cultures, but with the aim of freeing himself from paralyzing burdens: "Slavery has an aspect among Mexicans that is difficult to reproduce in other nations," Ramírez continues undeterred: "terror shook the whole of society."[15] Thus, in order to destroy the fetishes contained in this past, it is necessary, as a difficult and laborious task—not only historiographical, but also critical of the present—to bring those *also painful* times into dialogue with the arguments of the Enlightenment. The lesson is clear: one's own past, both social and personal, is not there to be rejected for its vices and fetishes, nor to be applauded for its virtues. It is there to learn from and thus to understand and explain the present, and to transform it.

To cap off the statement about how the indigenous people are oppressed, Ramírez continues to exhort them: "View with extreme distrust the owners of the estates, their stewards, the clergy, all the rich, and all those who let you kiss their hands, because most of these have an interest in leaving you poor and ignorant."[16] Such exhortations aroused fury at the time, and even fear in various social circles. There was fear of a possible indigenous rebellion. Because it never fails to provoke fear to expose what they want to hide with violence: to remember that social inequality is still there, that aggressive exclusion has not disappeared but confronts us like an open wound. (A strange paradox: they try to hide violence with violence). We can foresee that Ramírez was once again arrested and prosecuted. One testimony among others to this furious reaction is the letter by Mariano Riva Palacio published on the front page of the liberal newspaper *El siglo diez y nueve* (The nineteenth century): "Citizens who profess principles of all kinds and all cultured societies, are alarmed to see the propagation of foolish doctrines, whose application would result in plunging the world into barbarism, launching the human species into a crime run, and drowning in rivers of blood."[17] Perhaps the scandal would have multiplied had Ramírez's use of the strategy of transitions based on the quoted statements not been disregarded. I am referring to his proposal of universalizing the bitter circumstances suffered by the Indians. Indeed, it is not only the Indians of the Americas who suffer oppression. Ramírez universalizes his claims about freedom: because "the Russians are the Indians of the Czar, the Italians the Indians of the Pope, the Spanish, the Germans, the French are the Indians of their despots."[18] Whether or not one agrees with the examples, one should welcome the impulse indicated by this statement. Because a public claim that does not seek to universalize becomes a parody: of rage or resentment, or delusions, or their perverse mixture.

THE POLITICAL CLAIM FOR THE SOCIAL EXCLUSION OF WOMEN

According to Ramírez, women have historically been likened to machines and hence perceived to be in different social classes: a "machine of pleasures in some nations; a machine for making children and clothes and food in others; and in most, a positive piece of luxury furniture for the rich, and a dependent, the first of domestic animals for the poor."[19] But Ramírez proclaims that women are not machines. They are human animals. As such, they have human *capacities*: the *power* to do this or that. Consequently, they are capable of undertaking nomadic histories which cannot be foreseen. Specifically in his "notes" on women, Ramírez traces possible conjectural histories, between positivists and the Enlightenment, between republicans and liberals, and elaborates a narrative of the types of stages of women, based on patterns of initial ignorance and subsequent recognition. In this way, a possible teleology is reconstructed as follows: "Women have three historical and legal stages: 1. Slave; 2. Emancipated by means of man; 3. Emancipated by herself." Regarding this progressive encounter of woman with herself, of this process of the liberation of women, Ramírez says: "In the regime of force: slave, instrument, thing. Under the principle of authority: pupil, faithful, limitation of rights. In individual freedom: equality of rights."[20]

Like other teleologies postulated in the nineteenth century as liberating processes, teaching is proposed as the driving force for emancipation. (We are after all in the middle of the nineteenth century, that century that invested so much on education). In explaining why it is so important for women to be educated, Ramírez considers their emancipation as an end in itself, as the construction of their positive as well as negative autonomy. This is undoubtedly the primary moral purpose. But it is not the only one. Its social repercussions are also explored.[21] Because the education of women sets in motion an expanding circle of multiple goods:

> The instruction of women has a mission of primary importance in social relations; there is no need to extol the advisability of spreading sound knowledge to all classes of people; schools are not enough for this; the first ten years of human life are spent in the hands of mothers, relatives, and other women; at that early age much is learned, and much more can be learned; what a difference would result between a childhood spent among educated women and our present childhood, which is still being suckled on miserable advice![22]

One might criticize the excessively demanding tasks—the excessively heavy responsibilities—that seem to be attributed here only to women. It must be remembered that Ramírez is confronting the functions that women *already* had in the Mexican nineteenth century. However, even if one champions more egalitarian family structures, where the various adults collaborate in a more or less equal way, Ramírez's observations retain value. The environments in which we are raised and educated as the human animals we are—in very diverse family structures—constitute the first sphere of public life. This sensitive sphere, immensely receptive to influences, is often decisive in the good or bad construction of the other spheres of society. At the very least, it encourages human animals in formation to ingrain or discard certain desires, beliefs, and emotions early on. For example, in childhood, the desires for collaboration and necessary integration with others can become attractive, or we can assume attitudes proper to arrogant reason, and despise in advance those who "are not like us," without even allowing them to speak to us. (In some sectors of Latin America, those who have a different skin color, or different economic possibilities, or even those who speak a little differently than we do, are often considered to be "not like us.")

Furthermore, this first sphere of the public which is the family—any form of family—becomes a sounding box: It spreads the desires, beliefs, or emotions promoted within it, and propagates them, above all, in that second sphere of the public which is articulated by the neighborhood and schools, or any type of more or less formalized education. Thus, from these earliest stages of the construction of society—largely affective, but also inextricably epistemic—we construct ourselves as social multipliers of exclusion or integration. Moreover, for better or worse, the sounding boxes which are the various social spheres of the public not only transmit integrations or exclusions, they also strengthen them. Ramírez is right: for any society, what a difference there will be between a childhood spent within a family that promotes collaboration among its members and a childhood that only receives lessons in arrogant reason.

THE POLITICAL CLAIM FOR THE SOCIAL EXCLUSION OF "DAY LABORERS": CAMPESINOS OR WORKERS

Concerning the "day laborers," Ramírez suggests a teleology analogous, but not identical, to the one he proposed for women. The starting point is the same: like many groups of women, "day laborers" in the nineteenth century barely survived (only in the nineteenth century?) in a condition often close to slavery. Regarding the "day laborer," Ramírez observes that, "as a slave, nothing belongs to him, neither his family nor his existence; and food is not a right for this man-machine, but an obligation to preserve himself for the service of his owners."[23] Thus, in this intense preoccupation with exclusion—of indigenous people, women, and "day laborers"—we find the outlines of models for rethinking freedom as nonexclusion, or positively as social integration. These forms of exclusion are still part of Mexico today, and more generally of Latin America, so to continue elaborating models of nonexclusion and social integration, I will take just take a moment to review—extremely quickly, really—how the nomadic epistemology of one of the most important Mexican philosophers of the second half of the twentieth century, Luis Villoro (1922–2014), once again dissolves, with his claims, the false opposition between abstract universalism and cultural particularism.[24]

III

Whoever skims through the numerous writings of Villoro will immediately discover the nomadism of his thinking.[25] His first books start from urgent claims in those turbulent and hopeful years at the end of the first half of the twentieth century: *Los grandes momentos del indigenismos en México* and *El Proceso ideológico de la revolución de independencia*.[26] (One might say, somewhat arrogantly, "Two problems very much in the grip of 'cultural particularism' and not too promising for beginning a philosophical career!") But perhaps even more important was Villoro's claim about the injustices suffered by the indigenous peoples of Mexico, as well as the "impure" plurality of cultures. (The concern for the "purity" of a culture, of a tradition, of identity, of a bloodline, even of an academic discipline, is anything but pure. Sooner or later it is usually revealed as a sinister concern: as a tool of exclusion. And then one can persecute and annihilate the Other, and generally, any other that is considered "impure.") More precisely, it is noteworthy that general theories of social change and the mixing of cultures never lost Villoro's interest. Moreover, they were problems that tormented him throughout his life.

Despite his diverse concerns, Villoro did not confuse philosophy with the sentimental pamphlet, or what is worse, with that facile and strident culture of a lot of journalism that, in the mass media of Latin America, often wants to pass itself off as philosophy. In this regard, it is worth recalling some of the uses he deployed of the strategy of detours. In *El idea y el ente en la filosofía de Descartes* (1965), Villoro seeks to recover the "process of reason that goes from unfounded judgment to evident judgment," the epistemic process by which we abandon beliefs lacking sufficient support—among which false and biased beliefs have a decisive place—to acquire beliefs that possess it.[27] At the same time, *El concepto de ideología y otros ensayos*, opposes ideological beliefs, whose function is to ingrain the prevailing understandings that support power, to critical beliefs, or as he calls them "disruptive" beliefs.[28] These and other uses of the strategy of detours find a first culmination in his great book, *Creer, saber, conocer*, an original and meticulous epistemology, at least apparently in the most rigorous analytical tradition.[29] I indicated that "at least apparently" since, already in the prologue, Villoro formulates political claims that are uncommon in the epistemology of this tradition (at least up to the time of Villoro's writing). For example, he asks: "How does human reason work, throughout history, to reinforce situations of domination or, on the contrary, to free us from our restraints?"[30]

These and other uses of the strategy of detours led him to books with more direct moral and political claims: *El poder y el valor: Fundamentos de una ética política*; *Estado plural, pluralidad de culturas*; *Los retos de la sociedad por venir: Ensayos sobre justicia, democracia y multiculturalismo*; and his posthumous book, *La alternativa: Perspectivas y posibilidades de cambio*.[31] In these last writings, Villoro appeals once again to the strategy of transitions and resumes his concern for analyzing, from general perspectives, concrete claims. He had already made this strategy his own in his first two books and never stopped using it in his constant journalistic contributions.[32] (In these works, Villoro usually illuminates a concrete problem, e.g. social inequalities in Mexico, with abstract reflections and general theories about society and justice). But along with the situations of exclusion in Latin America—which he never ceased to attend to and often suffered from—Villoro was especially struck by uprising in Mexico, in 1994, of the Zapatista Army of National Liberation (EZLN) against indigenous exclusion. In this regard, I cannot forget the scandal that would arise in seeing the image of Villoro, one of the patriarchs of Mexican culture, in Zapatista videos, sitting next to Subcomandante Marcos and the other members of the EZLN discussing liberalism and communitarianism, even arguments and theories that are much appreciated in the Headquarters of Power and Thought, for example arguments and theories of Jürgen Habermas and John Rawls.[33] Against those thinkers, among other objections, Villoro insisted: in addition to a positive and abstract theory of justice, it is urgent to appeal to a negative and concrete path, and to bring both ways of thinking into dialogue. Because according to Villoro, it is not possible to think about justice without *simultaneously* elaborating theorizations, with nomadic thought, about diverse experiences of exclusion like the ones pointed out by Ramírez: for being an indigenous person, for being a woman, for being poor, for being a refugee, for being a disabled person. However, Villoro does not limit himself to pointing out this or that exclusion, but offers a nonstatic theory of justice. In this sense, I tend to disagree with Ambrosio Velasco, according to whom "Villoro's negative way does not presuppose any concept of justice in order to confirm the injustice existing in contemporary societies. It starts from the injustice suffered by human beings in contemporary societies, without questioning whether the sufferings endured by men and women of flesh and blood are truly 'injustices.'"[34] I suspect that one cannot qualify, and before that articulate, experiences without having some more or less precise, more or less vague concepts to articulate and qualify them. I recall the Kantian dictum: that intuitions without concepts are blind, and concepts without intuitions are empty. On the other hand, in Villoro *there is a theory of justice as nonexclusion but also as social collaboration*. It is inevitable: we have to think and apply the concept of justice, moving, with nomadic thought, between the negative and positive ways, a particular case of moving, with nomadic thought, between abstract universalism and cultural particularism.[35]

Let us examine for a moment some of the structures of this radical republicanism, in pursuit of justice as a *process* in several stages:

- *The experience of exclusion* is conceptualized as harm: an offense that oppresses. Because "to be excluded is not to be part of the totality just like anyone else, not to be fully recognized in the totality, not to have a place in it just like everyone else."³⁶ By these "totalities," Villoro means both societies and any social group whose fair integration is not incompatible with the freedom of its members.

- *Seeking to equate the excluded with "that which excludes,"* whether a certain organization of a society, a powerful group, or individuals (often a mixture of all of these). In seeking this equalization, the excluded person resists and makes demands.

- *Struggle or recognition.* When claims are made, a war may break out between the excluded and those who exclude them, or else the rights of the excluded may be recognized. If the latter happens, "the vindication of the excluded can then lead to the promulgation of universalizable norms," for example, the positive path of human rights.³⁷ Thus, norms of justice are established, at least as the legal structure of a society.

With the postulation of this scheme—analogous but not identical to Ramírez's teleologies—we seek to begin to respond to the claims of non-integration, which in various regions of Latin America, although not exclusively there, have been formulated since time immemorial, as Ramírez pointed out a century and a half ago, regarding indigenous peoples, women, and "day laborers," among others.

In this regard, it would be of the utmost importance to discuss step by step the detailed and acute article by Gregory Pappas, "The Limitations and Dangers of Decolonial Philosophies: Lessons from Zapatista Luis Villoro."³⁸ In what follows, I will only sketch some preliminary points. I will introduce a difference of emphasis from Pappas, rather than a real disagreement with him. Pappas points out:

> The Latin American approach shared by decolonialists and Villoro can be contrasted with an atomistic approach to problems of injustice. The atomistic approach is one that stresses the particularity of an injustice by neglecting history, and in general the relation of that event with others or with structural causes.³⁹

In other words, the atomistic perspective is typical of static epistemology and ignores the strategies of transitions and detours. Regarding the strategy of transitions, Pappas emphasizes the need to start from passages that articulate the most concrete experiences. Pappas quotes Villoro's second letter to

Subcomandante Marcos: "Our starting point should be our present particular experiences of marginalization and injustices."[40] Pappas opposes this perspective with that of decolonialists and their tendency to take general theories, about the world system and dependency, as a starting point. Thus, Pappas observes:

> The quest for a comprehensive explanation and a grand historical narrative is also in danger of not capturing the historical and concrete particularity (pluralism, complexity, uniqueness) of actual injustices. When we start at the broad level of globality and historicity as decolonialists often do, there is a risk of oversimplifying and encouraging blindness about concrete injustices.[41]

Pappas is partly right: Sometimes, remaining in a point of view that is too broad makes us blind to the particular. These extremely general "philosophies of history"—since they do have to be called something—that seem to explain everything, not only do not genuinely explain anything, but are also of little or no use for concrete action, for what matters most: the politics they claim to guide. However, with this reasoning Pappas seems to succumb to a version of the first false opposition we discussed, between abstract universalism and cultural particularism. Hence, perhaps many decolonialists attack Pappas by observing that introducing that form of arrogant reason that is colonial reason has—on the one hand—a certain explanatory power. But it will surely be pointed out, on the other hand, that concentrating too much on particular experiences brings us back to the atomistic conception that Pappas himself began by criticizing. It is not, therefore, a question of condemning oneself to a static epistemology and choosing between experiences and attention to concrete circumstances or else general and even universal theories; rather, starting from a nomadic epistemology, we can use the strategy of transitions to go from one to the other and vice versa: to dissolve this false opposition and to study the reciprocal determinations between the particular and the general, in an endless spiral.

However, where do we begin by gathering materials to build a just society?

In one of our last conversations, in the hallway of our Institute, where we warned about the danger of turning the exchange of arguments—so characteristic of philosophy—into a parlor game or a vice, that sort of "rationalizing" which sometimes turns into a merely ceaseless, aimless ruminating, the old professor pointed out that: "Sometimes you have to think and reason, but other times you have to look, listen and feel."[42] I cannot think of a more succinct way to summarize the principle of what I mean by nomadic thinking.

I will now formulate a further principle of this way of thinking as follows:

> *Investigate by going from living and self-understanding*
> *to thinking with rigor and reasoning with no less rigor;*
> *investigate also by looking, listening, and feeling*
> *with discernment here and there and vice versa.*
> *But do not neglect that between living,*
> *thinking, looking, listening, and feeling, complex*
> *counterpoints are often established.*

It is worth examining a little how the strategies of transitions and detours that were used in the brief discussion of some texts by Ignacio Ramírez and Luis Villoro, as well as the principles of nomadic thinking, noted in passing, are claims that have become "resources." Resources in what sense?

Caution: Following the resonances of the word "resources" in the next section, the direction of the reflection is completely modified, and other materials are introduced. This abrupt change, in some sense *methodological* (for lack of a better word to describe the change), returns to the reflections of the beginning of this chapter, to support once again the attempts to dissolve the false opposition between abstract universalism and cultural particularism.

IV

Once more we make use of the claim:

> *Be careful with words.*

I therefore propose, first of all, to carry out what might be called "a small exercise in ordinary language philosophy," comparing the use of the English word "resource," with the Spanish word "*recurso*," its usual translation. In English, a common use of the word "resource" refers to:

1. A means to achieve something, or

2. The ability to deal with a situation effectively.

The second sense can be understood as a refinement of the first: the ability to know how to use those means effectively. A third common use refers to:

3. An available supply, available capital.

In this sense, one refers to a rich country, a rich tradition, or a rich person, because it is a country, tradition, or person with many resources. Regarding the Spanish word *recurso*, we also find the uses already noted in relation to the English word "resource," but there is more. The word *recurso* is also used as

4. A demand against something.

This last use can be found in phrases like *"recursos de apelación,"* the complaint filed to revoke a decision: the resources of appeal. However, why should we focus on words like "resources," *recursos*, as well as other claims? Manuel Vargas has proposed that we think of philosophy in general, and therefore of Latin American and Mexican philosophy in particular, as a "cultural resource."[43] I would like to concentrate for a moment on his reasoning. Afterward I will reconstruct the observations of Robert Eli Sanchez Jr., understanding them not as objections to Vargas's argument, but as nomadic observations: important nuances and complements.[44]

Vargas starts from the truth of the following statements:

- There are cultural differences.
- Cultural differences can have consequences.[45]

Among these consequences, there is the fact that each culture has different resources (sense 3). Vargas characterizes a cultural resource as: "any entity, practice, pattern of judgment, or collection thereof whose nature and origin depends at least in part on the shared norms of a community of intentional agents."[46] He adds that cultural resources are means to achieve certain ends effectively (senses 1 and 2 of "resources"), namely: such resources "tend to have a *cultural utility*. Cultural utility is anything that assists in the flourishing, survival, or perpetuation of a given culture, understood in very broad ways."[47] As examples of this cultural utility, Vargas points to the humanities and, among them, to philosophy:

> The humanities, those oft-underestimated disciplines in the university system, are deeply interested in the production and preservation of complex cultural resources. The discipline of philosophy is a species of this more general project of producing and preserving complex cultural resources. Philosophy shares with other disciplines the general task of discovering, constructing, and preserving complex ideas with a wide degree of cultural utility.[48]

As already suggested by the title of his article, "On the Value of Philosophy: The Latin American Case," if good Latin American philosophy has value, it must have it like any good philosophy. Let me add: adopting a nomadic thinking, its principles, and its strategy of detours and transitions is a good way to *try* to do good philosophy *anywhere*. More precisely, as one goes back and forth between abstract universalism and cultural particularism, complex ideas are discovered and constructed beyond the usual problems and arguments.

Suppose—an assumption that Vargas does *not* have to make—that the "resources of cultural utility" are exclusively understood as what we can call "affirmative values" or resources that add to established theories: resources *added* to the arguments or existing methodologies, but without criticizing or questioning them. The "resources of cultural utility" would be reduced to introducing additions in a repertoire that is part, for example, of a static epistemology, in which there is no epistemic nomadism. We know in advance the types of questions to ask and the types of answers required, so formulating other types of questions and giving other answers is forbidden. (The anxiety to exclude, with hostility, everything that is not in direct continuity with what matters to *me*, given my beliefs, desires, and emotions, is also a general epistemic vice, not only a colonial one.)

In this way, not only is the fourth use of the Spanish term *recurso* being forgotten: as a demand against something. More importantly, it is suppressing a task that, as already noted, has been and is constitutive of philosophy: on the one hand, the critical thinking that affects a specific topic in a singular, focal way, sometimes coming from a cultural particularity; and, on the other hand, how philosophy also tends to affect things in a general way, as a challenge to a whole way of understanding knowledge, society, life, reality; claims that are often made when transitions are adopted toward universalistic perspectives.

These omissions and suppressions—these suicidal *fetishes* for philosophy—are precisely what Robert Eli Sanchez Jr. fears happen when the value of philosophy is introduced with the notion of "cultural resources." Thus, Sanchez points out that this is a way in which the emphatically critical, negative value that philosophy must have is neglected: "the value of radically destroying pretenses, traditions, and cultural norms and of injecting a sense of uncanniness, not-knowing, and solitude into our lives."[49] In this regard, Robert Sanchez rightly insists on understanding philosophy as epistemic nomadism that, from time to time, becomes extreme and branches out, and is formulated as a general challenge calling for what we considered, from our discussion of Carlos Sánchez in Chapter 1, as a "violent reading."

Or, according to Robert Sanchez: "philosophy as the disruption of an entire culture": "What is potentially valuable is not only what distinguishes it, but a challenge to the kind of question we ask about it or the kind of answer that satisfies us."[50] In this way, Robert Sanchez underlines the importance of the strategy of detours in philosophical work: "This awareness raises ... particular questions inside philosophy about the value of diversity."[51] But not only that; with this awareness, Robert Sanchez attends to the strategy of transitions, as he introduces in particular, "critically important questions about whether the nature of philosophy is determined in part by who participates, and how we should respond if it is."[52]

It is not by chance, then, that based on these observations, Robert Sanchez can conclude in part (although *only* in part) against Vargas, by pointing out that: "Philosophy does produce, preserve, and propagate complex cultural resources—certainly. But it can also disrupt and destabilize our grip on the manifestations of a tradition or a way of life."[53] In this passage, it is important to be careful with the words "disrupt,"[54] in the sense of producing disruptive thinking, and "destabilize." In this way, Robert Sanchez is right not to neglect the negative, critical, therapeutic value of philosophy or, in general, of culture. But he is not right in considering that this value cannot also be subsumed under the expression "cultural resources" or, more explicitly, "resources of cultural utility." We must not forget the comprehensive, extremely friendly, and even in some respects nomadic sense with which Vargas introduces the concept of cultural utility: "anything that assists in the flourishing, survival, or perpetuation of a given culture, understood in very broad ways." In addition, anomalous philosophers who were extremely challenging—such as Socrates, Kierkegaard, and Wittgenstein, or in Mexico, for example, Villoro, or in the rest of Latin America, Jose Martí or Carlos Vaz Ferreira—offered "resources" in the sense of claims for the "flourishing, survival, or perpetuation," not only of philosophical culture, but of their societies. Hence, the singular and general criticisms, as well as the challenges and therapies, are also essential "cultural resources." Taking up this lesson, we can then *re*-formulate that principle of nomadic thinking, the *maxim of data, fetishes, and materials*, as a *maxim of data, fetishes, resources, and demands*.

With an ascending passage, I will return for a moment to deal with the arrogant use of reason that I began to explore in Chapter 1.

V

At some points in this chapter I have explicitly alluded to an arrogant attitude. (But at other times, one may suspect arrogance is also lurking, manifest or latent). With arrogance, Mexican philosophy is cornered into adopting a static epistemology in the face of the false opposition between abstract universalism and cultural particularism. Arrogance was also assumed by those who consider it unpromising to begin a philosophical career using the strategy of transitions from studies as particular as indigenism in Mexico and the ideology of the Mexican Revolution.[55]

However, both attacks are, if I am not mistaken, only indications of a relatively common way of dealing badly with thought, and, more comprehensively, with culture and life. That is why I dared to propose as a basic mode of disorientation, not only in philosophy but in general, what I called "arrogant reason," and as one version, colonial reason. (There are other equally dangerous versions of arrogant reason, racial reason and technocratic reason, that are not necessarily identified with colonial reason). In *Los retos de la sociedad por venir*, Villoro opposes arrogant reason to *the reasonable*: "Beliefs and norms are reasonable, in fact, that do not express 'arrogant reason' (Carlos Pereda), but a reasonable exercise of justice; reasonable also is a political theory that leads to an effective democracy; and the relationship between cultures, isn't it supposed to be reasonable if it is not exclusionary?"[56]

In Chapter 1, I examined the maxims with which arrogant reason is actualized in practice. Repeating thoughts, even if their formulation is only slightly modified, sometimes constitutes a way of clarifying them and even of continuing to elaborate them. That is why I will take a moment—I hope it will not be too boring—to repeat these maxims.

One or several agents might fall prey to arrogant reasoning when they refuse to investigate unusual problems with the strategy of detours, for example, the authority of a philosophical canon, to call into question prestigious or at least traditional distinctions, to ponder arguments about social inequality and homophobia, or with the strategy of transitions, going from the particular, from concrete situations and even individual oppression, to the general—a radical change of political regime—and vice versa.

Alfonso Reyes (1889–1959) had already warned, some time before the philosophers that Orosco includes as "culturalists" (among others, several members of the Hyperion group): "the only way to be profitably national is to be generously universal."[57] According to the strategy of transitions, it is also worth taking into account, with Zea, the inverse warning: the only way to be profitably universal is to be generously national, and, perhaps, even generously personal.[58] With arrogant reason, instead of using these strategies, one only seeks to display a belonging. Of course, reducing one's identity to a "prestigious affiliation" represses deficiencies and protects us. This first maxim of arrogant reason commands: *Act by exhibiting an affiliation*. In turn, this affiliation receives, in support, emphatic disdain or contempt, and on occasion, militant persecution. For example, to anyone who proposes a course in Mexican philosophy, explicitly or implicitly some variation of the *license to marginalize* will be repeated. This second maxim of arrogant reason commands: *Act justifying yourself with disdain or contempt.*

On the other hand, arrogant uses of reason immunize one's own presuppositions as implicit. The agent firmly rejects, in advance, both local and general critical claims. Thus, the third maxim of arrogant reason commands: *Faced with difficulties about your affiliate identity, shield yourself.*

It is useful to put these last two maxims of arrogant reasoning directly (and the first one indirectly) in contact with the rejection of nomadism and the *pars pro toto* fallacy. Why? Justifying oneself with disdain or contempt, and shielding oneself from critical questions, is a way of fixating on the *part* that one is and overvaluing it (however small and unimportant it may be), believing or pretending to believe that it is the *whole*. Predictably, haughtily, it will be repeated that only *this* part matters, so you have to hold on to it. This holding onto is, of course, a way of preventing the very possibility of a vital and epistemic nomadism: a way of denying that beyond that *part* to which we cling, there is reality.

I return yet again to the concerns with which we began this chapter: "In what sense would it matter to teach courses in Mexican philosophy?" Or, even more generally, "Does Latin American philosophy have any importance?" The answer proposed to questions such as these is simple: Such courses are a matter of expanding the tradition, of enriching it. However, what are the grounds for this claim? Why would we be enriched by listening to different, even idiosyncratic voices with perhaps quite unique stories? As an example, two thinkers were briefly examined: Ignacio Ramírez and Luis Villoro. In both, we find reasons for the defense of a practical virtue: rejecting identity politics as a politics of exclusion. This was, of course, about the nonexclusion of social groups: indigenous people, women, day laborers, disabled people.... But as soon as we consider the demand for nonexclusion, especially once we rethink it with care and a nomadic, centrifugal imagination, its impetus becomes unstoppable.

Hence, on a level that I consider to be methodological, efforts toward nonexclusion are also found to be an epistemic virtue: "a resource of cultural utility," to use the words of Manuel Vargas. Moreover, the efforts of philosophy (in part) have been and will continue to be, on pain of committing suicide, to *re-found* and *transplant* voices. In this way we can revivify arguments that align with our beliefs, or are counterpoints to them, or are even harshly polemical of them. Moreover, one rarely knows in advance where the counterexamples will come from.[59] On the other hand, many of the criticisms, when added together, *interrupt* current discourses, and thus they produce something more than mere criticism: they generate freedom. In this way, as Robert Sanchez Jr. points out, we are invited to introduce other demands, different from those we are used to formulating and satisfying, which produce strangeness and can eventually destabilize an entire culture. This is another way of remembering that if we want to think deeply and rigorously, it is not a good method to refuse to *integrate* different positions, even marginal positions, or rather, positions that are degraded as such.

CHAPTER 3

Inconvenient Mexican Thinkers, and Irreverent Claims

In Mexico the question "Who are you when you are Mexican?," or even the claim of characterizing *the* Mexican, is ancient. There are those who vaguely place it years after the Spanish conquest, and *La grandeza mexicana* (Mexican greatness) by Bernardo de Balbuena (1562–1627) is already testimony to the concerns accentuated by the country's independence. However, as identity politics, the problem is usually raised beginning with the dictatorship of Porfirio Díaz and its aim of elevating Mexico, linking it to the *glamor* of Paris, and *Frenchifying* it: as expressing the consciousness of national unity, starting—paradoxically—with the flashiest philosophy of the time: Comte's positivism in various versions.[1] (Another symptom of colonial vices such as *subaltern fervor*, and so of that version of arrogant reason, colonial reason, which is still so strongly entrenched in some regions of Latin America, or at least in some behaviors of those regions.)

I

Within the group of *Porfirian scientists* in the cabinet of Porfirio Díaz (real addicts of technocratic reason), Justo Sierra (1848–1912) proposed that social problems in México must be attended by way of a specific cultural particularism: the study of Mexican nature and history.[2] Sierra's proposals, and even more so, the excitement caused by the Mexican Revolution of 1910 that overthrew Díaz, were the impetus for a young group to reflect on their national reality. They were called the "Ateneo de la Juventud" (Athenaeum of Youth, 1909–1914). Among those young people was the philosopher and educator Antonio Caso (1883–1946), and the philosopher, writer, politician, and educator, José Vasconcelos (1882–1959). According to Guillermo

Hurtado, "Mexican philosophy in those years is largely summarized by the work of both these thinkers."³ In the postrevolutionary period, a disciple of Caso, Samuel Ramos (1897–1959), continued these reflections in the then influential book, *El perfil del hombre y la cultura en México* (Profile of man and culture in Mexico).⁴ Ramos is inspired by the historicism—or perspectivism—of José Ortega y Gasset, and curiously by the psychology of Alfred Adler. Thus, Ramos discovers or diagnoses or proposes that "*the* Mexican" finds himself pierced by contradiction, between the indigenous past as traumatic history, and the superficial imitation of the West—what we have gathered from the reflections of Chapter 1, such as the crushing vices of *subaltern fervor* and *craving for novelty*—. This contradiction creates in *the* Mexican a serious "inferiority complex" that makes him distrust himself and everyone else. Ramos illustrates the ideal type or, to be more precise, the ghost that haunts *the* Mexican and often traps him and compels him to mimic "*el pelado*" or "*el peladito*." This character, which already appears in the literary work of the Novohispanic writer Fernández de Lizardi (1776–1827), becomes many years later a public icon of film. It is taken up with acuity, sometimes to the point of nausea, by the actor Mario Moreno, in his role as *Cantinflas*, with its unfortunately affected language, the *cantinfleo*, that confusion without saying anything, that evasion of the situation, but with many, many words: with a suffocating number of words. Nevertheless, in the films themselves (especially the earliest ones, filmed in black and white in the 1940s), the "relaxed" type (*relajiento*) personified by Cantinflas introduces a horizon of normality—and direct communication with the viewer—in contrast to the other characters, who all seem to be exaggerated updates of the "uptight" type—I am using the typology from Jorge Portilla's *Fenomenología del relajo*. The "uptight" type is one who is overwhelmed, and continues to overwhelm, not only in offices of the bureaucracy, but everywhere, encompassing many people who consider themselves to be "intellectuals."

There is no doubt: getting rid of these destructive ghosts, traumas from a past still present, superficial imitations of the West, etc., ... and renewing the politics of Mexican identity did not cease to be of interest to the generations following Ramos. However, those concerns were soon taken up from a different theoretical point of view: German phenomenology, with the study (or unintentionally imitative parody) of Heidegger and French existentialism, particularly Sartre. Although these and other phenomenologists and existentialists were not unknown in Mexico, an enormous effort to *transplant* these schools of thought was made by José Gaos, the illustrious teacher who fled the Franco dictatorship. Inspired by their teacher, a group of young professors and students, who were to some extent his disciples, organized themselves as a research group and called themselves *Hyperion* (*Hiperión*, 1948–1952).⁵ Why that name? According to Hesiod's *Theogony*, Hyperion is the titan son of Gaia and Uranus, who linked abstract universalism (Heaven) with cultural particularism (Earth). The philosophers of this group tried to do something similar in their reflections. The strategy of transitions, which I use in the reflections in this book, is also a way of achieving this purpose.

The group received a lot of publicity from the mass media of the time. From there it received *as a philosophical group* exceptional and lasting notoriety. On the other hand, as can be seen from some allusions, most of its members were public intellectuals and, to a greater or lesser degree, they became protagonists in the Mexican culture of that time, some with close relationships with writers, historians, journalists, anthropologists, economists, and also with important figures in politics and government. This situation can make one wonder: Does the growing "professionalization" of philosophy imply the isolation of those who practice it from other cultural activities and various social undertakings, as has often in fact happened in Mexico and other places?

But let us return to one of our concerns: Why is it thought that in philosophical reflection, and perhaps in any reflection, it is most useful to go from the concrete and particular to the abstract and general, and vice versa, from the abstract to the concrete, evaluating in each case what concreteness and what abstraction is appropriate? Without particular analyses of a situation, abstractions tend to become empty. But without the frames of reference of the abstractions, one tends not to fully grasp the meaning of concrete analyses, or even to understand why they are carried out.⁶ Did the *Hyperiones*, as they were often affectionately called, fulfill their purpose of uniting the abstractions of Heaven with the concreteness of Earth? Were they able to wander from one side to the other without losing their way? I will try to respond to these concerns a little—but only a little—by rereading the most controversial of the Hyperiones, Emilio Uranga, as well as a sharp critic of the movement, José Revueltas.

II

In a letter written on November 7, 1966, José Gaos tells Octavio Paz (1914–1998) that Paz has written "two books about *philosophy* [italics by Gaos], *The Bow and the Lyre* and *The Labyrinth of Solitude*, that are among the best, what the hell, they are the best, of two fruitful movements of our time: the philosophy of poetry and *la filosofía de lo mexicano*."⁷ In turn, shortly before his passing, Luis Villoro pointed out to me—in passing—that his contributions to *la filosofía de lo mexicano* had been minor and circumstantial, and that the only great contribution of the Hyperion group was the suggestive text by Jorge Portilla, and—in more or less these words—"perhaps we need to remember the disparate and not entirely concluded reflections of Uranga." Let us keep in mind that strong friendships, those that do not stop mattering even when they disappear or we critically abandon them, tend to follow us like shadows that we at times do and do not wish to go away forever. My suspicion: that casual remark by Villoro was too guided by humility, affectionate memories, and irritation of a friend who he had once appreciated so much.[8] What do I want to indicate with this suspicion?

There is no doubt that Villoro, out of modesty, did not want to acknowledge that beyond the proposals handled in the Hyperion group, in all his vast work, from his first book, *Los grandes momentos del indigenismo in México* (Great moments of indigenism in Mexico), until his posthumous work, *La alternativa* (The alternative), he makes very intelligent use of the strategies of detours and transitions.[9] In addition to other reflections that are important to retain, we are faced with a heartfelt meditation on Mexico and its problems. Still, I do not want to diminish the subtle and often magnificent descriptions by Jorge Portilla in *Fenomenología del relajo*.[10] Nevertheless, it may be worth examining whether there were other achievements in the Hyperion group as well. I am not referring to the historiographic work of Leopoldo Zea (1912–2004), and his tireless work of promoting the study of the history of ideas in Latin America, nor to his no less influential reflection on this subcontinent. This is a personal work with a separate value. In addition, Zea joined the group when it is already formed.[11] Instead, I am interested in interrogating the contributions of Emilio Uranga (1921–1988). At the time, these contributions were considered the most genuinely representative of the group; some classified his contributions as "extraordinary," even "brilliant." I would almost say, unfortunately, that these exaggerations, rather than describing or clarifying, only excite and briefly madden, or (negatively) scare and spread contempt. But they quickly evaporate without a trace.[12] In any case, why is the name of Uranga made to seem a *nobody*?[13]

Aurelia Valero Pie, in her review of the reissue of Uranga's book, *Análisis del ser del mexicano y otros escritos*, provides two explanations for the perceptions of this *nobody*.[14] The first refers, elegantly, specifically to Uranga: "Those who knew him usually bring to mind his genius and bad temper, the former wasted in the service of the powerful, and the latter expressed in the multiple insults he inflicted on his teachers and colleagues."[15]

Valero's second explanation of the silencing of Uranga is more inclusive: it encompasses all Mexican and (I would dare to generalize) Latin Americans philosophers. Valero cites Abelardo Villegas, according to whom Gaos commented one day, "In Europe, there were not only great philosophers, but also those who told them they valued them and gave them a suitable echo. Meanwhile, among the Mexican philosopher there was a kind of cannibalism, they devoured each other, or in the worst of cases, their works fell into a conspiracy of silence, as if nobody had written anything."[16]

Regarding Uranga's oblivion, another explanation could be added to these: the Heideggerian language that he uses. Indeed, in the years following Gaos's translation of *Being and Time*, this language unleashed in Latin American philosophy, even more than *subaltern fervor*, a *subaltern epidemic*. It became such jargon, such *cantinfleo*, that it was extremely difficult to distinguish between genuine contributions to thought, and those supposedly academic articles, which were, in reality, nothing more than parodies of Heidegger.[17]

In what follows, I will propose only a brief argumentative reading, one that is extremely tentative and far too unfriendly, as a first approximation to fragments of the obscure chapter 2—although central to Uranga's thought—of the previously mentioned *Análisis del ser del mexicano*, perhaps his most significant systematic text.[18] In my argumentative reading, I will resist two common temptations of explanatory history: a perverse use of the genetic fallacy (interpreting thoughts based on the worst aspects of biography) and the retrospective fallacy (interpreting thoughts using the author's later texts and positions). Sometimes thoughts, if they are strong, have a life of their own, beyond the one who thinks them and their history. Denying that certain thoughts have a life of their own makes us incapable of understanding why an explanatory history of thought and its no less explanatory glosses and readings are not enough: it makes us incapable of understanding why we can learn from past thought. Perhaps with respect to Uranga, his contemporaries overestimated the power of his thoughts, being carried away by the fascination with his celebrity (which is not uncommon in these regions).

In chapter 2 of *Análisis del ser del mexicano*, Uranga starts by signaling a certain "constitutional insufficiency in our manner of being," which is how Uranga reconstructs, ontologically, the "inferiority complex" to which Ramos referred.[19] From this reconstruction Uranga posits his well-known thesis about the ontology of the accident:

> Insufficiency, ontologically speaking, determines the accident in relation to substance. *Every modality of being grounded on accident is characterized by a lack of ground*, grounded on a shifting and fractured base. The accident is a *minus* of being, a being reduced or "fragmented" due to its mixture with nothingness.[20]

From that "fragmented" being, Uranga observes (but then, strangely, abandons the thought, although it would be useful to his project):

> In the accident there exists that *Werden* (*to become*), that transit and movement that Hegel elevated to the condition of "true" reality, inasmuch as the extremes as such, on their own and in their isolation, are "abstract and ideal." What is concrete is the movement itself.... On the other hand, substance is plenitude or fullness of being.[21]

Perhaps a way to translate and interpret this passage—which I consider important, but in which words like "history" or "historicity" are significantly missing—is as follows: what exists finds itself necessarily in "transit and movement." What there is are processes, and therefore never a finished substance. Furthermore, in several precarious processes, the wills of human animals intervene decisively, leaving, for better or worse, their sometimes deep tracks. Thus, these processes become stories; stories that humans develop in conditions not often of their choosing, and which in turn make them and break them. As a result, perhaps human animals are, at bottom, accidents that appear and wander from one place to another. They are nomads. Sometimes the stories of this nomadism involve crossing deserts or seas. Nomadism can become internalized and subjective at times. The mind wanders while the body remains still. Obviously: human animals are often unmoving travelers.

Shortly after the passage under discussion, Uranga signals that the being of humans is "ontologically accidental," which seems to confirm the previous observations. However, Uranga does not conceptualize the accidental character of being as that nomadic character that is its historicity. Instead, he makes a descending transition in his thought, a transition toward the concrete, and transforms an ontology into an anthropology, and even into a paralyzing politics of identity. Uranga writes: "The insufficiency of the Mexican is the insufficiency of his being as accidental."[22] It may be pointless to clarify this, but I do not think there are good reasons to criticize either the ascending or the descending uses of the strategy of transitions. I do not discredit political philosophers when, starting from certain abstractions, they use the descending strategy to carry out social criticism, even devastating social criticism, like those made by José Martí, Rosario Castellanos, the Frankfurt School, or Michel Foucault. I only object to the way Uranga uses that strategy in *this* case.

On the other hand, as a way of reaffirming his position, Uranga contrasts it with religious tradition. In this tradition, man is "being for substance":

being that must make itself substance. We define the being of the Mexican in precisely opposite terms. As a "being for accident," its being is a *having to be an accident*. . . . Similarly, if we say that the being of the human being is accidental, what we mean is that it must accidentalize itself, that the accident is not "given," but "proposed," as a project to be realized; we would say, "it must be realized." *To realize oneself as accident means that one must maintain oneself as accident.*[23]

Again, I formulate a translation or interpretation. Thinking of the human animal as a "being for accident" avoids thinking of it as a "given," entirely and once and for all, as a substance: a destiny. Instead, "with authenticity" one must think of it as a set of tasks that must be realized: an "open" and contingent reality that must not hide itself, deceiving itself by renouncing its freedom, and therefore becoming inhuman by thinking of itself as a "being for substance." The echoes of Jean-Paul Sartre are undeniable: we are not a complete being. We are animals marked by history. The essence of man consists in its unpredictable existence.

Surely, even among those who participate in the horizon this language opens up—in such a conceptual framework—an objection will have arisen, one which I already put forward (a possibly inappropriate use of the strategy of transitions), and that Uranga himself recognizes: "by affirming that the being of the Mexican is accidental, we have thereby defined the general human condition in which the Mexican participates." Uranga's response to this objection is that:

> we are not very certain of the existence of man in general and, second, that whatever passes itself off as man in general, namely, generalized European humanity, does not appear to us to define itself as accidental but precisely as arrogant substantiality.[24]

I find this response unsatisfactory. First, the expression "man in general" is an abstraction that is used in the strategy of transitions; an abstraction that may or may not be a useful tool for understanding and explaining processes and concrete entities. Therefore, it is not a question of judging the existence or non-existence of such abstractions, but their usefulness or uselessness in the task of theoretical elucidation or practical action—moral, legal, political—what is proposed in each situation. That is why the use of the expression "man in general," in addition to referencing a certain well determined species of animal (which is not a dispensable use at all, despite possible accusations of sexism and speciesism), can still retain other practical uses—moral, legal, political—, such as when one defends "human rights."

Second, criticizing the expression "man in general"—because with its usage one refers to a "generalized European humanity," which is not usually characterized as "being for accident" but as "arrogant substantiality"—moves too quickly from general ontology to social criticism (as already noted). Well, if as Uranga rightly points out, "man is constitutionally accidental," then hiding him, or rather, repressing him, and then praising him excessively, as the European does, as a "being for substance," is nothing more than succumbing to that form of arrogant reason that is colonial reason.[25] However, Uranga does not follow this path, and whoever thinks he does, has to de-ontologize him. (One would also have to politicize him in the opposite direction from what he himself chose in his later years. But is this observation not already falling victim to the retrospective fallacy?)

Third, I add yet another dissatisfaction linked to the first. By implicitly using the strategy of transitions, Uranga reconciles too quickly, and without the empirical examinations that such reconciliations would require, passages with high degrees of abstraction with others that include concrete observations. Thus, under the "originary phenomenon of accidentality of the Mexican," Uranga simply subsumes all the supposed properties that he and the other Hyperiones verified or believed themselves to have verified—or fantasized—in Mexicans (from which social class?, from which region in Mexico?, at what moment in history?): the inferiority complex, resentment, hypocrisy, cynicism.[26] Above all: *zozobra* and *nepantla*.[27] What is alluded to by these last beautiful, lovely little words? Uranga appropriates the word *zozobra* (anxiety, anguish) from the poetry of Ramon López Velarde, and turns it into a concept to refer to what he considers the temperament of *the* Mexican.[28] At the same time, Uranga takes up the Nahuatl word *nepantla*, which means inhabiting the contradiction without seeking to overcome it.[29] (Is it something like a Hegelian *Aufhebung* without synthesis?) Uranga indicates: "In the state of *zozobra* we do not know what to do, we vacillate between one 'law' and another, we are 'neutral,' 'in the middle,' '*nepantla.*'"[30] It is worth remembering that independently of Uranga, the indispensable poet and essayist Gloria Anzaldúa (1942–2004), also uses the word *nepantla* to refer to the "unknown land" in which emigrants and descendants of emigrants in the United States barely survive: an *always-in-transition space lacking clear boundaries*.[31] However, one difference should not be neglected. In Uranga the word *nepantla* directly expresses an *ontological structure* of *the* being of the Mexican. By contrast, Anzaldúa articulates, with immense acuity, a *historical condition* of women, men, and children obliged, often illegally, to cross a border. Of course, this condition that never ceases, as an extreme and even limiting condition, shows something of the human condition in general: an inevitably nomadic condition.

III

In his book on Revueltas, Álvaro Ruiz Abreu characterizes Revueltas as a "leftist nomad."[32] Indeed, the nomadism of Revueltas (1914–1976) applies to both his life and his thought. Like Ignacio Ramírez, Revueltas was imprisoned several times in appalling conditions.[33] In addition, at various periods of his life he also survived without a fixed home, moving from one place to another, often with friends and their charity.[34] But in this reflection, Revueltas's nomadic thought is just as important, if not more so. Although first and foremost a storyteller and, in particular, a novelist, Revueltas was also occupied with theoretical controversies as a member of various leftist groups, including the Mexican Communist Party, with which he was affiliated for some time.[35] Revueltas also detested the *cantinfleo* of Marxist language and shunned dogmas and impositions, which allowed him, contrary to various left-wing partisans, a vindication of the anarchist Ricardo Flores Magón.[36] Predictably, in this reflection I focus on his work, "Posibilidades y limitaciones del mexicano" (Possibilities and limitations of the Mexican), as a radical contrast to the reflections of the Hyperion group.[37] The text is not as complex as Uranga's, although it is no less acute. However, in what follows I propose as well a first approximation. I divide the reading into two parts: the critique of *la filosofía de lo mexicano*, which according to Revueltas, is mainly practiced by the Hyperiones, and the proposal itself.[38]

Let us consider the harsh critique. Revueltas observes:

> To speak of a particular "refinement" of the Mexican, or that the Mexican possesses a peculiar "feeling of rivalry," or in the same way a "voice, gesture, and silence" or an "amazement," or a way of feeling "the imaginary and the real," is to claim that certain invariant, universal phenomena are being expressed in an exclusive and differentiated way, due to who knows what mysterious factors, on a subject that in no way is or can be an exclusive and differentiated.[39]

A few pages later, Revueltas makes a similar criticism of the paralyzing identity politics that construct this character, "the Mexican," as described, or perhaps invented—with "light hypotheses" and not without frivolity, according to our author—, by the philosophers of the ontology of the Mexican:

> When intellectuals and professors try to define the Mexican by his sense of death, by his resentment, by his propensity for paradox and by his sexual inhibitions and exclusiveness, they create nothing more than cheap drawing-room fables.[40] The Mexican is not a single type for whom unique laws and definitions exist or ought to be invented, because such a type is to be found nowhere under any circumstances within the modern human conglomeration. The characteristics being passed off as unique to Mexicans (resentment, death consciousness, and so on) are features that have appeared and still appear in other peoples. Even more, these features, in the Mexican himself, are a changing surface, not only throughout history, but throughout a geographical range as well.[41]

The last statement may be confusing or at least misleading, since Revueltas does not argue that "the Mexican" does not exist. According to Revueltas, "the Mexican" does not exist as characterized by *la filosofía de lo mexicano*, because it has paid trifling attention to the "ephemeral data" of character. But then what is Revueltas's proposal?

It is about turning away from a psychology based on casual impressions and toward an actual investigation of the data of history, culture, sociology, and economics. "The Mexican" is the "national being" (like "the Frenchman," "the Swede," "the Chinese"), and according to Revueltas it is as such a construction:

> The national being of a human community cannot exist except on the condition that this community be united in itself by the same language, the same territory, the same economy, and the same culture. The absence of any of these factors causes the human community under discussion to lose its condition of being ... over the course of history the Mexican has not always been the national being (i.e., the Mexican nationality). This means that Mexican national being has an origin and a development.[42]

Revueltas therefore stops not only to examine economic developments—as perhaps a Marxist who has succumbed to that vice, static thinking, would do—but also considers the difficulties arising from the sex trade (the *mestizajes*, the "mixed-races") and, in general, the cultural and political problems that led to the constitution of the "being" of "*the* Mexican." Thus, contrary to what could be called "the white legend," according to Revueltas, the *mestizajes* did not appear because of the supposed nobility and generosity of Spanish domination, but, among other interests, because of "the need to preserve and reproduce the labor force."[43] However, the following statements are more than debatable:

The result of this is that, together with the old nationalities of the Anáhuac, which stands still and lacks historical perspective, and in opposition to the Spanish nationality, despoiler of the land and oppressor of other nationalities, a new nationality arose, a new being that, strictly speaking, can be called the Mexican.[44]

From this statement, Revueltas investigates Mexican attempts at independence from colonial reason (1810, 1910 . . .), and the peculiar contradictions that promote the frequent integrations and disintegrations of this "new being": of this new mestizo nationality. Among these contradictions, Revueltas points out:[45]

- The "dispersed indigenous nationalities," unable to draw on their own traditions and cultures, unify themselves using the Conquistador's weapons: Catholicism and the Spanish language.

- This new nationality is torn between a repressed and dispersed indigenous past, and a Spanish tradition representing oppression.

- Mexican nationality is developing with considerable historical delay: a great number of national states have already carried out their bourgeois revolution.

- Mexican nationality becomes "the national being of Mexico in a world where two phenomena coexist that had not existed in earlier times: imperialism and socialism."[46]

For Revueltas, the claims expressed by these contradictions will be resolved "in the socialist world of tomorrow."[47] Of course, these and other of Revueltas's reconstructions have rightly been discussed in relation to Mexico's historical, cultural, sociological, and economic developments, and its hopes as well. And even if it is assumed that some or many of these reconstructions are untenable, in this reflection what is crucial to emphasize is that the properties which were attributed to "Mexican being" in *la filosofía de lo mexicano* must, according to Revueltas, be redescribed—de-ideologizing them—as a product of "circumstances of economic, sociological, and historical character."[48] However, it is more important not to overlook his statement: those circumstances "are subject to transformation."[49] But why does Revueltas not continue with nomadic thinking regarding the process of social criticism? Why not conclude that *mestizaje* or "Mexican nationality" is *not* the "being of Mexico," whatever is supposed to be meant by that pompous expression? Or even more radically: Why does Revueltas not point out that "nationality" is merely the way in which, once the Mexican state is established, it recognizes its citizens and grants them rights and obligations, as well as an ID card and a passport for crossing borders if other states allow them to do so?

IV

To continue this exercise in nomadic epistemology around the politics of Mexican identity, I appeal again to the strategies of detours and transitions, in a different way—I would say an almost immeasurably different way—than I used them in relation to *la filosofía de lo mexicano*, although I continue to examine its anxieties. So another detour in our thinking. Indeed, in the first decade of the twenty-first century, some media outlets announced—and the news multiplied, backed even by the president of the Republic at the time—that in order to investigate Mexican identity, a transition was needed from ontology to genetics. Consequently, in Mexico it was no longer a question of asking oneself who one is, of scrutinizing "*the* Mexican" on the basis of outmoded speculations, more or less psychological or historical, but of the latest advances in nothing less than genomic science. Thus, if the "nationalization" of ontology was not alarming, perhaps the "nationalization" of genetics promoted by bureaucrats with the *craving for novelty* will be even less so. In few situations is nationalist rhetoric not a cause of confusion or worse, particularly when, as in these cases, judgment is clouded and the vice of *nationalist zeal* is used to hide difficulties, or rather, political setbacks.

What do I mean? For the time being, if you consult any more or less up-to-date biology textbook, you will obtain information such as the following: the genome of human animals is the DNA sequence contained in 23 pairs of chromosomes in the nucleus of each diploid cell. For example, one pair of these chromosomes determines sex (two X chromosomes in females, one X and one Y in males); others determine eye color, and so on. DNA contains the encoded but environmentally adaptable information of the set of proteins that are organized into functional networks of interactions. Hence, in addition to the theoretical interests in mapping the human genome, practical interests abound. For example, in preventive medicine, the aim is to discover predispositions to diseases in order to treat them in time, or even to be able to confront diseases that still have no cure. However, you might ask: In what sense can such an abstract map with universal pretensions—since it deals with research that concerns human animals as a species—shed light on something as supposedly concrete as the "Mexican identity"?

In a parallel way—although with a distant parallelism—to how a transition from general ontology to the ontology of the Mexican was attempted, an even more extravagant transition was attempted from the map of the human genome to the map of the Mexican genome. This project was launched, as Carlos López Beltran points out, "under the premise that the subject carrying that genome, the Mexican mestizo, is the bearer of idiosyncrasies and peculiarities that surpass the anecdotes of jokes, by delving into its most intimate structure, that of the molecules, that of the genes."[50] This new way of developing an ontology of the Mexican, this time with the vocabulary—and the prestige—of genetic science, implies, among other perilous consequences, a project for the *racialization* of biomedical research. Consequently, we are facing a repressive form of theorization. Why? On the one hand, identifying the body of all Mexicans with the body of *"the* mestizo" wrongly presupposes that *mestizajes* were and are *a single* process, and not a multiform variety. On the other hand, a politics of exclusion is practiced: With arrogant reason, the indigenous people are disdained—those eternally excluded—as well as, by the way, a huge group of people with diverse bodies *of different colors going from black to more or less white.*[51]

I will tally a provisional balance. With nomadic epistemology I examined how a philosopher and a storyteller, with elaborate theoretical concerns, discussed an ancient obsession of their own land: the politics of identity. Then I introduced—briefly, too briefly—an unexpected legacy, not only involuntary but irritating to the Hyperion group: the Mexican genome mapping project. What can be salvaged from these discussions? In response I once again embrace the contagious character of the claims: In this case, they are claims of political prudence that little by little distance us from the ghosts that populate the "ontology of the Mexican," but also from Uranga and Revueltas. Whoever thinks with nomadic thought never tires of thinking further.

V

First claim of political prudence: since people and societies are to some extent modifiable, this circumstance should not be ignored, as is often the case with colonial vices.

I have already said it: the reflections of Uranga, and also, as we observed, those of Revueltas, contain impure fetishes. As "impure fetishes," their destruction allows us to extract, at least, resources and claims to nourish thoughts of value, specifically, thoughts about the modifiable character of people and societies, although the two authors do it in opposite ways.

If we ignore Uranga's oscillations between general ontology and the allegedly particular anthropology of Mexicans, his efforts to *re-found* thoughts are illuminating: We can understand ontology as an ontology of accident and contingency, and so, of the modifiable. What is more, not doing so spreads violence large and small. On the one hand, violence against people if they seek to understand themselves as destinies already decided in advance. On the other hand, violence against society when it is regarded as something *already given*: what one has to endure or accept—applaud, reject—without having the option to change. As if, confronting society itself, we were faced with the alternative: take it *as is* or leave it.

On the contrary, if we take as a starting point the *modifiable* character—to a certain extent—of the processes that constitute the person or society themselves, then we rediscover another principle of nomadic thinking:

> *Life's processes are precarious, and therefore human animals and their theorizations and practices belong to this type of process.*

What do we mean by "precarious"? Let us once again do a little exercise in ordinary language philosophy, weaving a network of words. Maybe it will clarify some of their uses and indicate some of their repercussions:

> assailable, circumstantial, chance, changeable, context-dependent, fortuitous, fortune, historical, occasional, partial, what's possible, random, risky, lacking security or privileges, sensitive, temporary, transient, uncertain, unexpected, unfixed, unpredictable, vulnerable... And, once again, that precious Nahuatl word: *nepantla*.

Not by chance, the processes that shape people and societies are, like many of life's processes, including of course the various forms of identity politics, subject to various uses of words in this network. They are processes that are to some extent random, context-dependent, unpredictable, historical, vulnerable. An ontology of accidentality therefore generates a resource that must be taken into account in morality and politics as well. As Uranga observes: "*To realize oneself as accident means one must maintain oneself as accident, on the horizon of possibility of the accident itself.* Inauthenticity would be to flee the condition of accidentality and to substantialize oneself."[52]

"To escape from the condition of accidentality" is a common fantasy. It often remains long cherished in relation to one's own person. In relation to society, it is *nationalistic zeal*. In both cases these are acts of sabotage. Thus, at this point it is helpful to return to a principle of nomadic thought, the *imperative of life*:

> *Learn to know how to lose, to know how to resist, to know how to start over and act accordingly.*

In different language—perhaps closer to Uranga—, this imperative might be reformulated: "Oscillate between big and small adventures of all kinds, but don't forget that in part, and little by little, you yourself make them, you yourself enter into *nepantla*. Yes: if you get rid of colonial vices, often stumbling, and with many losses, resistances, and restarts, you can place yourself in the territory of *nepantla*."

Operating in the opposite direction, in Uranga's thought we can also extract a claim. So let us forget ontology, and let us maintain the impulse to think of Mexico, to gather the protests and losses of Mexicans, and their changing and often painful circumstances.[53] Uranga points out: "More than a clean and rigorous meditation on the being of the Mexican, *what brings us to this kind of study is the project of bringing about moral, social, and religious transformations with that being*."[54] How so?

In an argumentative reading at least—if one avoids, I repeat, the genetic fallacy and the retrospective fallacy—one can also use Uranga's *Análisis del ser del mexicano* as an *argument* against the arrogant reason of the Headquarters of Power and Thought, and therefore against our colonial vices. This claim is made because this Headquarters tends to ignore randomness, chance, uncertainty, good or bad fortune. These attributes permeate all institutions, and therefore remind us that as historical constructs they are modifiable or examples of "good" historicism. Because without question, history has not only been and is suffered by many Mexicans. It also builds a heavy legacy and a perplexity that persists in occupying even the passions, both of researchers and of our day-to-day reflections.[55] Thus, this protest operates as a decolonizing one. Why? From these often forsaken lands, it is a matter of *re-founding* a humanism of accident, of vulnerability. Its counterpart, the "arrogant" colonial humanism of substance, so sure of itself as being immutable; a process of *perpetuum mobile*. For this reason, "*any interpretation of man as a substantial creature seems to us inhuman.*"[56] Let us now apply the *maxim of data, fetishes, resources, and demands* to Revueltas. Liberating himself sharply from many *cantinfleos* with Marxist language, Revueltas proposes to reason with low degrees of abstraction, and consequently focuses on the modifiable character of the culture and economy of Mexico. However, his identity politics does not abandon the fetish: the identification of "Mexican nationality" with the Spanish-speaking mestizo. Thus, Revueltas violently excludes the "dispersed indigenous nationalities." Moreover, by making "Mexican nationality" the product of a society unified by a state, he tends to repress the rich, the exquisitely rich plurality—with many contradictions, as Revueltas himself recognizes in relation to his own person—of ways of life of Mexicans throughout their history and culture. However, one must be careful not to simply condemn his project as a pure fetish. Revueltas's concerns about "*the* Mexican" contain resources and claims for indicating that the colonial order of exclusions is fortuitous, an event like others in history that we can eventually be changed.

A NAGGING DOUBT

Faced with many of these considerations, perhaps one may ask—not without some discomfort— a question that could have been asked at the beginning of these reflections: Why insist on continuing to think only locally, for example to "think of Mexico" amid the current cosmopolitan tendency, fever, vertigo, vice . . .? Does the integration of Mexico—and this applies to almost any country—into the world markets still allow us to give any meaning to the expression "think of Mexico"? I suspect that advocating the need to think with nomadic thinking is already the beginning of an answer to these doubts.

VI

Second claim of political prudence, or not ignoring that theories and general rules of any kind—including our most cherished laws—are underdetermined, and in order to apply them, it is essential to cultivate the capacity for judgment.

For example, the general theory underlying invocations of the "bronze race" as a homogeneous "cosmic race" can in certain contexts support both just claims and unmet demands. But it can also become a new fetish that does not allow for considered judgment. Unfortunately, uncritical judgment leads to perverse uses of all-or-nothing logic.[57] The lesson is clear: giving blank checks to general theories is more than just a bad habit. If one does not know how to weigh things as indexed to place and time in relation to practical life, fanaticism soon spreads. For example, a policy that has been beneficial in a certain place and at a certain time can later mutate into forms of violence and terror. As indicated in the first claim of political prudence, life processes, and therefore also policies, are contingent: precarious. Thus, the iron from the hammers with which the old chains are broken, can be used to forge new ones. Hence the disasters when legal and political theories or agendas, which in the abstract would be most advisable, are applied in unsuitable situations. (Caution: one must not overlook an asymmetry:

there are very good political theories that, when applied in practice, can have bad or even horrible results. By contrast, there are bad political theories—an extreme example would be Nazism—that under no circumstances can have good results).

No perspective of abstract universalism avoids exploring—even in detail—the cultural particularities of each situation and seeing what they need. Even the most established generalities fail to eliminate the exercise of discernment. In this regard, let us consider uses of the strategy of transitions. Applying it well obviously implies knowing how to adjust it using the capacity for judgment. For example, I suspect that it does not take too much research to discover that expressions with intermediate degrees of abstraction, such as "the Mexican," "the Swede," or "the Chinese," are meaningless unless they boil down to statistics about a nationality. On the contrary, suppose we list the attributes that, among others, the Hyperiones have predicated of "the Mexican": inferiority complex, resentment, hypocrisy, cynicism, suspicion, hermeticism. As soon as one tries to contrast them empirically with a population of Mexicans, the result is predictable. There will be Mexicans—or Swedes, Chinese, etc.—to whom these attributes can be predicated, and many others to whom it is impossible.

In contrast, the strategy of transitions is useful in other ways: in research that predicates expressions with low degrees of abstraction, such as "the Mexican upper classes during the Porfiriato," "the Mexican university students in the strikes of 1968," or "the inhabitants of the San Angel neighborhood in Mexico City." There are even downward transitions that concern the very singular identity of a person, such as the changing identity of Emilio Uranga. These abstractions, which refer to groups (social classes, students, neighborhood residents) or to a singularity, are legitimate if they are used as the basis for surveys, empirical research, and statistics, as the social sciences do. At the same time, a singular identity can be the subject of various narratives, from psychological studies to autobiographies, biographies, or novels.

Also, the strategy of transitions becomes useful in relation to identity politics in which words with high degrees of abstraction are used, such as "man," in its generic equivalent sense of human animal. About such an animal, we can do various types of research, for example, in natural sciences, anthropology, and cognitive sciences. Likewise, the capacity for judgment must sometimes appeal to that word in moral, legal, and political debates, in which, with one false step, we are already in the midst of the worst violence. Like what?

Contrary to Uranga (and by the way contrary to Heidegger, his self-righteous reception in Latin America, and some of its numerous postmodern sequels, equally self-righteous), whether or not to attribute the predicate "man" has several normative consequences. Let us remember that in Spain, in the Debate of Valladolid (1550–1551), the "native controversy" confronted two ways of considering the conquest of America. In Europe there was a debate about the appropriate way to attribute the predicate "man": in an actual or potential way. Famously, Juan Ginés de Sepúlveda (1490–1573) justified the legitimacy of this conquest to subjugate the Indians, and if necessary, chain them by force to the "superior culture" of Spain. It was about the right of the dominator over the dominated, or of the (natural?) right to elevate these "inferior men"—maybe quasi-men or even potential-men-but-still-animals—to the "height of civilization." (Incidentally, or rather, above all, they defended the possession of docile servants, including terrifyingly docile indigenous women, and slaves who would work the land from sunrise to sunset.) In opposition, Bartolomé de Las Casas (1474–1566), the Bishop of Chiapas, defended the unrestricted attribution of the predicate "human," whether to the Spaniards or to the indigenous peoples.

However, it should be clarified that in this debate, there was *no* discussion—as it is sometimes assumed—as to whether the predicate "human" can be attributed to the indigenous people at all, or whether we are dealing with wild animals—"animals *without souls*"—which should be domesticated like other animals. With the papal bull *Sublimis Deus* of 1537 (inspired by the Dominicans), Pope Paul III put an end, at least in theory, or rather, at least in theological debates, to the colonial doubts of Europe (colonialistically interested in obtaining free labor) about whether to attribute the predicate "human" to the *natives* of America. In this regard, it is worth noting that until the end of the eighteenth century, similar discussions, both in philosophy and theology, both in Spain and Latin America, were framed in *diverse* versions of Aristotelianism.

I emphasize the word *diverse* because, indeed, there were many and disparate ways of reading Aristotle's general theories in the Hispanic traditions. We find proof of this in Virginia Aspe Armella's learned and meticulous book, *Aristoteles y la Nueva España* (Aristotle and New Spain).[58] With acute observations and subtle arguments, the author discovers an original Aristotelianism, a "differentiated Aristotelianism"—in her own expression—typical of the Mexico that was still known as New Spain. Despite the "common themes," the emphases that were introduced into their readings by Mexicans or residents of Mexico, reveal to us "heterodox mentalities": *creatively* heterodox. Precisely for this reason, we need to allude to a plurality of differentiated Aristotelianisms, which, depending on particular issues, are applied with the capacity for judgment, with *phronêsis*. We often find more than subtle contrasts, for example, in the Aristotelianism of De la Veracruz, or Las Casas, or Sor Juana, or Clavijero.

As a complement to Aspe's book, it is worth reading Noell Birondo's article, "The Virtues of Mestizaje: Lessons from Las Casas on Aztec Human Sacrifice."[59] Birondo shows that the colonialist use of Aristotle and his theory of the virtues to justify the conquest, such as the one made by Ginés de Sepúlveda, is far from being the only one. With Bartolomé de Las Casas we can also learn a liberating use of these general theories, what Birondo calls a "dialogical version" of Aristotle's moral and political philosophy.

One may still wonder how to educate the capacity for judgment in order to evaluate general theories of the human, in order to evaluate the use of "man" in the sense of human animal. Two struggles are the following:

THE ANTICOLONIAL STRUGGLE AGAINST THE SOCIAL DEGRADATION OF IDENTITIES

We need to make political use of the strategy of transitions for claims with even extreme degrees of concreteness, regarding very particular and even singular identities, using the capacity for judgment. Thus, starting from general theories, it is often a matter of defending minorities mistreated in the past, and frequently even in the present, for example various groups of women, people considered to have "deviant" sexuality, or the "disabled," or in some countries, "people of color." But isn't white also a color? Bolívar Echeverría sharply examined the metaphysics of whiteness—a second- or third-rate "metaphysics"—and rightly insisted: ultimately, it is only supported by the defense of completely illegitimate privileges.[60] In general, one should be wary of second- or third-rate "metaphysics" or "ontologies"—such as the "ontology of the Mexican"—, as one is wary, for example, of second- or third-hand automobiles that are actually a scam, since they stop working just a few days after naively being purchased.

Hence, it is important in certain circumstances, using the capacity for judgement, to give preferential treatment to identities that have been historically devalued. Taking this step, it may be possible to establish a growing equality of opportunities, hitherto unknown. Sometimes, such equality will have to be reached by indirect means, perhaps by introducing quotas for groups of women, for "people of color," for homosexuals, for trans people, for physically disabled people . . .[61] However, it is important to bear in mind that the lack of recognition that devalues certain identities forms a *continuum* between two poles:

- Individual ignorance is largely intentional, but often circumstantial and even without ramifications; and

- Structural discrimination is reified, for example in colonial vices which, with arrogant reason, are expressed in social systems resistant to change, and which often operate as manufacturers of ignorance.

Resisting structural discrimination by legal means is a beginning of resistance—an essential beginning—, but if these actions remain *merely* legal measures, the required changes will not occur. Therefore, in relation to this claim that seeks not to ignore the fact that universal norms are underdetermined, we must cultivate the capacity for judgment in order to apply them. There is also a second struggle:

THE ANTICOLONIAL STRUGGLE FOR THE DIVERSITY OF OVERLAPPING IDENTITIES

This struggle is a way to combat a ubiquitous tendency in institutions, and even in many societies: that of becoming "monotonous sects," to use a happy pleonasm of Borges. "Happy pleonasm": the participants of a cult are basically monotonous people who obey the rule that *more of the same is always good*. Consequently, it is always good to exclude the other. (For example, according to the perverse metaphysics of whiteness: *it is always good to have more and more white men in a society, in order to "whiten" the rest of the society, and thus to improve it*).

It may be intriguing: What, if any, relationships exist between the two struggles which seek to support this second claim of political prudence, about the need to adjust the capacity for judgment according to the situation? The justifications for the two struggles are different. *The anticolonial struggle against the social degradation of identities* is justified as a struggle for the dignity of each person; we are faced with struggles for the general recognition of the human. In this sense we also seek to achieve compensatory justice in the face of past or present ignorance. This struggle aims to destroy stigmas and establish social recognition that has been unjustifiably denied not only to certain singular identities, but also to types of identity (indigenous people, groups of women, people of color, workers, people with disabilities). On the other hand, *the anticolonial struggle for the diversity of overlapping identities* combats the tendency to turn institutions and societies into "monotonous sects." Using our capacity for judgment, the interrelationships between the two struggles are not difficult to establish: cultivating social diversity is, at the same time, bolstering the revaluation of perversely devalued identities. It is promoting a morality and politics of nonexclusion.

VII

Third claim of political prudence, or not ignoring the need to transform disputes between laws and customs into productive conflicts typical of radical republicanism.

We do not need to explore the situation, nor appeal to our capacity for judgment, every time we act. Although Uranga defends an ontology of accidentality, our fragility and that of our circumstances are not accidental at each and every step. For this reason, certain ways of acting become lasting and relatively fixed: We allow ourselves to be guided by reasonable habits and no less reasonable customs. We determine our conduct in compliance with law. Unfortunately, the forms of practice are often in conflict—habits and customs, on the one hand, and laws, on the other—, and the consequences form an ever-expanding circle of evils. An indication of the self-destructive nature of such quarrels is the sentence—in various senses of the term—, which is no less regrettable for its being repeated in Latin America: "It is decreed, but not enforced." With this sentence, many histories of generous legislation and just jurisprudence have been ruined and continues to be ruined. Why? If laws are decreed *and nothing else* is done to stop violence, to promote scientific and technological progress, and to integrate social groups, law is often used as magic. Law in this way becomes a parody of itself.

Let us consider for a moment the book *Nocturno de la democracía mexicana* (Nocturne of Mexican democracy) by Héctor Aguilar Camín.[62] The author rightly insists that in Mexico this dispute between laws and customs is serious and not new. As a persistent trauma, Aguilar Camín recalls how two thinkers of the first half of the nineteenth century, José María Luis Mora (1794–1850) and Lucas Alamán (1792–1853), have already been "driven mad" by this dispute:

> Mora, the reformist, deplored the absence of *customs* that could have given civic support to the liberal laws in which he believed, designed to govern a federal and democratic republic of industrious, enlightened, prosperous and independent citizens.[63] Alamán, the conservative, wanted rather the opposite: to adapt the laws to the existing customs and to found the new nation on their continuities, not on their illusions.[64]

Joshua Simon argues in his book, *The Ideology of the Creole Revolution: Imperialism and Independence in American and Latin American Political Thought*, that these conflicts were already tearing apart both "reformists" and "conservatives."[65] For example, in the chapter on "The Creole Conservatism of Lucas Alamán," Simon explores "the complexities of Creole conservatism, which was both revolutionary and reactionary, both egalitarian and elitist, and both anti-imperialist and imperialist."[66] It is well known that the lives of human animals are inevitably made and unmade by numerous and intertwined conflicts—small, serious, sometimes very serious. Furthermore, the reproduction of old conflicts and the production of new conflicts do not cease as long as there is human life. If these conflicts are not admitted and confronted, there is often no choice but to repress them. But it is rare, extremely rare, that this repression makes them disappear. On the contrary, sometimes they become ghosts that haunt us. Worse still, when reading with an itinerant reading that wonderfully decisive but also symptomatic Mexican novel *Pedro Páramo*, it becomes clear, sooner rather than later, that when there is harassment and repression, life is replaced by conversations between ghosts. Perhaps because its societies abound in exclusions, at more than a few moments in its history, the Mexican imagination never ceases to cram itself with ghosts.[67]

In addition, Mora might have slightly corrected the last expression of Aguilar Camín's quote. Perhaps Mora would have protested: "No, I am not invoking *my personal illusions*; it is a matter of defending just ideals." In any case, Aguilar Camín is right: this dispute between laws and customs, when it is decided exclusively in favor of the laws, tends to produce, among other evils, a "democracy without democrats."[68] Nevertheless, I repeat, the dispute and the conflicts which badly frame these hostilities remain. But let us not hurry. (Pressure and urgency are bad advisors for nomadic thinking).

For the time being, to give a fragment of ancient, very ancient genealogy to this dispute, I will appeal to the strategy of detours toward the past. Polemical analogies in various degrees, although *not* equal, have been recurrent in the history of thought. Centuries ago, Aristotle—not without emphasizing that he understood himself as a Platonist—pointed out that the Ideas (or Forms) proposed by Plato, such as the Idea of the Good, or Justice or Generosity, and the laws that actualize those Ideas, lacked sufficient content to determine concrete ways of acting. Hence, Aristotle focused his normative reflections—moral and political—not on laws and rules, but on good and bad habits, which he conceptualized as virtues and vices. These Aristotelian claims—variations on the first and second claims noted earlier, of precariousness and the need to cultivate the capacity for judgment—were renewed in modern times, though again in a particular variation. In the *Phenomenology of Spirit*, Hegel—a late and very original member of the crowded tradition of Western Aristotelianism—formulates a criticism not identical, but analogous, to Kant. Hegel thinks that something is missing in the formulations of the moral principles of universality, personal autonomy, and the kingdom of ends, which can be reconstructed as moral echoes of the political principles of the French Revolution: equality, liberty, fraternity. This absence is, for Hegel, difficult to make up. Like any general rule, such as the laws, these principles are underdetermined. Hegel points out, unfortunately and rightly, that the effectiveness of such principles in practice depends on how they are determined by the capacity for judgement, based on the customs of a society and the good or bad habits, the virtues and vices, of its citizens. Hence a central concept of Hegel's *Philosophy of Right* is that of *Sittlichkeit*, which I translate/paraphrase in a somewhat Aristotelian way as "normatively valued habits and customs of a people."[69] It is these habits and customs that in each historical situation ultimately guide the applications of both moral principles and laws, and even make us understand what they are about and why they should matter. For example, current customs help determine what is meant by autonomy with respect to people. Thus, in certain societies a woman's autonomy is not thought to include her right to work or her religious, sexual, and economic independence, while in other societies it includes all of these. In each case what is meant by "women's autonomy" will be different. Furthermore, these habits and customs form the context in which a moral principle or a law, and even more so, some of its applications, not only make sense but, above all, have value. Because it is already a relatively established anthropological fact: the only moral principles, laws, and political programs that take root in the lives of human animals are those which such animals understand (or misunderstand) as contributing to the shaping of spheres of goods—ranging from economic goods to that elusive good, happiness—from which they are *not* excluded.

Let us go back to Mexico and the dispute between laws and customs. I suspect that it is useful, that it clarifies something, to reconstruct it also as the false opposition between two persistent ghosts that tend not to give in to criticism: the previously noted desire to turn the law into magic, and the equally futile desire to revert to habits and customs, processes of *perpetuum mobile*. Two ghosts?

On the one hand, the laws, even the best laws, often produce neither immediate nor comprehensive effects. The best laws do not magically transport people, on a multicolored (multiculturalist?) flying carpet, away from the miseries reproduced by an economic system, social injustices and violence, to some counterfactual: republics with a plurality of conflicts and ways of resolving or dissolving them in peace. At best, if laws are effective, they contribute to setting in motion slow, reversible, and obstacle-ridden processes: they are *resources*.

Furthermore, the origin of these resources should not be neglected. They often result from the contingent and sometimes tragic balance between politics and the powers consolidated by an economic system. Of course, sometimes laws are a decisive cause in the civilizing process, though they are not the *only* cause. Let us bear in mind the decisive laws that in many countries abolished that awful ancient institution, whose damage and whose ghosts continue to oppress: namely, slavery. In many regions, notoriously, once this legality was abolished, many ways of treating former slaves remained unchanged. Sometimes it was not even encouraged to replace their self-understanding. Not only that. Sometimes abolitionist laws meant little or nothing, and even assisted lynchings. Why? Because this atrocious institution was immediately disguised in different clothes, while at the same time, in fact, the old structures of exploitation were reproduced outside the law.

On the other hand, social habits and customs are not *perpetuum mobile* processes, which once set in motion remain there, insensitive to the economies of societies or to the desires and beliefs of people. They are also *resources*. Some habits and customs—as resources used in food, in the constitution of families and their distribution of roles, in the complicated relations between the sexes and their numerous stigmas and secrets, in work and leisure habits—persist in many of society's structures. Well-known examples in Mexico, and in Latin America in general: we squander money tonight, even though we do not have resources to keep a roof over our heads tomorrow; we overeat what is notoriously harmful; we smoke; we despise, or rather, we are afraid of unconventional experiences and self-understandings described as "deviant" or "strange." We refuse to collaborate with others even for our own benefit. We waste our free time on nonsense that degrades and endangers the environment. More importantly still: driven by misery, bad habits, and the worst customs, we invent informal jobs as resources that become the only escape valves that the social system manages in the face of its own inability to bring about nonexclusion.[70]

Once again the question arises: What, if anything, can be done to transform this dispute between the resources of law and the resources of custom? Perhaps in order to pierce the shell of this nightmare, or to begin to do so, it may help to think nomadically, as it helped in the dispute between abstract universalism and cultural particularism. Let us resort once again, then, to the strategy of detours and explore *one* possible option, examining the construction of subjectivities. Let us look into *a resource*—one among others—to mediate in this conflict between laws and customs: emotional reeducation.⁷¹

In this regard, let us consider emotions that form habits and many customs, which are referred to with a network of words such as the following:

> Anger, annoyance, aversion, cantankerous, contradict, disgusted, enraged, exasperated, fed up, furious, fury, indignation, intolerable, ire, irritated, irritating, meltdown, mortified, offended, rancor, rant, resentment, seethe, strike, tantrum, violate, violence.

We often use the word "disgust" when faced with rotting food that might make us vomit: a rejection of the stomach. We also use the word derivatively to express moral rejection: "The death flights, in which the Argentine dictatorship of the 1970s threw its opponents from airplanes, disgust me." In this example feelings of disgust are reasonable. But perhaps articulating that experience as indignation is, morally, more beneficial. Why? Immediate rejections—"rejections of the stomach"—often inherit deep-seated prejudices and a lack of reflection. Hence the low moral reliability (much less the legal and political reliability) that the similar feelings of disgust and anger often have. Let us examine another word on the list: "rage" (*rabia*). First of all, we find a bodily reaction to a viral disease (*rabia*: rabies). However, we also use that word to express emotions of anger and mortification, which often make us lose control over our actions: "It enrages me that they discriminate against poor people, or those without white skin, or those who have sexual preferences that are not conventionally accepted." On the other hand, as indicated in the list, the degeneracies of enraged action are frequent. A clue: the words "tantrum" (*rabieta*) and "cantankerous" (*cascarrabias*). Thus, in the fury of some tantrums, one assumes a cantankerous character, incapable of clear judgment. Judith Butler is harsher: "If we forget to turn our anger into a demand for justice, we become pure destruction in the face of destruction."⁷²

Emotional reactive attitudes toward evils are therefore complex. In the case of rage, it is not only a matter of learning how to manage it, but also how to turn it into indignation. It should not be eliminated, then, or set aside. If we do, we lack *one* nutrient that—although there are others—nourishes us as citizens of a democratic republic; if we do without it, as Butler observes, "we lose the rage we need for the demand for justice and for the political future of freedom."⁷³

However, why do I consider that these reactive emotions in the face of evils—emotions that not only permeate habits and customs, but often shape them—should be re-educated as indignation if we want to avoid their degeneration? If I am not mistaken, indignation is the only *purely* moral reaction on the list. So, with respect to it, one can ask about its justification: about the reasons behind it. How is this?

I consult the very brief entry on "indignation" in a recent *Dictionary of Justice*.[74] The entry, written by Claudio Lomnitz, distinguishes two historical phases of the concept of indignation: in the Middle Ages "dignity referred both to a noble quality and to the attributes that represented a post." However, "dignity was not a general attribute, but only of some, of the deserving, of the noble." From the Enlightenment onward, and at this point, Kant's moral philosophy raises an unequivocal and implacable banner that universalizes dignity: each person is an end in themselves. In turn, the French Revolution politicizes this universal dignity. Observes Lomnitz: "'The rights of man and of the citizen' was a formula that meant that every human was worthy of recognition simply and straightforwardly for being human."

The resistance that these values arouse are perhaps a good symptom of the value involved in defending the equal dignity of human animals, and thus freedom as nonexclusion. As soon as these banners are raised, there are people who get nervous and, seized by arrogant reason, even despotic, and who, with imposing pride or desperation, insist on the *necessity* of this or that exclusion, even *for all time*. Once again, then, conversations between ghosts: the ghosts of the castes, of the blood with supreme courage and their honors —or rather, horrors—attributed to hierarchies invoked as eternal (thanks to their "noble lineage," to their "beautiful skin color," to their "abundant money," to their "prestigious tradition," to their "dominant sex," to the "influential" public posts they hold or offices they perform, to their "high culture . . . "). They are ghosts that do not want to say goodbye and cease harassing us.

But back to Lomnitz and the struggles for dignity. Lomnitz distinguishes between "the demand for dignity of those who have not had it" (and gives the example in Mexico of the Zapatista revolt in Chiapas) and "the demand of the 'indignant'" which can adduce generous or selfish reasons, impulses to recognize and integrate, or to exclude and subjugate, and whose political sign can and often does oscillate between the extreme left and the extreme right (as do reactions resulting from disgust and rage). Lomnitz concludes: "indignation does not in itself have a political meaning, while the demand for dignity from those who have not had it does." However, despite this ambiguity, why did I insist: that we do *not* need to empty ourselves completely of rage, nor disgust, much less indignation?

A complex answer: If the laws do not awaken corresponding emotions, they tend to become inert; they do not move us to action. Nevertheless, emotions—including those immediately reactive to what are considered evils—are blind if they are not reflected upon and weighed on the basis of evaluative judgments and the laws that govern a democracy. So, how can habits and customs *not* become blind in a democracy, for example, in Mexico, without eliminating, or at least weakening, the dispute between laws and customs? How, then, is it possible to transform this dispute into a productive conflict of porous reason, through which freedom as nonexclusion is multiplied?

Or more directly: How, starting from the *maxim of data, fetishes, resources, and demands*, can we rescue productive conflicts from this dispute? Here is a proposal: In every place, at all times, along with the best laws, it is urgent that the relevant habits and customs take root. But exclusion and its humiliations to human dignity are said in many ways. For example, among many others, there are humiliations of:

- Labor
- Finance
- Education
- Sanitation
- Law
- Politics
- Morality

SEVERAL REMAINING POINTS, PARTLY HISTORICAL, ON
THE DISPUTE BETWEEN LAWS AND HABITS AND CUSTOMS

I have not stopped repeating: it is a matter of establishing personal habits of collaboration that take root in social customs of nonexclusion. What exactly do I mean? By the word "habit," I refer to the bodily states of complex organisms—human animals—which, through familiarity and repetition, acquire dispositions and motivations to act with a similar purpose in similar circumstances. Consequently, habits and those social structures made of customary habits, even as they are formed by past experiences, build anticipations. These anticipations not only give stability to some life plans: they make them possible. Because they are not blind routines that oppose improvisation. They are dynamic processes of interacting circumstances that often call for improvisation. Hence the expressions "habits of freedom" and "customs of freedom" are hardly oxymorons. They are forms of equal treatment and respect for the autonomy of each person. In addition, they promote social collaboration.

As another link in the Aristotelian tradition, Montesquieu, in *The Spirit of the Laws* (1748), recognizes the importance of habits and customs for public life, which he calls "springs" (*resortes*). (Perhaps another word for the proposal by Manuel Vargas that I used in Chapter 2, "resources.") Thus, Montesquieu indicates that to maintain a monarchical and despotic government, the "springs"—the resources—of honor and fear "can rule or contain the whole. But in a popular state there must be an additional spring: which is virtue."[75] Montesquieu's sharp words about the social catastrophes produced by the neglect of that spring—of that resource—social virtue, seem to have been written in a Mexican newspaper or any other news source today, despite the centuries that have elapsed. I cannot bring myself to quote a mere fragment (ignoring the Greek nostalgia that perturbs Montesquieu, surely illusory, such as the false opposition between commerce and virtue, which we do not have to go into):

> The political men of Greece who lived under popular government recognized no other force to sustain it than virtue. Those of today speak to us only of manufacturing, commerce, finance, wealth, and even luxury. When that virtue ceases, ambition enters those hearts that can admit it, and avarice enters them all. Desires change their objects: that which one used to love, one loves no longer. One was free under the laws, one wants to be free against them. Each citizen is like a slave who has escaped his master's house. What was a *maxim* is now called *severity*; what was a *rule* is now called *constraint*; what was *vigilance* is now called *fear*. There, frugality, not the desire to possess, is avarice.[76]

Once again we are reminded: Moral and political degeneration and, in general, institutional corruption entails, as one of its steps, and not the last, twisting the uses of words so that they start to mean the opposite of what they used to. (As if the other powers, for example, the political and economic powers, necessarily had to subdue and repress, to make the language sabotage itself). Hence the civilizing value of not overlooking the demand:

Be careful with words.

Montesquieu, from his harsh critique of manners, concludes in a way that is no less harsh (maybe also desperate). In any case, he is not afraid to mix political and social issues in his discourse: "Formerly, the goods of individuals made up the public treasury; the public treasury has now become the patrimony of individuals. The republic is a cast-off husk, and its strength is no more than the power of a few citizens and the license of all."[77]

I will dwell for a moment on another thinker who also belongs to that corridor of republican thought of those who stress the importance of virtues and customs for good government. In *Democracy in America* (1835), Tocqueville reports on how collaboration became a habit of citizens in the early days of the United States, and how these habits and the corresponding customs not only influenced various ways of acting, but also the very construction of the new country and its laws. For example, in order to solve problems, according to Tocqueville, the inhabitants of the United States of the time, before turning to governmental bodies, associated freely to solve them. This author states: "In democratic countries the science of association is the mother science, and the progress of all the rest depends upon the progress of this one."[78] To a large extent, this "science" depends on how habits of freedom, such as personal autonomy and the willingness to collaborate and promote social integration, have been cultivated from childhood.

As David Bak Geler Corona points out:

> Apart from the permanent associations institutionalized by law, Tocqueville finds that Americans use association as an efficient means of solving all kinds of problems and guaranteeing all kinds of pleasures. The genesis of the "spirit of association" in citizens comes from birth: the inhabitant of the United States learns, according to Tocqueville, that he must rely on himself to face any obstacle that may arise.[79]

On the other hand, this whole series of promising words—"spirit of association," "social collaboration . . ."—alludes somewhat timidly to the battered political ideal of fraternity whose challenges (despite so much ill will) do not cease to disturb us. In this regard, it may be suggestive, as a contrast to Tocqueville's remarks, to consider a *Western* that portrays a supposedly later era in the United States than the one which Tocqueville considers to have been generated by the "spirit of association," and in which that spirit seems to have been lost. The film is *High Noon*.[80] Facing an attack by the film's villains, the hero, Sheriff Kane, finds himself without citizen cooperation. In the final battle he can only count on the precarious help of his wife, Amy, and she is a Quaker who detests violence. When Kane finally finishes off the attackers, the crowd rallies around him. However, in a gesture of contempt, Kane removes the Sheriff's badge, the representation of the law, and unceremoniously throws it in the mud. The couple immediately leaves the town that was unable to support them, and unable to come together in the "spirit of association" to support the law. But where can this lonely couple go *if they do not want to become ghosts as well*? More recently we have heard this question asked often and with some desperation, not only in the Unites States. But let us go back again to the dispute of which this third claim of political prudence is an indicator.

> *We are faced only with the productive conflict between laws and habits and customs, if, with nomadic thinking, we confront laws with habits and customs, again and again.*

If we accept some of the previous observations, those who favor nonhomogeneous but integrated societies, with productive interactions between laws, habits, and customs, must be accompanied by a porous reason capable of designing and implementing effective public policies. They must be able to eliminate the types of social inequalities that disintegrate societies into separate "worlds" (the rigorously closed elites, or at least with that pretension; the middle classes with aspirations that are often impossible to fulfill; the ghettos of poverty and misery, drug cartels and violence . . .). It is difficult to ignore that in the wake of these disintegrations, a crucial gamble by democratic republics becomes unbelievable: that it is a collective benefit that citizens comply with the law. But respecting the laws does not prevent seeing them—according to a principle of nomadic thought—as precarious processes: products of parliaments, of politics, of economic interests, of historical contingencies. Hence, from time to time, they must be re-examined, and eventually, replaced.

VIII

Fourth claim of political prudence, or the claim that leads us directly to think again about Latin America, and in particular, about Mexico, and to repeat, repeatedly: "No more social disintegration caused by violence. No more accumulation of corpses caused by violence. No more violence."

To address this claim, neither Uranga nor Revueltas are of any help. I resort once again to a nomadic aesthetic, to an itinerant reading, in this case, of a few fragments of the novel *Temporada de huracanes* (*Hurricane Season*) by Fernanda Melchor.[81] I am looking for one or two of its gruesome episodes to illustrate, by way of analogical projection, what has never ceased to be a concern in these claims of political prudence: *violence as a visible and invisible current that does not stop moving everything in the background.*

On the first page of the novel I come to a passage that insists on *not* abandoning the way forward. I translate this passage, or rather, generalize it, as the itinerant reader I am. It is a matter of moving forward everywhere. (Thinking is also often a matter of moving forward as one can):

> The elastic of his slingshot pulled taught in his hands, the rock snug in the leather pad, primed to strike anything that got in his way at the very first sign of an ambush, . . . the breeze warm and the almost white sky thick with ethereal birds of prey and a terrible smell that hit them harder than a fistful of sand in the face, a stench that made them want to hawk it up before it reached their guts, that made them want to stop and turn round.[82]

I omitted other obstacles that impede progress; the novel's prose stacks them up in a dizzying baroque.[83] However, the obstacles listed here already remind us that moving forward, in any sense, is often arduous. That is why, with every step we take, *we lose the desire to continue moving forward*. As in my reading of *El ejército iluminado*, in Chapter 1, I will skip some pages and attend to the end of the novel. It presents an account of a monstrous piling up of corpses, or rather, the remains of corpses. (It is *monstrous*. But it is a pile of corpses like the ones that television news and newspapers have led us to believe are part of the norm in Latin America. In Mexico, for example, we are accustomed to piles of corpses; not accustomed, but rather, domesticated, so that we do not even feel that something urgent needs to be done). I quote the account, which details

> the faceless, sexless remnants of people: the calloused foot of some peasant who'd probably tried to clear the hillside brush while drunk; fingers and lumps of liver and strips of skin, post-op scraps from the Oil Company clinic. The first intact corpse they brought out was clearly a tramp: his skin was sallow and shrivelled like someone who'd spent half his life on a driftless rant under the harsh sun. Next, the young lady who'd been chopped to pieces. At least she wasn't naked, poor thing, but wrapped in sky-blue cellophane; presumably . . . to prevent her severed limbs from sloshing out all over the ambulance floor. Then came the newborn, the little creature with a tiny head like a custard apple, almost certainly abandoned by its parents in some clinic before the little lamb had even finished dying.[84]

The accumulation of corpses continues without respite. Worse: outside of the novels, we live with these "scenes of corpses" every day, as if we were in front of old pictures that are kept in the family, and in which new "pictures of corpses" do not bother us enough to stop drinking our coffee among ghosts. But how can we become bothered, how can we shake ourselves off and stop being ghosts? How can we respond in practice to this urgent fourth complaint: *no more violence*? What political, legal, economic, and cultural measures should be taken?

IX

Caution: Do not forget that we were reading the novel *Temporada de huracanes*. What more is happening in these pages? A mysterious character walks among them, the Grandfather, of whom it is said that he was "hearing voices and had lost his marbles," when he only wanted to explain "that you had to talk to the bodies as you buried them."[85] A grandfather who talks to the bodies as he buries them? This should not alarm us: The various forms of mourning, both private and public, are a strange way of talking to the dead, so that when one is ready one can say goodbye to them once and for all, and in this way release resentment and hatred, or the infinite, paralyzing sadness and melancholy caused by these losses. A person or society that dares not to engage in such excruciating rituals runs the risk of living more and more each day among ghosts, compulsively repeating that resentment or hatred, or the paralyzing sadness and melancholy.

But to continue simply talking to the dead like the Grandfather, does it not *also* condemn us to dwell among ghosts? Are we now resigned to living *definitively* among ghosts? Is there no other option to violence than to turn our backs and continue talking only among ghosts? We should not despair so soon. It should not be overlooked that, using a nomadic aesthetic, the kind of itinerant reading I am attempting at the moment *moves to the reader's horizon and interprets it*. So although the Grandfather in the novel consoles the dead, the reader might be made to ponder, in order to work out a reflection that drove him to want to continue thinking with nomadic thought, and above all, to cling to living. In the text of the novel, the Grandfather says, to the pile of corpses still lying uncovered in the grave: "The darkness doesn't last forever. See there? See that light shining in the distance? The little light that looks like a star? That's where you're headed, he told them, that's the way out of this hole."[86]

"That's the way?" they might ask themselves, those who read no further, who lift their heads from the book and look anxiously at the helplessness of their surroundings, those who continuously hear noises near and far, the desperate silences and the sounds of violence. So is that a good way to go? Over there? But where are we headed?

Notes

PREFACE

1. In these reflections I return to the description of these vices that I gave about the field of philosophy in particular: see my "Latin American Philosophy: Some Vices," *Journal of Speculative Philosophy* 20, no. 3 (2006) 192–203. However, in these essays I establish such vices as general afflictions. They are vices that operate outside of philosophy as well, in public policy, law, economics, international relations, and even people's customs.
2. Materials to enrich the analogy are everywhere. Amy Reed-Sandoval, in a discussion of my book, *Los aprendizajes del exilio*, makes various distinctions regarding these social "nomadisms" (displaced persons, immigrants, exiles, refugees . . .): see her "'Immigrant' or 'Exiled'? Reconceiving the Desplazada/os of Latin American and Latina/o Philosophy," *APA Newsletter on Hispanic/Latino Issues in Philosophy* 15, no. 2 (2016): 11–14. That book is also discussed in the essays by Mariflor Aguilar, Griselda Gutierrez, and Nora Rabotnikof in Miguel Ángel Fernández and Guillermo Hurtado, eds., *Normatividad y argumentación: Carlos Pereda y sus críticos* (Mexico City: Instituto de Investigaciones Filosóficas, Universidad Nacional Autónoma de México, 2013). It is also useful to consult José Jorge Mendoza's book *The Moral and Political Philosophy of Immigration: Liberty, Security, and Equality* (Lanham, MD: Lexington, 2016).
3. Emiliano Monge, *No contar todo* (Mexico City: Random House, 2018), 16; Emiliano Monge, *What Goes Unsaid: A Memoir of Fathers Who Never Were*, trans. Frank Wynne (Melbourne: Scribe, 2022).

CHAPTER 1

1. Guillermo Bonfil Batalla, *México profundo: Una civilización negada* (Mexico City: Grijalbo, 2003 [1987]), 130; Bonfil Batalla, *México Profundo: Reclaiming a*

Civilization, trans. Philip A. Dennis (Austin: University of Texas Press, 1996). Bonfil Batalla asks: "What does it mean for our history, and our present, and above all for our future, the coexistence of the two civilizations, the Mesoamerican and the Eastern?" His challenge: "Any decisions taken to orient the country ... implies an option in favor of one of those projects" (9). Bonfil Batalla defends the view that we must choose the Mesoamerican civilization: the "México profundo" instead of the "México imaginario." I think that with nomadic thinking we must do justice to both projects, as suggested by Luis Villoro. See also Iver A. Beltrán García, "Luis Villoro: El desafío de una nueva comunidad y las tareas de la razón critica" [Luis Villoro: The challenge of a new community and the tasks of critical reason], *Ideas y valores* 69, no. 173 (2020): 103–22.

2. Perhaps it will useful to compare these suggestions with those theories that use words like "postcolonialism" or "decolonial." An initial introduction to these proposals can be found in the well-known book *A Companion to Postcolonial Studies*, eds. Henry Schwarz and Sangeeta Ray (Malden: Blackwell, 2000). Among other works in the volume, it would be useful for this reflection to reread carefully, with a relentless argumentative reading, "Imperialism, Colonialism, Postcolonialism," by Neil Larsen (23–52), and "Human Understanding and (Latin) American Interests—The Politics and Sensibilities of Geohistorical Locations," by Walter D. Mignolo (180–202). As a useful and almost essential companion, a more specific anthology should also be taken into account: *Decolonial Voices: Chicana and Chicano Cultural Studies in the Twenty-First Century*, eds. Arturo J. Aldama and Naomi H. Quiñonez (Bloomington: Indiana University Press, 2002). These works discuss very specific mistreatment of bodies along the border between Mexico and the United States, in particular the mistreatment of women, but in general of any migrant or refugee. However, they also portray and examine audible resistances, desperate silences, which must not be forgotten either.

3. Bonfil Batalla, *México profundo*, 106.
4. Bonfil Batalla, *México profundo*, 109.
5. With a variation of Ortega's sentence, "I am myself and my circumstance," Roberto Sánchez Benítez summarizes the vice of *craving for novelty* as: "Strange tendencies foreign to creativity, to the formulation of relevant arguments and ideas for a context like ours and that we could also summarize under the motto, 'I am me and my trends or author of fashion,'" Roberto Sánchez Benítez, "Review of Carlos Pereda, *La filosofía en México en el siglo XX: Apuntes de un participante*," *Nóesis: Revista de ciencias sociales y humanidades* 24, no. 47-2 (2015): 152.
6. David Toscana, *El ejército iluminado* (Mexico City: Tusquets, 2006); *The Enlightened Army*, trans. David William Foster (Austin: University of Texas Press, 2019).
7. See Carlos Pereda, *Patologías del juicio: Ensayos sobre literatura, moral y estética nómada* [Pathologies of judgment: Essays on literature, morals, and nomadic aesthetics] (Mexico City: CENART-Institute for Philosophical Research, Universidad Nacional Autónoma de México, 2018).

8. Toscana, *El ejército iluminado*, 35.
9. Toscana, *El ejército iluminado*, 121.
10. Toscana, *El ejército iluminado*, 58.
11. Toward the end of the play "Galileo Galilei" by Bertold Brecht, after the renunciation of Galileo, harassed by the Inquisition (the renunciation of one of his strongest astronomical beliefs), an assistant of Galileo loudly laments: "Unfortunate are those who have no heroes." Undeterred, Galileo replies: "Unfortunate are those in need of heroes."
12. Toscana, *El ejército iluminado*, 176. In other Toscana novels, such as *Santa María del circo* [Saint Mary of the circus] (Mexico City: Plaza y Janes, 1998), we find the same insistence, of Toscana disbelieving the stories of the official history of Mexico. Does Toscana doubt the stories narrated by the walled-in historians in Mexico City? For example, in *Santa María del circo*, various other stories from the history of Mexico are parodied—stories about the Artillery Boy, the eagle and the cactus, the national anthem.
13. Toscana, *El ejército iluminado*, 192.
14. In July 1968, marches began in Mexico City, first student marches, which soon brought together other sectors of the population, calling for more freedoms and less authoritarianism on the part of the state. On October 2, a public action was called in the historic Plaza de las Tres Culturas in Tlatelolco. During the demonstration, a helicopter launches flares on the crowd. Was an order given? Immediately military, paramilitary, and snipers open fire. See Elena Poniatowska, *La noche de Tlatelolco: Testimonios de historia oral* [The night of Tlatelolco: Oral history testimonies] (Mexico City: Era, 1971); *Massacre in Mexico*, trans. Helen R. Lane (Columbia: University of Missouri Press), and Jorge Volpi, *La imaginación y el poder: Una historia intellectual de 1968* [Imagination and power: An intellectual history of 1968] (Mexico City: Era, 1998). Susana Draper transgresses the normal perspective on these events, a perspective too obsessed with male leaders, and reintegrates, with singular mastery, the wishes and affections of the figures and voices left in the shadows: see her *México 1968: Experimentos de la libertad: Constelaciones de la democracia* (Mexico City: Siglo Veintiuno, 1998); *Mexico 1968: Constellations of Freedom and Democracy* (Durham, NC: Duke University Press, 2018). Two memorable *meta*-testimonials of that horror are the poems *La limpidez* [Clarity] by Octavio Paz, and *Memorial de Tlatelolco* [Tlatelolco memorial] by Rosario Castellanos.
15. Recently, Paola Vázquez Almanza has made a valuable journey of half a century with regards to Mexican identity in her book, *Aquellos que dejamos de ser: Ficción y nación en México* [What we cease to be: Fiction and nation in Mexico] (Mexico City: Siglo Veintiuno), 201.
16. José Martí, *Our America: Writings on Latin America and the Struggle for Cuban Independence*, ed. Philip S. Foner, trans. Elinor Randall (New York: Monthly Review Press, 1977), 84.
17. Carmen Boullosa, *La patria insomne* [The sleepless homeland] (Madrid: Poesía Hiperión, 2011). See also Carlos Pereda, "Ten cuidado con las palabras 'patria,'

'violencia,' e 'insomne,' pero en México también con la palabra 'suave'" [Be careful with the words 'homeland,' 'violence,' and 'sleepless,' but in Mexico also with the word 'smooth'], *Debate feminista* (Feminist debate) 46, no. 23 (2012): 219–24.

18. To elaborate some of these problems, and letting myself be carried away by an emphatically anticolonial virtue—that of arguing seriously with the people around us—I will take into account several reflections stimulated by my book *La filosofía en México en el siglo XX: Apuntes de un participante* [Philosophy in Mexico in the twentieth century: Notes from a participant] (Mexico City: Conaculta, 2013). In the discussion of that book, José María Espinasa observes that: "it has already become commonplace in our historical and artistic descriptions [to produce] an inadvisable fact: the theme justifies the argument and not the other way around. . . . [By contrast] Pereda dissolves the nationalist falsehoods in the central idea—this or that philosophy is important because a Mexican thinks it—, by emphasizing the content that matters for the argument and not for its nationality. This is how to understand the expression 'Philosophy in Mexico' in the title, rather than 'Mexican Philosophy,'" *Estudios* 12, no. 108 (2014): 185. Reaffirming the first expression ("philosophy in Mexico"), Rodolfo Suárez indicates more ambitiously: "By its nature and objectives, philosophical work would seem to point to the universal, or to its borders, to questions that go beyond national spheres," *Diánoia* 59, no. 73 (2014): 158.

19. For example, Ambrosio Velasco reasonably protests: "I do not agree that it would be dangerous to recognize certain vague and general, but distinctive features of philosophical work in Mexico," "Review of Carlos Pereda, *La filosofía en México en el siglo XX: Apuntes de un participante*," *Tópicos: Revista de filosofía* 45 (2013): 345–51.

20. I introduce these distinctions in my book, *Razón e incertidumbre* [Reason and uncertainty] (Mexico City: Siglo Veintiuno, 1994), 95–107. I elaborate these distinctions in "Explanatory and 'Argumentative' History of Philosophy," in *The Role of History in Latin American Philosophy: Contemporary Perspectives*, eds. Arleen Salles and Elizabeth Millán-Zaibert, 43–56 (Albany: State University of New York Press, 2005). I also touch on these distinctions in my previously cited book on Mexican philosophy.

21. A traditional form of explanatory history has sometimes been called "antiquarian," or "antiquarianism," by its advocates, perhaps poking a little fun at themselves. See Daniel Garber, "Towards an Antiquarian History of Philosophy," *Rivista di storia della filosofia* [Journal of the history of philosophy] 58, no. 2 (2003): 207–17.

22. Carlos Alberto Sánchez, *Contingency and Commitment: Mexican Existentialism and the Place of Philosophy* (Albany: State University of New York Press, 2016).

23. Sánchez, *Contingency and Commitment*, 5.

24. Sánchez, *Contingency and Commitment*, 5.

25. Sánchez, *Contingency and Commitment*, 43.

26. In his discussion, "Why historians of philosophy should also read the classics

of the historical sciences," Alejandro Estrella González asks "whether the opposition posed by Carlos Pereda between explanatory history and argumentative history implies an opposition between historical or social sciences (which would account for the former) and philosophy (which would fit in with the latter). In this regard, the book is not clear." Estrella González continues: "the capacity of the social sciences to construct an argumentative history" is great, because when reading a text—or taking into account any document—part of the task of historians and social scientists is "to understand its meaning, to evaluate it critically and to discuss its actuality, and in so doing to try to mobilize some of the tools provided by the social sciences. Does this background contribute to an argumentative reading of philosophy? Would this operation be justified? My thesis says 'yes.'" See Alejandro Estrella González, "Por qué los historiadores de la filosofía también deberían leer a los clásicos de ciencias históricas: Reseña de Carlos Pereda, *La filosofía en México en el siglo XX: Apuntes de un participante*" [Why historians of philosophy should also read the classics of the historical sciences: Review of Carlos Pereda, *Philosophy in Mexico in the Twentieth Century: Notes from a Participant*], *Signos Filosóficos* 16, no. 31 (2014): 208–9. Contrary to what Estrella González suggests, I actually agree with him, as I believe is evident in this discussion.

27. This account is based on my book, *La filosofía en México en el siglo XX*.
28. About these three thinkers, as in general about the various traditions of Marxism in Mexico, it is useful to consult the work of Carlos Illades, *El Marxismo en México: Una historia intellectual* [Marxism in Mexico: An intellectual history] (Mexico City: Taurus, 2018). On Sánchez Vázquez, see the collection *En torno a la obra de Adolfo Sánchez Vázquez* [On the work of Adolfo Sánchez Vázquez], ed. Gabriel Vargas Lozano (Mexico City: Universidad Nacional Autónoma de México, 1995); see also *Repensar la 'Filosofia de la praxis': Homenaje a Adolfo Sánchez Vázquez* [Rethinking the 'Philosophy of Praxis': Tribute to Adolfo Sánchez Vázquez], eds. Gilberto García, Ambrosio Velasco, and Victor Hernándes (Ciudad Juárez: Universidad Autónoma de Ciudad Juárez, 2017). (Perhaps it is worth remembering that unlike José Gaos, who understood himself as a "transplant" ["change of land, that's all"], Adolfo Sánchez Vázquez, although he spent most of his life in Mexico, never stopped thinking of himself as "banished," as "exiled." "I did not change lands, but I was violently torn away from my homeland," he insisted in one of his last lectures).
29. Roberto Sánchez Benítez recalls, in his review of a book about philosophy in Mexico, that the metaphor of the archipelago is "very much in the style of the *Contemporáneos*," that important group of great critical poets of the Mexican Revolution. Sánchez Benítez, "Review of Carlos Pereda, *La filosofía en México*," 152. On this group it is worth consulting the work of Guillermo Sheridan, *Los contemporáneos ayer* [Contemporaries, yesterday] (Mexico City: Fondo de Cultura Económica, 2015). At the same time, Ambrosio Velasco applauds the use of the metaphor of the archipelago in my book to refer to this generation, as

it introduces "a breath of fresh air and liberating wind in the face of the hegemony of the big blocs." Velasco, "Review of Carlos Pereda, *La filosofía*," 348.
30. Guillermo Hurtado, *Dialéctica del naufragio* [Dialectic of the shipwrecked] (Mexico City: Fondo de Cultura Económica, 2016).
31. Hurtado, *Dialéctica del naufragio*, 89. Hurtado proposes such a dialogue, but also "an archeology of hope" (107). In this way, Hurtado perhaps qualifies the diagnosis (already announced in the title) of his book *México sin sentido* [Senseless Mexico] (Mexico City: Siglo Veintiuno, 2011). As María Antonia González Valerio acutely points out: "Historical work, then, is not work done just because we can; it is work in which the very shape of something, as well as its possibilities for becoming something different, is at stake." A new beginning, then. A paragraph later she rightly adds: "History—which one, ours?—does not want to be finished." González Valerio, "Review of Carlos Pereda, *La filosofía en México en el siglo XX: Apuntes de un participante*," *Intersticios* 18, no. 39 (2013): 167–68.
32. Rodolfo Suárez observes: "Certainly, as Pereda emphasizes in the case of Samuel Ramos, belonging to this or another category is debatable, and sometimes, not very significant." Suárez had already wondered in the previous paragraph: "Could it be, for example, that Carlos Pereyra would have felt more comfortable in one of the large blocs? Or that a certain part of Luis Villoro's work finds a better place in the middle of the archipelago, and even on the edges of philosophy where it would surely meet Ambrosio Velasco or one of the versions of Guillermo Hurtado which Pereda himself recognizes." Rodolfo R. Suárez, "Review of Carlos Pereda, *La filosofía en México en el siglo XX: Apuntes de un participante*," *Diánoia* 73 (2014): 157.
33. In this sense Estrella González is right when he stresses that "there are arguments used by philosophers of the same type as those used by social scientists" (see his "Por qué los historiadores," 214).

CHAPTER 2

1. José-Antonio Orosco, "The Philosophical Gift of Brown Folks: Mexican American Philosophy in the United States," *APA Newsletter on Hispanic/Latino Issues in Philosophy* 15, no. 2 (2016): 23–28. Orosco's title is a suggestive and inspiring variation of W. E. B Du Bois's book *The Gift of Black Folk* (1924) which highlights the cultural, political, and economic contributions from the African American community.
2. See Orosco, "Sobre la actualidad filosófica de Ramos" [On the philosophical relevance of Ramos], in Aureliano Ortega Esquivel, *Filosofía mexicana* (Guanajuato: University of Guanajuato, 2018), 125–32. Samuel Ramos's most influential work is *El perfil del hombre y la cultura en México* (Mexico City: Espasa-Calpe, 1992 [1943]); *Profile of Man and Culture in Mexico*, trans. Peter G. Earle (Austin: University of Texas Press, 1963). Among the many works of Leopoldo Zea, consider especially *En torno a una filosofía americana* [Regarding American philosophy] (1946); *La filosofía como compromiso* (1952) (a selection is available as

"Philosophy as Commitment (1952)," in Sánchez and Sanchez, *Mexican Philosophy*, 125–40); *América como conciencia* [America as consciousness] (1953); *La filosofía en México* [Philosophy in Mexico] (1955); *América en la historia* (1957) (*The Role of the Americas in History*, ed. Amy Oliver, trans. Sonja Karsen [Savage, MD: Rowman & Littlefield, 1992]); and *Latinoamérica en la formación de nuestro tiempo* [Latin America in the shaping of our time] (1965). Nor should we forget Jorge Portilla's *Fenomenología del relajo, y otros ensayos* (Mexico City: Ediciones Era, 1966). (Available in English in *The Suspension of Seriousness: On the Phenomenology of Jorge Portilla, With a Translation of the Fenomenología del relajo*, trans. Carlos Alberto Sánchez [Albany: State University of New York Press, 2012]).

3. Among other works by Gracia, consult "Identity and Latin American Philosophy" for an introduction to his ideas, in *A Companion to Latin American Philosophy*, ed. Susana Nuccetelli, Ofelia Schutte, and Otávio Bueno, 253–68 (Malden: Wiley-Blackwell, 2010). A volume that discusses and deepens these aspects of Gracia's philosophical thought is Ivan Jaksic, ed., *Debating Race, Ethnicity, and Latino Identity: J. E. Gracia and His Critics* (New York: Columbia University Press, 2015). I think it is fair to quote from Stephanie Rivera Berruz's review of this book. She rightly points out that "there is no doubt that Gracia's contributions to philosophy have been great and influential, and this book is a true testimony to that fact." Stephanie Rivera Berruz, "Debating Race, Ethnicity, and Latino Identity: Jorge J. E. Gracia and His Critics," *APA Newsletter on Hispanic/Latino Issues in Philosophy* 15, no. 2 (2016): 28.

4. Augusto Salazar Bondy, *¿Existe una filosofía de nuestra América?* [Is there a philosophy of our America?] (Mexico City: Siglo Veintiuno, 1968). Among other critics, the well-known attacks of José Mariátegui in his *Siete ensayos de interpretación de la realidad peruana* (1928) (*Seven Interpretive Essays on Peruvian Reality*, trans. Marjory Urquidi [Austin: University of Texas Press, 1971]) move in a direction analogous to that of Salazar Bondy. I will also take this opportunity to say that I probably expressed myself poorly, because I do not consider my article, "Latin American Philosophy: Some Vices"—or, for that matter, Chapter 1 of this book—to be contrary to Orosco, or to be defending an abstract universalism, but as the critical work of another participant in Latin American philosophy concerned about some of its colonial vices. So I do not consider myself very far from the critiques of Salazar Bondy or Mariátegui. It is a critical work employing the perspective of epistemic nomadism. In any case, we must not forget the polemical context in which such critiques are introduced.

5. Salazar Bondy's critiques (or other analogous or different ones) can be made whether one defends an abstract universalism or a culturalist particularism, or other positions.

6. Ignacio Ramírez, *Ignacio Ramírez "El nigromante": Obras completas*, compiled by David R. Maciel and Boris Rosen Jélomer (Mexico City: Centro de Investigación Científica Jorge L. Tamayo, 1984–1985), 3 vols., I:114.

7. Ignacio Ramírez, *La palabra de la reforma en la república de las letras: Una*

antología general [The word of reform in the republic of letters: A general anthology], ed. and with a "Preliminary Study" by Liliana Weinberg (Mexico City: Fondo de Cultura Económica, 2009), 28.

8. Weinberg, "Preliminary Study," in Ramírez, *La palabra de la reforma*, 20.
9. Weinberg, "Preliminary Study," 19. In this regard, Weinberg alludes to a "disruptive necromancy," 19. If I understand it correctly this is a "necromancy" that destabilizes the current bad habits and bad customs of society, and one of its main supports, established corruption.
10. Ramírez, *Obras completas*, vol. III, prologue by Carlos Monsiváis, v–vi. Regarding Ramírez's declaration "There is no God," pronounced in 1837, when he entered the Academy of San Juan de Letrán at a very young age, Monsiváis notes: "The declaration of atheism would mark Ramírez for the rest of his life. In today's age, where religious experience has been lost and rediscovered many times, it is perhaps useless to imagine even approximately the scope of a pronouncement of a century and a half ago, and only possible to stick to the testimonies of his time. So, Ramírez is literally the devil." A few paragraphs later Monsiváis notes, "What Ramírez introduces by his example is not religious doubt (which, socially, will take time to occur), but the initial respect for diversity. A single act advances central debates of the Reform generation: freedom of worship and freedom of conscience." Ramírez, *Obras completas*, III:vii.
11. Weinberg, "Preliminary Study," 60. Once again we find, then, an example of how to go from certain general knowledge to particular cultural knowledge: already to the very title *Ensayo sobre las sensaciones* Ramírez adds: "dedicated to the Mexican youth" because—so he seems to be suggesting—the work is much needed by them, educated as they have been in late Spanish scholasticism.
12. The liberal republicans of the restored republic of the Mexican nineteenth century—Guillermo Prieto, Ignacio Manuel Altamirano, Manuel Payno, Tomás de Cuellar, Vicente Riva Palacio, Juan A. Mateos, Francisco Zarco, Florencio M. del Castillo, Pantaleón Tovar, Alfredo Chavero, and of course, the radical Ignacio Ramírez, none of whom distinguished between republicanism and liberalism—thought of freedom as integration into a participatory society, and so, as incorporating nonexclusion. As we will see later, this proposal was taken up and elaborated in philosophical detail in the latter part of the twentieth century by Luis Villoro. In that way, this avenue of radical republican thought in Mexico is more promising, because of its tendency toward social integration, than Philip Pettit's late twentieth-century republicanism, which thinks of freedom as non-domination. See Philip Pettit, *Republicanism: A Theory of Freedom and Government* (Oxford: Clarendon Press, 1997); especially chapter 2, "Liberty as Non-domination." This tendentiously individualistic conception of freedom more or less identifies with what Kant, and the Kantian tradition in general, including Habermas and Rawls, think of as negative autonomy. However, for Kant and some parts of the Kantian tradition, this is only a first step toward the concept of positive autonomy—being a co-legislator—and the need

to contribute to a well-integrated society, which Kant understands as a "Kingdom of Ends." With the third formula of the Categorical Imperative, freedom is no longer mere freedom as nondomination, but becomes freedom as the capacity for social collaboration.
13. Ramírez, *Obras completas*, vol. III.
14. Ramírez, *Obras completas*, III:400.
15. Ramírez, "Historia política de México: Las naciones primitivas" [Political history of Mexico: Primitive nations], in *Obras Completas*, II:23.
16. Ramírez, *Obras completas*, III:402.
17. Quoted by David R. Maciel, in Ramírez, *Obras completas*, I:xlv. Faced with statements like the ones mentioned, would we not also witness similar reactions today, in the first quarter of the twenty-first century?
18. Ramírez, *Obras completas*, III:403.
19. Maria Teresa Bermúdez de Brauns, *Bosquejos de educación para el pueblo: Ignacio Ramírez e Ignacio Manuel Altamirano* [Sketches of education for the people: Ignacio Ramírez and Ignacio Manuel Altamirano] (Mexico City: El Caballito, 1985), 28.
20. Ramírez, *Obras completas*, III:403.
21. For this reason, Ramírez also advocates for the legalization of divorce, in Ramírez, *Obras completas*, II:206–11.
22. Ignacio Ramírez, *Escuelas laicas* [Secular schools] (Mexico City: Empresas Editoriales, 1967), 145–49; quoted by David R. Maciel, in Ramírez, *Obras completas*, I:cvii.
23. Ramírez, *Ensayos*, 49–50, quoted by David R. Maciel, in Ramírez, *Obras completas*, I:lviii. Commenting on the previous paragraph of Ramírez, Maciel points out that "the real problem consists in emancipating the workers from the capitalists; in his opinion, the solution was simple: it was only a matter of converting labor into capital, and this will assure the worker with not only a salary to subsist, but also a right to divide the profits with the employer proportionally. This utopian, socialist feature of Ramírez's ideology would find an extension in the anarchist activity of the Flores Magón brothers." Ramírez, *Obras completas*, I:cviii–lix.
24. In the report by the organization Afluentes, S. C., Mexico, 2018, for example on page 38 (but almost any other page could be consulted with no more encouraging information found) we read: in Sinaloa "an elementary school located in a Campo Agrícola and a technical high school in the Sindicatura of Villa Juárez were visited. In these places, discrimination and cultural shock affected the rights of day laborers arriving in the agricultural fields from Guerrero or Oaxaca. Children, adolescents, and young people, as well as adult women and men, are discriminated against because of their skin color, because they are indigenous, do not speak Spanish or speak with an indigenous accent, or come from very poor areas.... All these migrants are mistreated and branded as 'Oaxacans' or 'Paisas' ... women, adolescents, and girls are often violated and face

new dangers: abuse and harassment by campers, forced prostitution, the risk of becoming pregnant or contracting sexually transmitted diseases."

25. In this very brief rereading of Villoro, I revisit ideas found in my earlier works about this thinker: "Luis Villoro: Un Ulises del recomenzar" [Luis Villoro: A Ulysses of new beginnings], in *Luis Villoro: conocimiento y emancipación: Homenaje póstumo del Instituto de Investigaciones Filosóficas* [Luis Villoro: Knowledge and emancipation: Posthumous tribute of the Institute for Philosophical Research], ed. Pedro Stepanenko (Mexico City: Instituto de Investigaciones Filosóficas, UNAM, 2017). Additionally, in my book *Debates* (Mexico City: Fondo de Cultura Económica, 1987), I discuss in some detail Villoro's book *Creer, saber, conocer* (Mexico City: Siglo Veintiuno, 1982). (Luis Villoro, *Belief, Personal, and Propositional Knowledge*, trans. David Sosa and Douglas McDermid [Amsterdam-Atlanta: Brill Rodopi, 1998].) Also, in *La filosofía en México en el siglo XX*, I include four works about Villoro: "Del saber y de la servidumbre en Luis Villoro" [Of knowledge and servitude in Luis Villoro], "Respuestas y preguntas a Villoro" [Responses and question to Villoro], "Villoro y sabiduría" [Villoro and wisdom] and "Villoro, Muguerza y el combate a la razón arrogante" [Villoro, Muguerza, and the fight against arrogant reason]. For excellent introductions to Villoro, see Mario Teodoro Ramírez, *La razón del otro: Estudios sobre el pensamiento de Luis Villoro* [The reason of the other: Studies in the thought of Luis Villoro] (Mexico City: Insituto de Investigaciones Filosóficas, UNAM, 2010) and *Humanismo para un nueva época: Nuevos ensayos sobre el pensamiento de Luis Villoro* [Humanism for a new era: New essays on the thought of Luis Villoro] (Mexico City: Siglo Veintiuno, 2011). See also Gabriel Vargas Lozano, "La evolución filosófica de Luis Villoro" [The philosophical evolution of Luis Villoro], in *Luis Villoro, Filosofía, historia y política* [Luis Villoro: Philosophy, history, and politics], ed. Gustavo Leyva and Jorge Rendón Alarcón (Mexico City: Gedisa-Universidad Autónoma Metropolitana, 2016).

26. Luis Villoro, *Los grandes momentos del indigenismo in México* (Mexico City: El Colegio de México, 1950); a selection of this work is available as "The Major Moments of Indigenism in Mexico: Conclusion (1950)," in Sánchez and Sanchez, *Mexican Philosophy in the Twentieth Century*, 156–64. Luis Villoro, *El proceso ideológico de la revolución de independencia* [The ideological process of the revolution of independence] (Mexico City: Universidad Nacional Autónoma de México, 1953).

27. Luis Villoro, *La idea y el ente en la filosofía de Descartes* [Idea and entity in the philosophy of Descartes] (Mexico City: Fondo de Cultura Económica, 1965), 13.

28. Luis Villoro, *El concepto de ideología y otros ensayos* [The concept of ideology and other essays] (Mexico City: Fondo de Cultura Económica, 1985).

29. Villoro, *Creer, saber, conocer*.

30. Villoro, *Creer, saber, conocer*, 9.

31. Luis Villoro, *El poder y el valor: Fundamentos de una ética política* [Power and value: Foundations of a political ethics] (Mexico City: Fondo de Cultura

Economica-El Colegio de México, 1997); Luis Villoro, *Estado plural, pluralidad de culturas* [Plural state, plurality of cultures] (Mexico City: Paidós-Facultad de Filosofía y Letras, UNAM, 1998); Luis Villoro, *Los retos de la sociedad por venir: Ensayos sobre justicia, democracia y multiculturalismo* [The challenges of the society to come: Essays on justice, democracy, and multiculturalism] (Mexico City: Fondo de Cultura Económica, 2007); Luis Villoro, *La alternativa: Perspectivas y posibilidades de cambio* [The alternative: perspectives and possibilities for change] (Mexico City: Fondo de Cultura Económica, 2015). In this last book Villoro discusses proposals by the Zapatistas, and the book includes correspondence between Villoro and Subcomandante Marcos.

32. See Guillermo Hurtado, "Luis Villoro en *La Jornada*: Crónica de una conversión" [Luis Villoro in *La Jornada*: Chronicle of a conversion], in Stepanenko, *Luis Villoro*, 267–86. Here I disagree somewhat with Hurtado: in Villoro's works we find not a "conversion," but a radicalization of his old positions. On the other hand, it is worth remembering the Mexican liberal republicans of the nineteenth century, their constant collaboration, and their founding of newspapers and magazines. Since then, and until recently, this has been a frequent tradition among Latin American intellectuals. Their guiding concern was clear: to influence and to reinvigorate the public sphere by these interventions. In the first quarter of the twenty-first century, the channels for intervening in the public sphere have branched out: In addition to television, we have the Internet, social media, and other mass media.

33. Radio Zapatista, http://radiozapatista.org.
34. Stepanenko, *Luis Villoro*, 100.
35. The concerns of Iris Marion Young arguably include a theorization of justice as social nonexclusion: see her *Justice and the Politics of Difference* (Princeton, NJ: Princeton University Press, 1990).
36. Villoro, *Los retos de la sociedad*, 22.
37. Villoro, *Los retos de la sociedad*, 34.
38. Gregory Fernando Pappas, "The Limitations and Dangers of Decolonial Philosophies: Lessons from Zapatista Luis Villoro," *Radical Philosophy Review* 20, no. 2 (2017): 265–95.
39. Pappas, "The Limitations and Dangers," 268.
40. Villoro, *La alternativa*, 105.
41. Pappas, "The Limitations and Dangers," 271.
42. About Villoro's emphasis on knowing how to listen, I am reminded of some comments by Ángeles Eraña with Socratic echoes: "From my perspective, the most important legacy that [Villoro] leaves us has to do with his role as a student in the Zapatista school. A teacher who is a student.... To be a student, one must know how to listen (or learn to do so), and for that one needs humility. We need to recognize that there are other ways, that light comes from many directions, that we know little, that we understand less" (Stepanenko, *Luis Villoro*, 287–88). In this way, we can conclude that Villoro's nomadic epistemology is

a consequence of his vital, personal nomadism: the events of history teach the great professor to resist and to shed old desires and beliefs in order to start over as an attentive apprentice who knows how to listen. In the beautiful and heartfelt memory of his father, the writer Juan Villoro notes something similar: "the student of Sahagún, Las Casas, Clavijero and Vasco de Quiroga, became an interlocutor of the indigenous communities, not with the desire to advise or enlighten them, but to learn from them." Stepanenko, *Luis Villoro*, 334.

43. Manuel Vargas, "On the Value of Philosophy: The Latin American Case," *Comparative Philosophy* 1, no. 1 (2010): 33–52.
44. Robert Eli Sanchez Jr., "Strengthening the Case for Latin American Philosophy: Beyond Cultural Resources." *APA Newsletter on Hispanic/Latino Issues in Philosophy* 13, no. 2 (2014): 2–9.
45. Vargas, "On the Value of Philosophy," 34.
46. Vargas, "On the Value of Philosophy," 37.
47. Vargas, "On the Value of Philosophy," 38.
48. Vargas, "On the Value of Philosophy," 41.
49. Sanchez, "Strengthening the Case," 5.
50. Sanchez, "Strengthening the Case," 4, 6.
51. Sanchez, "Strengthening the Case," 7.
52. Sanchez, "Strengthening the Case," 7.
53. Sanchez, "Strengthening the Case," 7.
54. A different philosopher, Bernard Williams, also highlights the disruptive character that the best philosophy can—or ought to?—have. See Bernard Williams, "Descartes and the Historiography of Philosophy," in *The Sense of the Past: Essays in the History of Philosophy*, ed. Myles Burnyeat, 257–64 (Princeton, NJ: Princeton University Press, 2007). In particular, the disruptive way of doing the *history* of philosophy is often opposed to what in Chapter 1 was mockingly described as "antiquarian." Both approaches involve the distinction between argumentative and explanatory history of philosophy. In a complex continuation of various aspects of the distinction, it is useful to consider Robert B. Brandom's contrast between intellectual historiography "*de dicto*" and textual interpretations "*de re*" in his book, *Tales of the Mighty Dead: Historical Essays in the Metaphysics of Intentionality* (Cambridge, MA: Harvard University Press, 2002), 102, and in general, his discussion of "hermeneutics" under the title "Pretexts," 90–118. These and other converging contrasts are variations—each with its own commitments—between being in the position of observer, that is, in the third-person point of view, or intervening as a participant, and thus oscillating between the first- and the second-person point of view. However, I suspect that when one works in the history of philosophy, or even in history in general— and even when reading a past text that discusses thought *to any degree*—one needs to inquire in both directions, even if the primary intention is to argue in a "disruptive" way, or to explain in an "antiquarian" way.
55. Another example of the strategy of transitions comes from the following claims by Leopold Zea: "The starting point of those who think is always the concrete

man.... This is the golden rule of philosophy: to start from your own, specific problems, and then look for the universal that may exist in them.... I mean: in my identity I come across other similar identities, I find that other men have problems like me: problems like those that all men have in all times." Pereda, *La filosofía en México*, 88–89.
56. Villoro, *Los retos de la sociedad por venir*, 11.
57. Alfonso Reyes, "A vuelta de correo," in *La "X" en la frente* [The x on the forehead] (Mexico City: Porrúa y Obregón, 1952).
58. See Guillermo Hurtado, ed., *El Hiperión: Antología* [Hyperion: An anthology], introduction and selections by Guillermo Hurtado (Mexico City: Universidad Nacional Autónoma de México, 2015). On the importance of this group, see also Alexander Stehn, "Latin American Philosophy," *Internet Encyclopedia of Philosophy*, https://iep.utm.edu/latin-am/.
59. Thoughts moving in a similar direction to these observations are found in Samuel C. Rickless, "Brief for an Inclusive Anti-Canon," *Metaphilosophy* 49, nos. 1–2 (2018): 167–81, regarding courses on the history of philosophy.

CHAPTER 3

1. The dictatorship of Porfirio Díaz lasted for thirty-four years (1876–1911). As Guillermo José Mañon Garibay points out, the philosophy supporting the Porfirista project was "the French positivism of Auguste Comte, introduced in Mexico by Gabino Barreda (1818–1881)." "Historia de las ideas en México: El grupo Hiperión: reflexiones sobre el problema de la obediencia y el cumplimiento del deber" [History of ideas in Mexico: The Hyperion group: reflections on the problem of obedience and the fulfillment of duty], *Revista Mexicana de historia del derecho* (Mexican journal of legal history), second issue, 34 (2016): 54. On positivism in Mexico, the studies by Leopoldo Zea are pioneering: *El positivismo en México: Nacimiento, apogeo y decadencia* (Mexico City: Fondo de Cultura Economica, 1968) (*Positivism in Mexico*, trans. Josephine H. Schulte [Austin: University of Texas Press, 1974]), and *El positivismo y la realidad mexicana* [Positivism and Mexican reality] (Mexico City: Universidad Nacional Autónoma de México, 1985).
2. Samuel Ramos, *Historia de la filosofía en México* [History of philosophy in Mexico] (Mexico City: Universidad Nacional Autónoma de México, 1990), 204 ff.
3. Guillermo Hurtado, *La Revolución creadora: Antonio Caso y José Vasconcelos en la Revolución Mexicana* [The innovative revolution: Antonio Caso and José Vasconcelos in the Mexican Revolution] (Mexico City: Universidad Nacional Autónoma de México, 2016), xi. Hurtado's proposal in this book is openly polemical. The "official idea," traditionally defended—by Alfonso Reyes, Octavio Paz, and Leopoldo Zea, among others—is that the Mexican Revolution, in contrast with others, was born "without ideas." That is why this revolution "could change its trajectory in accordance with the needs of the Mexicans at each moment; it could shift from left to right." Hurtado, *La Revolución creadora*, xv.

Against this thesis, the so-called "revisionist historians" appeared around 1960; for example, Arnaldo Córdova, who insists in his book *La ideología de la Revolución Mexicana* [The ideology of the Mexican Revolution] (Mexico City: Era, 1973) that the ideology in question is *"social positivism"*—maybe a variation of Porfirian positivism? As opposed to that, Hurtado argues (in a post-revisionist way?) that the Revolution "was influenced not by one, but by several philosophies or ideologies: nineteenth-century liberalism, twentieth-century reformist liberalism, anarchism, socialism, Christian social doctrine, social positivism and *the spiritualist humanism of Caso and Vasconcelos*." Hurtado, *La Revolución creadora*, xviii. In support of his proposal, Hurtado studies various stages of the thought of Caso and Vasconcelos, and underlines their links with the Mexican Revolution. As one example among many, we might consider these remarks by Vasconcelos: "Poverty and ignorance are our worst enemies, and it is up to us to solve the problem of ignorance. I am at this time more than a new rector who succeeds the previous ones, a delegate of the Revolution who does not come to seek refuge to meditate in the calm atmosphere of the classroom, but to urge you to go out with him to fight, to share with us the struggles and responsibilities." See José Vasconcelos, "Discurso en la Universidad con motivo de la toma de posesión del cargo de Rector" [Speech at the University on the occasion of taking office as President], *Obras completas* (Mexico City: Libreros Mexicanos Unidos, 1959), 2:773. In addition, a fresh and very welcome approach to the varied work of this thinker can be found in *Los retornos de Ulises: Una antología de José Vasconcelos* [The resurgence of Ulysses: An anthology of José Vasconcelos], ed. Christopher Domínguez Michael (Mexico City: SEP-Fondo de Cultura Económica, 2010). In this anthology we find, in addition to the acute preface, many excellent representative texts, and several excellent essays about Vasconcelos's work.

4. Samuel Ramos, *El perfil del hombre*.

5. As an excellent introduction to these thoughts, see Roger Bartra, *La jaula de la melancholía: Identidad y metamorfosis del mexicano* (Mexico City: Grijalbo, 1987). (*The Cage of Melancholy: Identity and Metamorphosis in the Mexican*, trans. Christopher J. Hall [New Brunswick: Rutgers University Press, 1992])

6. The reflections of the Hyperion group on one's own "circumstance" were marked by a sought-after ontological register, which did not prevent their being related to a robust tradition of the Ibero-American essay on the subject. For example, among others, recall the Spaniards Miguel de Unamuno and his sorrow for Spain, and Ortega y Gasset and his celebrated *dictum*, "I am myself and my circumstance"; the Cuban Jose Martí in *Nuestra América*; the Argentinian Ezequiel Martínez Estrada in *Radiografía de la pampa* (*X-Ray of the Pampa*), trans. Alain Swietlicki (Austin: University of Texas Press, 1972); José Carlos Mariátegui and his *Siete ensayos de interpretación de la realidad peruana*; as well as Borges in some of his earliest books. In an oblique and perhaps anomalous way, but often with analogous effects on its readers, José Enrique Rodó's *Ariel* can also be considered as belonging to this tradition of writings, so famous and influential in its time, and so difficult to reread.

7. Octavio Paz, *El arco y la lira* (Mexico City: Fondo de Cultura Económica, 1956); Octavio Paz, *The Bow and the Lyre: The Poem, the Poetic Revelation, Poetry and History*, trans. Ruth L. C. Simms (Austin: University of Texas Press, 1973); Octavio Paz, *El laberinto de la soledad* (Mexico City: Cuaderno Americanos, 1950); Octavio Paz, *The Labyrinth of Solitude: Life and Thought in Mexico*, trans. Lysander Kemp (New York: Grove Press, 1961). See also José Gaos, *Materiales para una autobiografía filosófica* [Materials for a philosophical autobiography], foreword and selection by Adolfo Castañon (Mexico City: Bonilla Artigas, 2015), 367.
8. Villoro writes the prologue to the government reissue of *Análisis del ser del mexicano* (Guanajuato: Gobierno de Guanajuato, 1990); *Emilio Uranga's Analysis of Mexican Being: A Translation and Critical Introduction*, trans. Carlos Alberto Sánchez (New York: Bloomsbury Academic, 2021). It is a prologue that is both complimentary and critical, exhibiting a cultured attitude frequently used by Villoro. Years later Villoro included this prologue in his collection of papers: *En México, entre libros: Pensadores del siglo xx* [In Mexico, among books: Thinkers of the twentieth century] (Mexico City: Fondo de Cultura Económica, 1995). Villoro's criticism of Uranga indicates, on the one hand, that it is not possible to formulate the project of an ontology of being, in general, from some particular, the Mexican; and, on the other hand, that "the Mexican" suggests something homogenous that does not exist. In my reading of Uranga, I reiterate these criticisms. However, unlike Villoro, I think these are serious difficulties for Uranga that cannot be made to disappear if the theoretical framework of "ontology" is replaced by another one, the "philosophy of culture."
9. Luis Villoro, *Los grandes momentos*; Luis Villoro, *La alternativa: Perspectivas y posibilidades de cambio* (Mexico City: Fondo de Cultura Económica, 2015).
10. Portilla, *Fenomenología del relajo*. Victor Flores Olea, Alejandro Rossi, and Luis Villoro, Portilla's editors, used to tell stories that show Portilla to be a sharp and brilliant speaker, a welcome participant in the coffee gatherings of the time and, simultaneously, a man torn between a deep and visceral Catholicism and a poorly controlled hedonism. In his *Manual del distraido* [Manual of the distracted] (Mexico City: Joaquín Mortiz, 1978), Rossi first describes Portilla as a "dissatisfied, anarchistic, and confused man" (67), but ends by indicating he was a "mixture of moralist and social critic" (70). Additionally, it seems that Carlos Fuentes once confessed that Portilla was the inspiration for the character López Wilson in his novel *La región más transparente* (Mexico City: Fondo de Cultural Económica, 1958); *Where the Air is Clear*, trans. Sam Hileman (New York: Farrar, Straus and Giroux, 1988), a figure eager for pleasures, as well as a witness to social collapses and the end of a political regime (or what Fuentes fantasizes as the end of a political regime).
11. *El Hiperión*, introduction and selections by Guillermo Hurtado (Mexico City: Universidad Nacional Autónoma de México, 2006), ix. In addition to the participants of the Hyperion group mentioned in this work, we must also include other participants such as Ricardo Guerra (1927–2007), Joaquín Sánchez McGregor (1925–2008), and Fausto Vega (1922–2015).

12. Given his personality, it is not by chance that Uranga appears as a character in various works of literature, for example, in the only novel by Sergio Avilés Parra (1924–1975), *El tiempo muerto en el tiempo* [The dead time in time] (Mexico City: Editorial Latina, 1950). There were rumors that Héctor Aguilar Camín was inspired by Uranga in his creation of Galio Bermúdez, a slightly comical character in his novel, *La Guerra de Galio* [Galio's war] (Mexico City: Cal y Arena, 1991). Many years later Uranga returns in José Manuel Cuéllar Moreno's story "El consejero presidencial" [The presidential advisor], published in the magazine, *Punto de Partida* [Point of departure], new issue, no. 211, 2018, which, more than a mere story, is a series of probable observations about this character. I cite two observations by Cuéllar, which, if I am not mistaken, characterize Uranga: "He rejected the designation that an entire generation be placed on his back. He was not and did not want to be the conscience of the republic" (17). I also recall the reconstruction of this moment of lucidity: "He corrects himself: he is not fed up, but rather lethargic. 'It sounds hollow': in this expression a whole metaphysics, morality, and aesthetics is contained" (19); perhaps those of Uranga, I would like to add.
13. About "ninguneo," see Carlos Pereda, *Critica de la razón arrogante* [Critique of arrogant reason] (Mexico City: Taurus, 1999).
14. Emilio Uranga, *Análisis del ser del mexicano y otros escritos sobre la filosofía de lo mexicano (1949–1952)*, selections, notes, and prologue by Guillermo Hurtado (Mexico City: Bonilla Artigas, 2013). The review by Valero was published in *Diánoia* 59, no 72 (2014): 155–61.
15. For example, Pedro Salmerón Sanginés, "La *mexicanidad* al servicio del PRI" [*Mexicanness* in the service of the PRI], *La Jornada*, August 9, 2016. José Manuel Cuéllar Moreno in his book *La revolución inconclusa: La filosofía de Emilio Uranga, artífice oculto del PRI* [The unfinished revolution: The philosophy of Emilio Uranga, hidden architect of the PRI] (Mexico City: Ariel, 2018) does a better job than the title promises. The first chapter, "Emilio Uranga, philosopher of the hollow and accidental," already constitutes a brief introduction to Uranga's thought. On the other hand, Jacinto Rodríguez Munguía, in his polemical book *La conspiración del 68: Los intelectuales y el poder: así se fragüó la matanza* [The conspiracy of '68: Intellectuals and power: How the massacre was planned] (Mexico City: Debates, 2018)—although harsher regarding the political role of Uranga, who is accused of being an ideologist for Díaz Ordaz and his crimes—clearly admires the intelligence of this celebrity. I quote passages from his book: "From the shadows of the corridors of the old Bucareli Palace, a thinker surfaced of 'the kind Europe produces every 100 years,' as some of his contemporaries defined him at the time; a discreet man, a philosopher overflowing with knowledge, who also had the ear of at least three presidents of the Republic. . . . That brilliant mind decided to operate from the darkness and serve political power" (16); "President Gustavo Díaz Ordaz even said: 'We are facing a rare case of lucidity, which I have to be careful around, because as soon as I open my

mouth, Emilio finds it problematic" (126). "Uranga talked much of Díaz Ordaz. One time he went to visit him in Cuernavaca, where he found him watering his flowers and reading a biography of Hitler" (126). Rodríguez Munguía also remembers the words of Uranga's great friend, the writer Ricardo Garibay: "He returned from Europe lazy, drunk, slothful, inattentive, and starved of wellbeing. He devoted himself to editorial journalism with contempt for the truth, for clarity, and for language, as a way to curry favor with politicians, to prosper, to receive financial protection: he became the unconditional spokesman for government regimes. He was blamed for having written *El móndrigo*, a filthy libel, on the subject of 68" (291). Rodríguez Munguía's conclusion about Uranga lies in this scandalous question: "Was Emilio Uranga perhaps—as Viktor Reinmann said about Goebbels—'the spiritual director of terror' in Mexico?" (302). Valero, in *Diánoia* 59, no. 72 (2014): 155. In the *Excelsior* newspaper, January 4, 2015, Ricardo Sevilla Gutiérrez includes a reference to "Emilio Uranga: The father of insidiousness." As a further cause for the neglect of Uranga, we can join Hurtado in observing that "Uranga's personal twilight, increasingly isolated and ill, coincided with the total discrediting of *la filosofía de lo mexicano*." See the prologue by Hurtado in *Análisis del ser del mexicano y otros escritos*, 14.

16. Abelardo Villegas, "Polémica de las mafias," *Proceso*, no. 798, February 17, 1992, 39.

17. See Carlos Pereda, "La contaminación heideggeriana," *Vuelta* 12 (1988): 55–57. I would add: Uranga could be imaginative and irreverent in his occasional writings. Full of insightful observations, these writings were published in the leading cultural supplements of the day: *México en la cultura*, from the newspaper *Novedades*, and *La revista mexicana de cultura*, from *El nacional*, as indicated in the third part of Hurtado's reissue, *Análisis del ser del mexicano y otros escritos*: "Artículos en suplementos culturales." Such publications explain his controversial but important and sometimes influential presence in public life. We also find novelty and sensitivity in his *Diario de Alemania*. Unfortunately, I do not think such qualities are present when Uranga proposes to do "serious philosophy," which can be confirmed by anyone who studies the treatise (*Análisis del ser del mexicano*) included in the first part of Hurtado's reissue, whose chapter 2 we comment on in this reflection. But I would almost say, also unfortunately, that doing "serious philosophy" was, notoriously, an obsession that Uranga never abandoned; for example, this obsession is present at every step of his still unedited *Diario de Alemania*.

18. In *El laberinto de la solidad*, Paz classified Uranga as the "primary inspiration" of *la filosofía de lo mexicano*. At the same time, Uranga dedicated his *Análisis del ser del mexicano* to Paz, and classified Paz's book to be of "priceless value" (*Análisis del ser del mexicano*, 39). However, years later, in order to defend the government's horrible and repressive treatment of the student rebellion of '68, including the tragedy of October 2nd, almost as if it were a different person, Uranga attacked Paz in a manner that was derisive, furious, and—it is hard to

find any other expression—*stupid*: "Examen de una postdata: La poca Paz de Octavio" [Examination of a postscript: The little Peace of Octavio] (in three parts), *Revista de América*, 1970. This was not his only malicious indulgence: he broke with Juan José Arreola, and, by the way, with Juan Rulfo; also with Carlos Fuentes and his fellow group members, Jorge Portilla and Leopoldo Zea, and his teacher José Gaos; he called Daniel Cosío Villegas "an old gossip." On this, see also Gerardo de la Concha, *La razón y la afrenta: Antología del panfleto y la polémica en México* [Reason and insult: An anthology of pamphlets and controversies in Mexico] (Toluca: Instituto Mexiquense de Cultura, 1995). I emphasize that my reading will be an "unfriendly reading." For a more respectful interpretation of Uranga, consult *Filosofía mexicana* [Mexican philosophy] by Aureliano Ortega Esquivel (Guanajuato: Universidad of Guanajuato, 2018). Ortega Esquivel distinguishes four periods in Uranga's output. The first, which I consider in this work, takes place in his two books *Ensayo de ontología del mexicano* and *Análisis del ser del mexicano* (141–42). The second consists in what Ortega Esquival calls his "Marxist *interregnum*" (although he clarifies that it is a Marxism "more declarative than real") with books such as, *Mi camino hacia Marx* [My path to Marx], *El pensamiento filosófico* [Philosophical thought], and *¿De quién es la filosofía?* [Who owns philosophy?] (143). The third period represents his encounter with analytic philosophy and the philosophy of language, and the most important work of this period is *Astucias literarias* [Literary tricks]. Ortega Esquivel adds a final period, "the most rambling, the most gloomy, and the most personal" (144). In the last three periods, Uranga alternates between philosophical reflection and journalism. Ortega Esquivel emphasizes Uranga's good advice, especially for those whose thinking is far from the Headquarters of Power and Thought: "What's urgent is not to let yourself be stupefied." *El pensamiento filosófico*, 169. Contrary to Ortega Esquivel, I humbly submit that Uranga frequently ignored this wise advice.

19. Uranga, *Análisis del ser del mexicano*, 40.
20. Uranga, *Análisis del ser del mexicano*, 40.
21. Uranga, *Análisis del ser del mexicano*, 40.
22. Uranga, *Análisis del ser del mexicano*, 41.
23. Uranga, *Análisis del ser del mexicano*, 41–42.
24. Uranga, *Análisis del ser del mexicano*, 43.
25. Uranga, *Análisis del ser del mexicano*, 45.
26. Uranga, *Análisis del ser del mexicano*, 53–54.
27. Emilio Uranga, "Optimismo y pesimismo del mexicano" [The Mexican's optimism and pessimism], *Historia Mexicana* 1, no. 3 (Jan.-Mar. 1952): 397.
28. On Ramón López Velarde it is worth remembering Octavio Paz's lucid and imaginative lectures in *Cuadrivio* (Mexico City: Joaquín Mortiz, 1965); Guillermo Sheridan's *Un corazón adicto: La vida de Ramón López Velarde* [An addicted heart: The life of Ramón López Velarde] (Mexico City: Fondo de

Cultura Económica, 1989); and José Emilio Pacheco's *La lumbre inmovil* (Mexico City: Era, 2018).

29. Javier Garibay indicates that "to be in *nepantla*" means to be in transition, to be on the way: see *Nepantla situades en medio: Estudio histórico-teológico de la realidad indiana* [Nepantla positioned in between: A historical-theological study of indigenous reality] (Mexico City: Centro de Reflexión Teológica, 2000), 227.

30. In "La idea mexicana de la muerte" [The Mexican idea of death], in *México en la cultura*, a supplement of the newspaper *Novedades*, September 3, 1950. Sor Juana was born—by one of those chance happenings we sometimes call "destiny"?—in San Miguel Nepantla.

31. From the words "it is worth remembering that independently of Uranga," or better yet, taking these words as a pretext and continuing with some of the critical observations already made about Uranga, it would be most useful to write an *explanatory history of bewitchment by malignant thought*. It is notorious how theorists with a tendency to the perverse have aroused, and continue to arouse, an almost irresistible seduction in many intellectual circles, or those which describe themselves as such. In this possible history of theoretical snake charmers, perhaps a place will be reserved, albeit a very minor one, for the attraction that the late Uranga aroused, and arouses, in many people. Instead we should study the enchantment that the Marxist neopositivism of Althusser arouses in the Academy, and above all, the fascination that the Nazi theorist Carl Schmitt (along with some of his contemporaries) still arouses in a major way. Perhaps by digging into the explanatory history of this kind of enchantment, we may discover two of its causes: on the one hand, the feeling of radical impotence to act, or even to make criticisms with any impact on society (even a minor one) by those who become addicted to evil, and, on the other hand, the need so typical of the Academy, to continue accumulating words and theory to avoid revealing that it no longer knows where to go. In contrast, see Gloria Anzaldúa and her wonderful *Borderlands/La Frontera: The New Mestiza* (San Francisco: Aunt Lute, 1987).

32. Álvaro Ruiz Abreu, *José Revueltas: Los muros de la utopía* [José Revueltas: The walls of utopia] (Mexico City: Cal y Arena, 1992), 416. Revueltas was a nomad in several ways. For example, Carlos Illades observes in *El marxismo en México*: "While he was imprisoned by the state for dissent, the Mexican communist party expels Revueltas . . . also for dissent."

33. Juan Carlos Galdo compares how these two writers elaborate their traumatic prison experiences in the novels he discusses: "Nacionalismo y disidencias en la narrativa carcelaria latinoamericana: *Los muros del agua* de José Revueltas and *El sexto* de José María Arguedas" [Nationalism and dissidence in Latin American prison narrative: *The walls of water* by José Revueltas and *The sixth* by José María Arguedas], *Lucero: A journal of Iberian and Latin American Studies* 12, no. 3 (2001): 57–64. Regarding the novel by Revueltas, Galdo points out: "*Los muros*

del agua is a novel dating back to 1941. It is well known that the novel recreates the double prison experience on the Marias Islands [by Revueltas], a penal colony where he was successively deported, first in 1932 and later in 1943." In turn, the philosopher Juan Cristóbal Cruz Revueltas, his grandson, fifty years after the tragedy of October 2nd [1968], published an emotional article in the newspaper *El universal*, titled "October 2nd and Jose Revueltas: A Remembrance." I quote two passages: "I remember that on that October 2nd my mother Andrea, sharing her father's convictions, went to the Three Cultures rally and it would take forever to return for her children; then, my grandfather in prison comes to mind, the two or three times I went to visit him in jail, and above all, the feeling of oppressive authoritarianism that was in the air at that time in Lecumberri." Further on, Cruz Revueltas adds: "the Revueltas that I had the fortune of knowing, though briefly, seems to me to be a writer who sought to defend the individual and society against ideological dogmatism and state power," available at "El 2 de octubre y José Revueltas, una evocación," *El Universal*, May 10, 2018, https://www.eluniversal.com.mx/columna/juan-cristobal-cruz-revueltas/cultura/el-2-de-octubre-y-jose-revueltas-una-evocacion. Among other terrible situations Revueltas experienced in prison, Illades recalls: "On New Year's Eve of 1970, the authorities of the Lecumberri Preventive Prison relaxed the security of the political prisoners, giving common prisoners an opportunity to attack them and loot their cells. They received a dreadful beating, and books, desks, typewriters, watches, mattresses, and clothes disappeared or are destroyed. Revueltas is stripped of his typewriter and 'a cardboard box with more than 15 folders of notes.'" Illades, *El marximo en México*, 120.

34. See Carlos Monsiváis, *Amor perdido* (Mexico City: Era, 1977), 102.
35. In his book *José Revueltas: Una literatura del "lado moridor"* [José Revueltas: A literature of the "dying side"] (Mexico City: Fondo de Cultura Económica, 2014), Evodio Escalante observes: "Revueltas can only be fully understood if one pays attention to what he says in his political and philosophical texts. There is an intimate connection between them and his narrative works." Escalante gives the following examples: "The ideas advanced in a novel like *Los días terrenales* (1949) [*Earthly Days*, trans. Matthew Gleeson (Mexico City: Archive 48, 2020)] are explained and formulated theoretically in the *Ensayo sobre un proletariado sin cabeza* [Essay on a headless proletariat; 1962], a true political-philosophical manifesto of the Spartacist Leninist League. Similarly, the argumentative background of *Los errores* [Mistakes; 1964] becomes more evident when compared with certain passages from *Dialéctica de la conciencia* [Dialectic of consciousness; 1982]. With this parallelism, however, I do not mean to suggest that the 'truth' of the two narrative works must be sought elsewhere.... What I mean is that the interplay of the literary sign is corroborated and clarified in proximity to these other texts" (103–4). Illades also points out: "Revueltian narrative is full of passages about the tumultuous relationship with official communism and imprisonment, crudely exposed in his novels. 'Free' on an island in *Los*

muros del agua [The walls of water; 1941] or condemned to the immobility of a punishment cell in *El apando* [The hole; 1969], prisoners are dehumanized, prison democracy makes them equal. The only thing that contains the hopelessness of political prisoners—that omnipresent minority in the universe of Revueltas—is fraternity and the sense that someday the revolutionary project will be realized." Illiades, *El marxismo en México*, 85. Additional observations about some of the novels' assumptions can be found in Edith Negrín, *Entre la paradoja y la dialéctica: Una lectura de la narrative de José Revueltas* [Between paradox and dialectic: A reading of José Revueltas's narrative] (Mexico City: El Colegio de México, 1995).

36. Ruiz Abreu points out: Revueltas "receives his provenance from socialist realism, and then rebels, criticizes his origin, surpasses it, and walks on at his own risk. It is a heartbreaking work, full of contrasts, in which there are few intermediate stations, only one track that reaches the terminals. One of these led Revueltas to his thesis of failure. Communists should seek new forms of social participation, strengthen the Party's democracy. Premonition? Simply a desperate and at the same time lucid and sincere vision of socialism in the world." Ruiz Abreu, *José Revueltas: Los muros de la utopía*, 418.

37. José Revueltas, "Posibilidades y limitaciones del mexicano," in *Obras Completas*, 26 vols., ed. Andrea Revueltas and Philippe Cheron (Mexico City: Era, 1978–1987), vol. 19; "Possibilities and Limitations of the Mexican," in Sánchez and Sanchez, *Mexican Philosophy*, 216–32. Max Parra contrasts Revueltas not with the Hyperion group but with Paz: see Max Parra, "El nacionalismo y el mito de 'lo mexicano' en Octavio Paz y José Revueltas," *Confluencia* 12, no. 1 (1996): 28–37. According to Parra, Paz's *Labyrinth* "marks a culminating moment, both conceptually and stylistically, in the construction of the myth of 'the Mexican'"; this myth "maintains an intimate relationship, although not always immediate or evident" with the nationalist discourse of the post-revolutionary Mexican state (28). Further on Parra insists: "what Paz passes off as *natural* to the Mexican is above all a mythical construction" (31). Regarding Revueltas, Parra observes: "In comparison to Paz, the essay by Revueltas is modest, even schematic, and not without problems, but it adopts a position that is unique for its time: it maintains that the idea of 'lo mexicano' is a mystification that only serves to obscure understanding of the problem of nationality in Mexico" (32). Among these problems, according to Parra, is "his positivist vision of history . . . [this] makes him see the social evolution of the country as an ascending and integrative progress, a vision that is conceptually similar to that of the ideologists of nationalism and their sense of the inevitability of this process. In this sense, the essay maintains a critical, but also ambiguous, relationship with the hegemonic nationalist thought of the time" (35).

38. Although in this work Revueltas does not explicitly cite any of the Hyperion group, he is clearly engaging in polemics with them. Besides, the work was originally published where most of the Hyperion group's works were published,

Filosofía y letras: Revista de la facultad de filosofía y letras [Philosophy and literature: Journal of the faculty of philosophy and literature]. The editors of his *Obras completas* confirm this antagonistic relationship in the preface to volume 19: "In 'Posibilidades . . . ,' Revueltas took a position in the debate about 'the Mexican,' a theme that, after the publication of *El perfil del hombre y la cultura en México* by Samuel Ramos in 1934, and until the 1950s, exercised and motivated the work of many intellectuals" (10). On the other hand, in an interview with O. Díaz Ruanova in *México en la cultura* [Mexico in culture], May 28, 1950, regarding the representation of his play, *El cuadrante de la soledad* [The quadrant of solitude], Revueltas himself—emphatically separating himself from the colonial vice of the *craving for novelty*—states: "I am not an existentialist. Neither Uranga nor Zea nor the other philosophers who study fashionable theories have included me among those who disseminate them. They consider me a heterodox Marxist, but in reality they do not know what I am: a product of Mexico, a monstrous country that we could symbolically represent as a being that simultaneously has the forms of a horse, a snake, and an eagle. Everything among us is contradiction" (3). See also Díaz Ruanova, *Los existencialistas mexicanos* (Mexico City: Rafael Jiménez Silés, 1982), where it is mentioned as well that Uranga succumbs to the *glamour* of Paris.
39. Revueltas, "Posibilidades y limitaciones," 43. For example, regarding "refinement," Revueltas may be implicitly referring to chapter 1 of *El amor y la amistad en el mexicano* [Love and friendship in the Mexican] (Mexico City: Porrúa y Obregón, 1952), a book by the Hyperion member Salvador Reyes Nevares (1922–1993). On the other hand, when Revueltas refers to the "voice, gesture, and silence" characteristic of Mexican being, he may have in mind passages like those of Emilio Uranga when he points out, for example: "'Sorrow' is the voice of conscience in the Mexican, a voice that in turn must be interpreted as arising from the very same being that constitutes us. . . . In the Mexican there is a feeling of burden that is never overcome. . . . Life becomes difficult, and, more than joy or a feeling of power before the difficulty, a vague and obscure suffering presides over it. It is certainly not one of our characteristics to be light-hearted or easygoing in life. We are situated at the antipodes of a 'sportive' and 'festive' conception of man and world." Uranga, *Análisis del ser del mexicano*, 28. Regarding this observation by Uranga, some readers might wonder: Aren't parties, food varieties, and festive atmospheres *also* a characteristic, at least, of many occasions in Mexican society? Despite so many problems, the lives of many Mexicans of all social classes, even in the midst of the violence of the early twenty-first century, are not usually so bleak—not so reminiscent, *à la* Heidegger, of the German chiaroscuros of the pre-war period—as they were sometimes depicted by some of the participants in the philosophy of "the Mexican."
40. It is worth preserving Revueltas's criticism of the supposed metaphysics of death present in Mexico throughout its history. Like all explanations that overextend themselves, this metaphysics explains nothing: in this case, a second- or

third-rate metaphysics purports to explain everything from Aztec sacrifices to the crimes of drug traffickers! Even worse, like many cars bought second- or third-hand, this metaphysics only causes difficulties; among others, it generates bafflement and confusion when the actual causes are investigated in each context, past and present, of crimes committed in Mexico.

41. Revueltas, "Posibilidades y limitaciones," 45.
42. Revueltas, "Posibilidades y limitaciones," 46.
43. Revueltas, "Posibilidades y limitaciones," 51.
44. Revueltas, "Posibilidades y limitaciones," 52.
45. Revueltas, "Posibilidades y limitaciones," 56–58.
46. Revueltas, "Posibilidades y limitaciones," 57.
47. Revueltas, "Posibilidades y limitaciones," 58.
48. Revueltas, "Posibilidades y limitaciones," 58.
49. Revueltas, "Posibilidades y limitaciones," 58.
50. Carlos López Beltrán, ed., *Genes (&) mestizos: Genómica y raza en la biomedicina mexicana* [Genes (&) mestizos: Genomics and race in Mexican biomedicine] (Mexico City: Universidad Nacional Autónoma de México, 2011), "Introducción," 12. See also Sergio Armando Gallegos-Ordorica, "*Mestizaje* as an Epistemology of Ignorance: The Case of the Mexican Genome Diversity Project," in *Making The Case: Feminist and Critical Race Philosophers Engage Case Studies*, ed. Heidi Grasswick and Nancy Arden McHugh (Albany: State University of New York Press, 2021), 260–92.
51. See Federico Navarrete, *México racista: Una denuncia* [Racist Mexico: A denunciation] (Mexico City: Grijalbo, 2017); Federico Navarrete, *Alfabeto del racismo mexicano* [Alphabet of Mexican racism] (Barcelona: Malpaso, 2016).
52. Uranga, *Análisis del ser del mexicano*, 42.
53. In Mexico, around sixty different indigenous languages survive in addition to Spanish. This fact alone would complicate the projects of a unitary ontology of "the Mexican," if someone, misusing the strategy of transitions, were to require such an ontology.
54. Uranga, *Análisis del ser del mexicano*, 34.
55. Manuel Vargas, in his article "Disagreement and Convergence on the Case of Latin American Philosophy, For Example: Reply to Carlos Pereda and Robert Sanchez" (*Comparative Philosophy* 10, no. 1 (2019): 208–12), responds to an earlier, abbreviated version of Chapter 2 of this book, published in *Comparative Philosophy* 10, no. 1 (2019): 192–207, and raises a difficulty related to these passions. Maybe *there is* a version of the debate between abstract universalism and cultural particularism that resists resolution, or dissolution, with nomadic thought, namely, the debate in Mexico between historicism and anti-historicism. In this regard, Vargas cites the work of Carlos Alberto Sánchez, "The Gift of Mexican Historicism," *Continental Philosophy Review* 51, no. 3 (2018): 439–57. In this instance I tend *not* to be convinced by Vargas. Why? In any debate, part of the discussion depends on how words are used. Let us understand by "historicism"

the belief that all human activities—including the truths of math and logic—are in some sense related to context. In the final pages of his book *Word and Object* (Cambridge, MA: MIT Press, 1960), W. V. Quine points out: "there is no cosmic exile." If there is no cosmic exile, a question arises: *in what sense* do the beliefs we consider true *depend* on a particular context? Hardly anyone would deny that even those beliefs that are considered most true arise in one or more places and times. Furthermore, it would seem that with explanatory history and sufficient information, we can explain the causes of this emergence, both socially and psychologically. Nevertheless, we can also ask ourselves: Why do we assert that *this* belief is true? To respond, we need to provide *justifications* in the form of reasons. Of course, with nomadic thought, I have to remain *forever open* to the possibility that, in the future, however unlikely it may be, opposing reasons might be found in the midst of research, that defeat the belief that, until that moment, I have held to be true. I suspect that in his work, Carlos Alberto Sánchez dissolves the controversy between historicists and anti-historicists in a direction perhaps not very far from what I suggest. Sánchez distinguishes between "good" and "bad" historicism—between a "perspectivism" that is open—more or less in the style of Ortega—and a "perspectivism" that is progressively closing, as in the case of the mature Gaos. As Sánchez suggests, this distinction also applies to historicism. On one side, we have "bad" historicisms which eliminate any use of the concept of truth; but there are also "good" historicisms, "open historicisms," with "the power to transcend their moment" and "explain objectivity," as proposed by Leopoldo Zea, and recalled by Sánchez, quoting *La filosofía de lo mexicano* by Abelardo Villegas in "The Gift of Mexican Historicism," 452. Consequently, the defense of "good" or "liberatory" historicism can perhaps be understood as a tactic—with nomadic thought—for downplaying the importance of the use of the words "historicism" and "anti-historicism," and forgetting about the fruitless debates that tend to arise.

56. Uranga, *Análisis del ser del mexicano*, 45.
57. This invocation had an influence in several countries in Latin America; see Marilyn Grace Miller, *Rise and Fall of the Cosmic Race: The Cult of Mestizaje in Latin America* (Austin: University of Texas Press, 2004).
58. Virginia Aspe Armella, *Aristóteles y la Nueva España* (San Luis de Potosí: Universidad Autónoma de San Luis de Potosí, 2018); Virginia Aspe Armella, *Aristotle and New Spain*, trans. Juan Carlos González (New York: Routledge, 2025).
59. Noell Birondo, "The Virtues of Mestizaje: Lessons from Las Casas on Aztec Human Sacrifice," *APA Studies on Hispanic/Latino Issues in Philosophy* 19, no. 2 (2020): 2–8.
60. See Bolívar Echeverría, *Modernidad y blanquitud* [Modernity and whiteness] (Mexico City: Era, 2010).
61. The term "quotas" refers, in this case, to the need to promote a group that has been *ignored*, and therefore, underrepresented in the past. Consequently, this group must be taken into consideration in positions of responsibility, in access to higher levels of education such as the university or technical institutes, and

in important public positions. Nevertheless, and contrary to those who attack quota policy, a clarification is needed: such policy does not aim to favor unqualified groups over pseudo-majorities—white men—who are more qualified, but rather seeks to remedy persistent structural flaws, often ancient legacies of terrible social inequalities.

62. Héctor Aguilar Carmín, *Nocturno de la democracia mexicana* (Mexico City: Debate, 2018).
63. With respect to Mora's environment, it is worth consulting Charles Hale, *El liberalismo mexicano en la época de Mora, 1821–1853* [Mexican liberalism in the time of Mora, 1821–1853], 7th ed. (Mexico City: Siglo Veintiuno, 1977).
64. Aguilar Carmín, *Nocturno de la democracia mexicana*, 93.
65. Joshua Simon, *The Ideology of Creole Revolution: Imperialism and Independence in American and Latin American Political Thought* (Cambridge: Cambridge University Press, 2017).
66. Simon, *The Ideology of the Creole Revolution*, 133.
67. Years after *Pedro Páramo*, among other texts, ghosts circulate again—*other* ghosts—in the novel of a Mexican writer (read also with an itinerant reading, at least in some circles) apparently having nothing to do with *Pedro Páramo*. It does not even take place in the lands of Mexico, although surely in its imaginary. I refer to *Los ingrávidos* [The weightless] by Valeria Luiselli (Mexico City: Sexto Piso, 2011). So that when a child asks the mother who is writing, "What's your book about, mommy?," she immediately answers: "It's a novel about ghosts." It is because the ghost of Gilberto Owen, the poet, repeatedly appears and disappears, and even spends time in a phantasmagorical New York: "that was the first night I had to spend with the ghost of Gilberto Owen," the narrator's voice suddenly confesses, and adds: "It was from then on that I began to exist as I did in another possible life that was not mine, but that was enough to imagine to completely abandon myself to it." It is not just about *that* ghost. At some point also, "the middle child speaks with the ghost of the house."
68. Aguilar Camín, *Nocturno de la democracia mexicana*, 12. Regarding the Mexican nineteenth century, this proposal was explored by Fernando Escalante Gonzalbo in his important book *Ciudadanos imaginarios* [Imaginary citizens] (Mexico City: El Colegio de México, 1992). However, the expression "imaginary citizens" can be understood in several ways. According to one of them, we would once again be facing ghosts that continue to disturb social life. It would be about some of the obsessions that a political elite of a certain country projects onto a population that has little or nothing to do with such desires. Consequently, the expression refers to ghosts that mask realities and disorient. (if I am not mistaken, this is the sense that Escalante has in mind). On the contrary, in the opposite direction, with the expression "imaginary citizens," ghosts are set aside and the horizon of citizenship that is painstakingly sought to be achieved is reconstructed; the one that not only Mora strove to build, but also until today, the corridor of republican thought for which we must fight fervently. In this latter sense, imaginary citizens are not ghosts to be destroyed,

but ideals, in the best sense of the word "ideal." They are the "counter-factual citizens" of the Enlightenment, that arduous, conflictive, and very slow civilizing process according to Kant, which, according to Habermas, despite so much tragedy and no less constant failures and regressions, we must not renounce—just as we must not renounce the renewed conflict between the factual and the horizon of the counter-factual—if we do not want to give up the best goods—moral, legal, political—of human life. See Jürgen Habermas, *Facticidad y validez: Sobre el derecho y el Estado democrático de derecho en términos de teoría del discurso*, trans. M. Jimenez Redondo (Madrid: Trotta, 1998); *Between Facts and Norms: Contributions to a Discourse Theory of Law and Democracy*, trans. William Rehg (Cambridge, MA: MIT Press, 1996).

69. Literally, the German word *Sittlichkeit* would have to be translated with an unattractive word like "customariness." The most common translations often prefer an enigma just as unsightly: "ethicality" (Spanish: *eticidad*). I recommend, in this case, resorting to a paraphrase as often as possible.

70. Here are some quirky but extreme everyday instances of the wide continuum of informal employment in Mexico: "jobs" are invented, such as taking out a shovel on a public street and demanding money to repair potholes—and even sinkholes—in the streets, or youngsters go door to door asking for money to unclog sewers. Of course, there is no question that engaging in these and other "informal jobs"—which should be the responsibility of the authorities—is preferable to theft and similar crimes. Nevertheless, one might ask, surely, and not without a hint of bitter irony: In these miserable conditions, does the indispensable porous reason—which prevents falling into blind habits and no less blind customs—not lack both space and motivations to develop?

71. An exploration of reactive attitudes—with different purposes—can be found in the influential work of P. F. Strawson, *Freedom and Resentment and Other Essays* (London: Methuen, 1974).

72. Judith Butler, "Vulnerabilidad y resistencia revisitadas." Lecture presented at the Programa Universitario de Estudios de Género (PUEG) and the Facultad de Filosofía y Letras, Universidad Nacional Autónoma de México, March 23, 2015, available on YouTube. Commenting on and extending this conference, Rosaura Martínez Ruiz points out that this space of vulnerability and resistance is "the space where the paradox between subjection and agency is played out." This paradox is what makes the animals we are into persons. They make us, we make ourselves, and also, we just make. Rosaura Martínez Ruiz, *Eros: Más allá de la pulsión de muerte* [Eros: Beyond the death drive] (Mexico City: Siglo Veintiuno, 2018), 155. A page later, Martínez Ruiz adds: "The problem in sociopolitical terms, in collective terms, is how we resist violence and how we manage vulnerability; and that vulnerability is not a weakness to overcome, but an opening to the other and to alter-action" (156–57). However, let us not forget that vulnerability, or better, vulnerabilities, in addition to being psychological and affective characteristics, are also, on the other hand, political, legal, and

economic characteristics, which Martínez Ruiz will not deny.
73. Judith Butler, "Vulnerabilidad y resistencia revisitadas."
74. Carlos Pereda, ed., *Diccionario de justicia* [Dictionary of justice] (Mexico City: Siglo Veintiuno, 2017).
75. Montesquieu, *Del espíritu de las leyes* [The spirit of the laws], trans. Mercedes Blázquez y Pedro de Vega (Barcelona: Atalaya, 1993), Part I, ch. 3, 27.
76. Montesquieu, *Del espíritu de las leyes*, Part I, ch. 3, 28.
77. Montesquieu, *Del espíritu de las leyes*, Part I, ch. 3, 28.
78. Alexis de Tocqueville, *La democracia en América* [Democracy in America] (Mexico City: Fondo de Cultura Económica, 2005), 476. I suspect that a parallel reading of two almost contemporary books, at the same time belonging to the varied tradition of modern Aristotelianism, although extremely different and often conflicting, *Democracy in America* (1835) and Hegel's *Philosophy of Right* (1821), provides *resources* to transform the dispute between laws, habits, and customs into conflicts that multiply the claims of freedom as nonexclusion.
79. David Bak Geler Corona, "Improvisación práctica: Una reconsideración de la espontaneidad para la teoría democrática" [Practical improvisation: A reconsideration of spontaneity for democratic theory], in *Conceptos políticos: Herramientas teóricas y prácticas para el siglo XXI* [Political concepts: Theoretical and practical tools for the twenty-first century], ed. Melissa Amezcua Yépiz and David Bak Geler Corona (Guadalajara: Universidad de Guadalajara, 2019), 188.
80. *High Noon*, directed by Fred Zinneman (United Artists, 1952), 1:25, with Gary Cooper as Will Kane and Grace Kelly as Amy Fowler.
81. Fernanda Melchor, *Temporada de huracanes* (Mexico City: Random House, 2017); Fernanda Melchor, *Hurricane Season*, trans. Sophie Hughes (New York: New Directions, 2020).
82. Melchor, *Temporada de huracanes*, 11.
83. The torrential prose of *Hurricane Season* sometimes makes one think (or think the worst?) that Melchor is attempting to rewrite with malice—from the point of view of trash, filth, and the bloodiest violations—the torrential, luminous, and somehow reconciliatory prose of Gabriel García Márquez in *One Hundred Years of Solitude*.
84. Melchor, *Temporada de huracanes*, 219.
85. Melchor, *Temporada de huracanes*, 221.
86. Melchor, *Temporada de huracanes*, 222.

Bibliography

Aguilar Camín, Héctor. *La Guerra de Galio*. Mexico City: Cal y Arena, 1991.

———. *Nocturno de la democracia mexicana*. Mexico City: Debate, 2018.

Alcoff, Linda Martín. "Philosophy and Philosophical Practice: Eurocentrism as an Epistemology of Ignorance." In *The Routledge Handbook of Epistemic Injustice*, edited by Ian James Kidd, José Medina, and Gaile Pohlhaus Jr., 397–408. New York: Routledge, 2017.

Aldama, Arturo J., and Naomi H. Quiñonez, eds., *Decolonial Voices: Chicana and Chicano Cultural Studies in the Twenty-First Century*. Bloomington: Indiana University Press, 2002.

Amezcua Yépiz, Melissa, and David Bak Geler Corona, eds., *Conceptos políticos: Herramientas teóricas y prácticas para el siglo XXI*. Guadalajara: Universidad de Guadalajara, 2019.

Anzaldúa, Gloria. *Borderlands/La Frontera: The New Mestiza*. San Francisco: Aunt Lute Books, 1987.

Aspe Armella, Virginia. *Aristóteles y Nueva España*. San Luis Potosí: Universidad Autónoma San Luis Potosí, 2018.

———. *Aristotle and New Spain*. Translated by Juan Carlos González. New York: Routledge, 2025.

Avilés Parra, Sergio. *El tiempo muerto en el tiempo*. Mexico City: Editorial Latina, 1950.

Bartra, Roger. *La jaula de la melancolía: Identidad y metamorfosis del mexicano*. Mexico City: Grijalbo, 1987.

———. *The Cage of Melancholy: Identity and Metamorphosis in the Mexican Character*. Translated by Christopher J. Hall. New Brunswick, NJ: Rutgers University Press, 1992.

Beuchot, Mauricio. "The Study of Philosophy's History in Mexico as a Foundation for Doing Mexican Philosophy." In *The Role of History in Latin American*

Philosophy: Contemporary Perspectives, edited by Arleen Salles and Elizabeth Millán-Zaibert, 109–29. Albany: State University of New York Press, 2005.

Beltrán García, Iver A. "Luis Villoro: El desafío de una nueva comunidad y las tareas de la razón crítica." *Ideas y Valores* 69, no. 173 (2020): 103–22.

Bermúdez de Brauns, María Teresa. *Bosquejos de educación para el pueblo: Ignacio Ramírez e Ignacio Manuel Altamirano.* Mexico City: El Caballito, 1985.

Birondo, Noell. "Kantian Reasons for Reasons." *Ratio* 20, no. 3 (2007): 264–77.

———. "Virtue and Prejudice: Giving and Taking Reasons." In *Virtue's Reasons: New Essays on Virtue, Character, and Reasons*, edited by Noell Birondo and S. Stewart Braun, 189–202. New York: Routledge, 2017. Originally published in *The Monist* 99, no. 2 (2016): 212–23.

———. "Patriotism and Character: Some Aristotelian Observations." In *Handbook of Patriotism*, edited by Mitja Sardoč. Cham: Springer, 2020.

———. "The Virtues of Mestizaje: Lessons from Las Casas on Aztec Human Sacrifice." *APA Studies on Hispanic/Latino Issues in Philosophy* 19, no. 2 (2020): 2–8.

———, ed., *The Moral Psychology of Hate.* Lanham, MD: Rowman & Littlefield, 2022.

Bonfil Batalla, Guillermo. *México profundo: Una civilización negada.* Mexico City: Grijalbo, 2003 [1987].

———. *México Profundo: Reclaiming a Civilization.* Translated by Philip A. Dennis. Austin: University of Texas Press, 1996.

Boullosa, Carmen. *La patria insomne.* Madrid: Ediciones Hiperión, 2011.

Brandom, Robert B. *Tales of the Mighty Dead: Historical Essays in the Metaphysics of Intentionality.* Cambridge: Harvard University Press, 2002.

Butler, Judith. "Vulnerabilidad y resistencia revisitadas." Lecture presented at the Programa Universitario de Estudios de Género (PUEG) and the Facultad de Filosofía y Letras, UNAM, March 23, 2015.

Cassam, Quassim. *Vices of the Mind: From the Intellectual to the Political.* Oxford: Oxford University Press, 2019.

Castro-Gómez, Santiago. *Critique of Latin American Reason.* Translated by Andrew Ascherl, introduction by Eduardo Mendieta, foreword by Linda Martín Alcoff. New York: Columbia University Press, 2019 [1996].

———. *Zero-Point Hubris: Science, Race, and Enlightenment in Eighteenth-Century Latin America.* Translated by George Ciccariello-Maher and Don T. Deere. Lanham, MD: Rowman & Littlefield, 2021 [2005].

Córdova, Arnaldo. *La ideología de la Revolución Mexicana.* Mexico City: Era, 1973.

Cruz Revueltas, Juan Cristóbal. "El 2 de octubre y José Revueltas, una evocación." *El Universal* (Mexico City, Mexico), October 5, 2018.

De la Concha, Gerardo. *La razón y la afrenta: Antología del panfleto y la polémica en México.* Toluca: Instituto Mexiquense de Cultura, 1995.

Díaz Ruanova, Oswaldo. *Los existencialistas mexicanos.* Mexico City: Editorial Rafael Giménez Siles, 1982.

Draper, Susana. *México 1968: Experimentos de la libertad: Constelaciones de la democracia*. Mexico City: Siglo Veintiuno, 1998.

———. *1968 Mexico: Constellations of Freedom and Democracy*. Durham: Duke University Press, 2018.

Echeverría, Bolívar. *Modernidad y blanquitud*. Mexico City: Era, 2010.

Escalante, Evodio. *José Revueltas: Una literatura del "lado moridor."* Mexico City: Fondo de Cultura Económica, 2014.

Escalante Gonzalbo, Fernando. *Ciudadanos imaginarios*. Mexico City: El Colegio de México, 1992.

Espinasa, José María. "Review of Carlos Pereda, *La filosofía en México en el siglo XX: Apuntes de un participante*," *Estudios* 12, no. 108 (2014): 185.

Estrella González, Alejandro. "Por qué los historiadores de la filosofía también deberían leer a los clásicos de ciencias históricas: Reseña de Carlos Pereda, *La filosofía en México en el siglo XX: Apuntes de un participante*," *Signos Filosóficos* 16, no. 31 (2014): 205–214.

Fernández, Miguel Ángel, and Guillermo Hurtado, eds., *Normatividad y argumentación: Carlos Pereda y sus críticos*. Mexico City: Instituto de Investigaciones Filosóficas, Universidad Nacional Autónoma de México, 2013.

Fuentes, Carlos. *La región más transparente*. Mexico City: Fondo de Cultura Económica, 1958.

———. *Where the Air is Clear*. Translated by Sam Hileman. New York: Farrar, Straus and Giroux, 1988.

———. Foreword to *The Underdogs: A Novel of the Mexican Revolution*, by Mariano Azuela, trans. Sergio Waisman. New York: Penguin Books, 2014, vii–x.

Gaos, José. *Materiales para una autobiografía filosófica*. Foreword and selection by Adolfo Castañón. Mexico City: Bonilla Artigas, 2015.

Galdo, Juan Carlos. "Nacionalismo y disidencias en la narrativa carcelaria latinoamericana: Los muros del agua de José Revueltas y El sexto de José María Arguedas." *Lucero: A Journal of Iberian and Latin American Studies* 12, no. 3 (2001): 57–64.

Gallegos-Ordorica, Sergio Armando. "*Mestizaje* as an Epistemology of Ignorance: The Case of the Mexican Genome Diversity Project." In *Making The Case: Feminist and Critical Race Philosophers Engage Case Studies*, edited by Heidi Grasswick and Nancy Arden McHugh, 260–92. Albany: State University of New York Press, 2021.

Garber, Daniel. "Towards an Antiquarian History of Philosophy." *Rivista di Storia della Filosofia* 58, no. 2 (2003): 207–17.

García, Gilberto, Ambrosio Velasco, and Víctor Hernández, eds., *Repensar la filosofía de la Praxis. Homenaje a Adolfo Sánchez Vázquez*. Juarez City: Universidad Autónoma de Ciudad Juárez, 2016.

Garibay, Javier. *Nepantla: Situados en medio: Estudio histórico-teológico de la realidad indiana*. Mexico City: Centro de Reflexión Teológica, 2000.

González Valerio, María Antonia. "Review of Carlos Pereda, *La filosofía en México en el siglo XX: Apuntes de un participante*," *Intersticios* 18, no. 39 (2013): 167–75.

Habermas, Jürgen. *Between Facts and Norms: Contributions to a Discourse Theory of Law and Democracy*. Translated by William Rehg. Cambridge, MA: MIT Press, 1996.

Hale, Charles. *El liberalismo mexicano en la época de Mora, 1821–1853*. Mexico City: Siglo Veintiuno, 1977.

Hegel, G. W. F. *Elements of the Philosophy of Right*. Edited by Allen W. Wood. Translated by H. B. Nisbet. Cambridge: Cambridge University Press, 1991.

Hurtado, Guillermo, ed., *El Hiperión: Antología*. Mexico City: Universidad Nacional Autónoma de México, 2006.

———. *México sin sentido*. Mexico City: Siglo Veintiuno, 2011.

———. *Dialéctica del naufragio*. Mexico City: Fondo de Cultura Económica, 2016.

———. *La Revolución creadora: Antonio Caso y José Vasconcelos en la Revolución Mexicana*. Mexico City: Universidad Nacional Autónoma de México, 2016.

———. *Biografía de la verdad*. Mexico City: Siglo Veintiuno, 2024.

Illades, Carlos. *El marxismo en México: Una historia intelectual*. Mexico City: Taurus, 2018.

Jaksić, Iván, ed., *Debating Race, Ethnicity, and Latino Identity: Jorge J. E. Gracia and His Critics*. New York: Columbia University Press, 2015.

Leyva, Gustavo, and Jorge Rendón Alarcón, eds. *Luis Villoro, Filosofía, historia y política*. Mexico City: Gedisa–Universidad Autónoma Metropolitana, 2016.

López Beltrán, Carlos, ed., *Genes (&) mestizos: Genómica y raza en la biomedicina mexicana*. Mexico City: Universidad Nacional Autónoma de México, 2011.

Luiselli, Valeria. *Los ingrávidos*. Mexico City: Sexto Piso, 2011.

Lukács, Georg. *Mi camino hacia Marx*. Introduction, translation, and notes by Emilio Uranga. Mexico City: Federación Editorial Mexicana, 1971.

Mañón Garibay, Guillermo José. "Historia de las ideas en México. El grupo Hiperión: Reflexiones sobre el problema de la obediencia y el cumplimiento del deber." *Revista Mexicana de Historia del Derecho* 34 (2016): 51–80.

Mariátegui, José Carlos. *Siete ensayos de interpretación de la realidad peruana*. Lima: Editorial Minerva, 1928.

———. *Seven Interpretive Essays on Peruvian Reality*. Translated by Marjory Urquidi. Austin: University of Texas Press, 1971.

Martí, José. "Nuestra América." New York: Revista Ilustrada, 1891.

———. *Our America: Writings on Latin America and the Struggle for Cuban Independence*. Edited, with an Introduction and Notes, by Philip S. Foner. Translated by Elinor Randall. New York: Monthly Review Press, 1977.

Martínez Estrada, Ezequiel. *Radiografía de la pampa*. Buenos Aires: Editorial Losada, 1974 [1933].

———. *X-Ray of the Pampa*. Translated by Alain Swietlicki. Austin: University of Texas Press, 1971.

Martínez González, Victor Hugo, Sergio Ortiz Leroux, and Álvaro Aragón Rivera, eds. *La imaginación ilustrada: El ensayo filosófico, político y cultural de Carlos Pereda*. Mexico City: Gedisa Editorial, 2024.

Martínez Ruiz, Rosaura. *Eros: Más allá de la pulsión de muerte*. Mexico City: Siglo Veintiuno, 2018.

Medina, José. "Epistemic Border-Crossing: Polyphonic Decolonial Resistance and Collective Epistemic Self-Empowerment." International Conference on Epistemic Oppression and Decolonization, May 29–31, 2024, Université du Québec à Montréal.

Melchor, Fernanda. *Temporada de huracanes*. Mexico City: Random House, 2017.

Mendoza, José Jorge. *The Moral and Political Philosophy of Immigration: Liberty, Security, and Equality*. Lanham, MD: Lexington Books, 2016.

Miller, Marilyn Grace. *Rise and Fall of the Cosmic Race: The Cult of Mestizaje in Latin America*. Austin: University of Texas Press, 2004.

Monge, Emiliano. *No contar todo*. Mexico City: Penguin Random House, 2018.

———. *What Goes Unsaid: A Memoir of Fathers Who Never Were*. Translated by Frank Wynne. Melbourne: Scribe, 2022.

Monsiváis, Carlos. *Amor perdido*. Mexico City: Era, 1977.

———. Prologue to *Ignacio Ramírez "El Nigromante": Obras Completas*, vol. III, by Ignacio Ramírez, compiled and revised by David R. Maciel and Boris Rosen Jélomer. Mexico City: Centro de Investigación Científica Jorge L. Tamayo, 1984.

Montesquieu. *Del espíritu de las leyes*. Translated by Mercedes Blázquez y Pedro de Vega. Barcelona: Atalaya, 1993.

———. *The Spirit of the Laws*. Edited and translated by Anne M. Cohler, Basia Carolyn Miller, and Harold Samuel Stone. New York: Cambridge University Press, 1989.

Navarrete, Federico. *Alfabeto del racismo mexicano*. Barcelona: Malpaso, 2016.

———. *México racista: una denuncia*. Mexico City: Grijalbo, 2017.

Negrín, Edith. *Entre la paradoja y la dialéctica: Una lectura de la narrativa de José Revueltas*. Mexico City: El Colegio de México, 1995.

Nuccetelli, Susana, Ofelia Schutte, and Otávio Bueno, eds. *A Companion to Latin American Philosophy*. Malden: Wiley-Blackwell, 2010.

Ocampo, Anthony Christian. *The Latinos of Asia: How Filipino Americans Break the Rules of Race*. Stanford, CA: Stanford University Press, 2016.

Orfila Reynal, Arnaldo. *En México: 50 años de Revolución*. Mexico City: Fondo de Cultura Económica, 1960.

Orosco, José-Antonio. "The Philosophical Gift of Brown Folk: Mexican American Philosophy in the United States." *APA Newsletter on Hispanic/Latino Issues in Philosophy* 15, no. 2 (2016): 23–8.

Ortega Esquivel, Aureliano. *Filosofía mexicana*. Guanajuato: Universidad de Guanajuato, 2018.

Pacheco, José Emilio. *Ramón López Velarde: La lumbre inmóvil*. Mexico City: Era, 2018.

Pappas, Gregory Fernando. "The Limitations and Dangers of Decolonial Philosophies: Lessons from Zapatista Luis Villoro." *Radical Philosophy Review* 20, no. 2 (2017): 265-95.

Parra, Max. "El nacionalismo y el mito de 'lo mexicano' en Octavio Paz y José Revueltas." *Confluencia* 12, no. 1 (1996): 28-37.

Paz, Octavio. *El laberinto de la soledad*. Mexico City: Cuadernos Americanos, 1950.

———. *El arco y la lira*. Mexico City: Fondo de Cultura Económica, 1956.

———. *The Labyrinth of Solitude: Life and Thought in Mexico*. Translated by Lysander Kemp. New York: Grove Press, 1961.

———. *Cuadrivio*. Mexico City: Joaquín Mortiz, 1965.

———. *The Bow and the Lyre: The Poem, the Poetic Revelation, Poetry and History*. Translated by Ruth L. C. Simms. Austin: University of Texas Press, 1973.

Pereda, Carlos. *Debates*. Mexico City: Fondo de Cultura Económica, 1987.

———. "La contaminación heideggeriana." *Vuelta* 12, no. 142 (1988): 55-7.

———. *Razón e incertidumbre*. Mexico City: Siglo Veintiuno, 1994.

———. *Crítica de la razón arrogante*. Mexico City: Taurus, 1999.

———. "Explanatory and 'Argumentative' History of Philosophy." In *The Role of History in Latin America*, edited by Arleen Salles and Elizabeth Millán-Zaibert, 43-56. Albany: State University of New York Press, 2005.

———. "Latin American Philosophy: Some Vices." *Journal of Speculative Philosophy* 20, no. 3 (2006): 192-203.

———. *Los aprendizajes del exilio*. Mexico City: Siglo Veintiuno, 2008.

———. "Ten cuidado con las palabras 'patria,' 'violencia,' e 'insomne,' pero en México también con la palabra 'suave.'" *Debate feminista* 46, no. 23 (2012): 219-24.

———. *La filosofía en México en el siglo XX: Apuntes de un participante*. Mexico City: Conaculta, 2013.

———, ed., *Diccionario de justicia*. Mexico City: Siglo Veintiuno, 2017.

———. *Lessons in Exile*. Translated by Sean Manning. Leiden: Brill-Rodopi, 2018.

———. *Patologías del juicio: Ensayos sobre literatura, moral y estética nómada*. Mexico City: CENART-Instituto de Investigaciones Filosóficas, 2018.

———. "Assertion, Truth, and Argumentation." In *Perspectives on Habermas*, ed. Lewis Edwin Hall, 51-70. LaSalle, IL: Open Court, 2020.

———. *Pensar a México: Entre otros reclamos*. Mexico City: Universidad Nacional Autónoma de México, 2021.

———. *Practical Holism and Nomadic Thought*. Translated by Sean Manning. Lanham, MD: Lexington Books, 2023.

Pettit, Philip. *Republicanism: A Theory of Freedom and Government*. Oxford: Clarendon Press, 1997.

Poniatowska, Elena. *La noche de Tlatelolco: Testimonios de historia oral*. Mexico City: Era, 1971.

———. *Massacre in Mexico*. Translated by Helen R. Lane. Columbia: University of Missouri Press, 1975.
Portilla, Jorge. *Fenomenología del relajo*. Mexico City: Fondo de Cultura Económica, 1984.
———. *The Suspension of Seriousness: On the Phenomenology of Jorge Portilla*. Translation of *Fenomenología del relajo*. Translated by Carlos Alberto Sánchez. Albany: State University of New York Press, 2012.
Quine, Willard Van Orman. *Word and Object*. Cambridge, MA: MIT Press, 1960.
Ramírez, Ignacio. *Ignacio Ramírez "El Nigromante": Obras Completas*. Compiled and revised by David R. Maciel and Boris Rosen Jélomer. Mexico City: Centro de Investigación Científica Jorge L. Tamayo, 1984.
———. *La palabra de la reforma en la república de las letras: Una antología general*. Edited and with a "Preliminary Study" by Liliana Weinberg. Mexico City: Fondo de Cultura Económica, 2009.
Ramírez, Mario Teodoro. *La razón del otro: Estudios sobre el pensamiento de Luis Villoro*. Mexico City: Instituto de Investigaciones Filosóficas, Universidad Nacional Autónoma de México, 2010.
———. *Humanismo para una nueva época: nuevos ensayos sobre el pensamiento de Luis Villoro*. Mexico City: Siglo Veintiuno, 2011.
Ramos, Samuel. *El perfil del hombre y la cultura en México*. Mexico City: Espasa-Calpe, 1992 [1934].
———. *The Profile of Man and Culture in Mexico*. Translated by Peter G. Earle. Austin: University of Texas Press, 1963.
———. *Historia de la filosofía en México*. Mexico City: Universidad Nacional Autónoma de México, 1990 [1943].
Reed-Sandoval, Amy. "'Immigrant' or 'Exiled'? Reconceiving the Desplazada/os of Latin American and Latina/o Philosophy." *APA Newsletter on Hispanic/Latino Issues in Philosophy* 15, no. 2 (2016): 11–14.
Reséndez, Andrés. *The Other Slavery: The Uncovered Story of Indian Enslavement in America*. Boston: Houghton Mifflin Harcourt, 2016.
Revueltas, José. *Los muros de agua*. Mexico City: Era, 1941.
———. *Los días terrenales*. Mexico City: Editorial Stylo, 1949.
———. Interview with O. Díaz Ruanova. *México en la cultura* (Mexico City, Mexico), May 28, 1950.
———. *Ensayo sobre un proletariado sin cabeza*. Mexico City: Liga Leninista Espartaco, 1962.
———. *Los errores*. Mexico City: Fondo de Cultura Económica, 1964.
———. "Posibilidades y limitaciones del mexicano." In *Obras Completas*, edited by Andrea Revueltas and Philippe Cheron. Mexico City: Era, 1978–1987.
———. *Dialéctica de la conciencia*. Mexico City: Era, 1982.
———. *El cuadrante de la soledad (y otras obras teatrales)*. Mexico City: Ediciones Era, 1984.
———. *Earthly Days*. Translated by Matthew Gleeson. Mexico City: Archive 48, 2020.

Reyes, Alfonso. *La "X" en la frente*. Mexico City: Porrúa y Obregón, 1952.
———. "Possibilities and Limitations of the Mexican." Translated by David W. Bird. In *Mexican Philosophy in the Twentieth Century: Essential Readings*, edited by Carlos Alberto Sánchez and Robert Eli Sanchez Jr., 216–32. New York: Oxford University Press, 2017.
Reyes Nevares, Salvador. *El amor y la amistad en el mexicano*. Mexico City: Porrúa y Obregón, 1952.
Rickless, Samuel C. "Brief for an Inclusive Anti-Canon." *Metaphilosophy* 49, no. ½ (2018): 167–81.
Rivera Berruz, Stephanie. "Debating Race, Ethnicity, and Latino Identity: Jorge J. E. Gracia and His Critics," *APA Newsletter on Hispanic/Latino Issues in Philosophy* 15, no. 2 (2016): 28–30.
Rodríguez Munguía, Jacinto. *La conspiración del 68: Los intelectuales y el poder: así se fraguó la matanza*. Mexico City: Debates, 2018.
Rossi, Alejandro. *Manual del distraído*. Mexico City: Joaquín Mortiz, 1978.
Ruiz Abreu, Álvaro. *José Revueltas: Los muros de la utopía*. Mexico City: Cal y Arena, 1992.
Rulfo, Juan. *Pedro Páramo*. Mexico City: Fondo de Cultura Económica, 1955.
Salazar Bondy, Augusto. *¿Existe una filosofía de nuestra América?* Mexico City: Siglo Veintiuno, 1968.
Salles, Arleen, and Elizabeth Millán, eds., *The Role of History in Latin American Philosophy: Contemporary Perspectives*. Albany: State University of New York Press, 2005.
Salmerón Sanginés, Pedro. "La mexicanidad al servicio del PRI." *La Jornada* (Mexico City, Mexico), August 9, 2016.
Sánchez, Carlos Alberto. *Contingency and Commitment: Mexican Existentialism and the Place of Philosophy*. Albany: State University of New York Press, 2016.
———. "The Gift of Mexican Historicism." *Continental Philosophy Review* 51, no. 3 (2018): 439–57.
———. *Mexican Philosophy for the Twenty-First Century: Relajo, Zozobra, and Other Frameworks for Understanding Our World*. London: Bloomsbury Academic, 2023.
———. *Blooming in the Ruins: How Mexican Philosophy Can Guide Us toward the Good Life*. New York: Oxford, 2024.
Sanchez, Robert Eli, Jr. "Strengthening the Case for Latin American Philosophy: Beyond Cultural Resources." *APA Newsletter on Hispanic/Latino Issues in Philosophy* 13, no. 2 (2014): 2–9.
Sánchez Benítez, Roberto. "Review of Carlos Pereda, *La filosofía en México en el siglo XX: Apuntes de un participante*." *Noésis: Revista de Ciencias Sociales y Humanidades* 24, no. 47-2 (2015): 151–3.
Saslow, Eli. *Rising Out of Hatred: The Awakening of a Former White Nationalist*. New York: Anchor Books: 2018.
Schwarz, Henry, and Sangeeta Ray, eds., *A Companion to Postcolonial Studies*. Malden: Blackwell, 2000.

Sheridan, Guillermo. *Un corazón adicto: la vida de Ramón López Velarde*. Mexico City: Fondo de Cultura Económica, 1989.

———. *Los contemporáneos ayer*. Mexico City: Fondo de Cultura Económica, 2015.

Simon, Joshua. *The Ideology of Creole Revolution: Imperialism and Independence in American and Latin American Political Thought*. Cambridge: Cambridge University Press, 2017.

Stehn, Alexander. "Latin American Philosophy." In *Internet Encyclopedia of Philosophy*.

Stepanenko, Pedro, ed., *Luis Villoro: Conocimiento y emancipación. Homenaje póstumo del Instituto de Investigaciones Filosóficas*. Mexico City: Instituto de Investigaciones Filosóficas, Universidad Nacional Autónoma de México, 2017.

Strawson, P. F. *Freedom and Resentment and Other Essays*. London: Methuen, 1974.

Suárez, Rodolfo R. "Review of Carlos Pereda, La filosofía en México en el siglo XX: Apuntes de un participante." *Diánoia* 59, no. 73 (2014): 155–9.

Tocqueville, Alexis de. *La democracia en América*. Mexico City: Fondo de Cultura Económica, 2005.

Toscana, David. *Santa María del circo*. Mexico City: Plaza y Janes, 1998.

———. *El ejército iluminado*. Mexico City: Tusquets Editores, 2006.

———. *The Enlightened Army*. Translated by David William Foster. Austin: University of Texas Press, 2019.

Uranga, Emilio. "Optimismo y pesimismo del mexicano." *Historia Mexicana* 1, no. 3 (1952): 395–410.

———. "Examen de una postdata: La poca Paz de Octavio." Mexico City: Revista de América, 1970.

———. *Astucias literarias*. Guanajuato: Federación Editorial Mexicana, 1971.

———. *Análisis del ser del mexicano*. Foreword by Luis Villoro. Guanajuato: Government of the State of Guanajuato, 1990.

———. *¿De quién es la filosofía?: sobre la lógica de la filosofía como confesión personal*. Guanajuato: Gobierno del Estado de Guanajuato, 1990.

———. *Análisis del ser del mexicano y otros escritos sobre la filosofía de lo mexicano (1949-1952)*. Selections, notes, and prologue by Guillermo Hurtado. Mexico City: Bonilla Artigas, 2013.

———. *Emilio Uranga's Analysis of Mexican Being: A Translation and Critical Introduction*. Translated by Carlos Alberto Sánchez. New York: Bloomsbury Academic, 2021.

Valero Pie, Aurelia. "Emilio Uranga, *Análisis del ser del mexicano* y otros escritos sobre la filosofía de lo mexicano (1949-1952)." *Diánoia* 59, no. 72 (2014): 155-61.

Vargas, Manuel. "On the Value of Philosophy: The Latin American Case." *Comparative Philosophy* 1, no. 1 (2010): 33–52.

———. "Disagreement and Convergence on the Case of Latin American Philosophy, For Example: Reply to Carlos Pereda and Robert Sanchez." *Comparative Philosophy* 10, no. 1 (2019): 208–12.

———. "The Philosophy of Accidentality." *Journal of the American Philosophical Association* 6, no. 4 (2020): 391–409. Now reprinted in *The Latinx Philosophy Reader*, edited by Lori Gallegos, Manuel Vargas, and Francisco Gallegos. New York: Routledge, 2025.

Vargas Lozano, Gabriel. *En torno a la obra de Adolfo Sánchez Vázquez*. Mexico City: Universidad Nacional Autónoma de México, 1995.

Vasconcelos, José. *Obras Completas*. 2 Vols. Mexico City: Libreros Mexicanos Unidos, 1959.

———. *Los retornos de Ulises: Una antología de José Vasconcelos*. Edited by Christopher Domínguez Michael. Mexico City: Secretaría de Educación Pública-Fondo de Cultura Económica, 2010.

Vázquez Almanza, Paola. *Aquellos que dejamos de ser: Ficción y nación en México*. Mexico City: Siglo Veintiuno, 2019.

Velasco, Ambrosio. "Review of Carlos Pereda, *La filosofía en México en el siglo XX: Apuntes de un participante*," *Tópicos: Revista de Filosofía* 45 (2013) 345–51.

Villegas, Abelardo. *La filosofía de lo mexicano*. Mexico City: Fondo de Cultura Económica, 1960.

———. "Polémica de las mafias." *Proceso*, no. 798, February 17, 1992: 39.

Villoro, Luis. *Los grandes momentos del indigenismo en México*. Mexico City: El Colegio de México, 1950.

———. *El proceso ideológico de la revolución de independencia*. Mexico City: Universidad Nacional Autónoma de México, 1953.

———. *La idea y el ente en la filosofía de Descartes*. Mexico City: Fondo de Cultura Económica, 1965.

———. *Creer, saber, conocer*. Mexico City: Siglo Veintiuno, 1982.

———. *El concepto de ideología y otros ensayos*. Mexico City: Fondo de Cultura Económica, 1985.

———. *En México, entre libros: Pensadores del siglo XX*. Mexico City: Fondo de Cultura Económica, 1995.

———. *El poder y el valor: Fundamentos de una ética política*. Mexico City: Fondo de Cultura Económica-El Colegio de México, 1997.

———. *Estado plural, pluralidad de culturas*. Mexico City: Paidós-Facultad de Filosofía y Letras, Universidad Nacional Autónoma de México, 1998.

———. *Belief, Personal, and Propositional Knowledge*. Translated by David Sosa and Douglas McDermid. Amsterdam-Atlanta: Brill Rodopi, 1998.

———. *Los retos de la sociedad por venir: Ensayos sobre justicia, democracia y multiculturalismo*. Mexico City: Fondo de Cultura Económica, 2007.

———. *La alternativa: Perspectivas y posibilidades de cambio*. Mexico City: Fondo de Cultura Económica, 2015.

———. "The Major Moments of Indigenism in Mexico: Conclusion (1950)." Translated by Kim Díaz. In *Mexican Philosophy in the Twentieth Century: Essential Readings*, edited by Carlos Alberto Sánchez and Robert Eli Sanchez Jr., 156–64. New York: Oxford University Press, 2017.

———. *La razón disruptiva: Antología compilada por Guillermo Hurtado*. Mexico City: Penguin Random House, 2023.
Volpi, Jorge. *La imaginación y el poder: Una historia intelectual de 1968*. Mexico City: Era, 1998.
Williams, Bernard. *The Sense of the Past: Essays in the History of Philosophy*. Edited by Myles Burnyeat. Princeton: Princeton University Press, 2006.
———. "Why Philosophy Needs History." In his *Essays and Reviews 1959–2002*, 405–12. Princeton, NJ: Princeton University Press, 2014.
Young, Iris Marion. *Justice and the Politics of Difference*. Princeton: Princeton University Press, 1990.
Zavala, Oswaldo. *Drug Cartels Do Not Exist: Narco-Trafficking and Culture in the US and Mexico*. Translated by William Savinar. Nashville, TN: Vanderbilt University Press, 2022.
Zea, Leopoldo. *En torno a una filosofía americana*. Mexico City: El Colegio de México, 1945.
———. *La filosofía como compromiso*. Mexico City: Tezontle, 1952.
———. *América como conciencia*. Mexico City: Universidad Nacional Autónoma de México, 1953.
———. *La filosofía en México*. Mexico City: Libro-Mex, 1955.
———. *América en la historia*. México City: Fondo de Cultura Económica, 1957.
———. *Latinoamérica en la formación de nuestro tiempo. Cuadernos*. Mexico City: Cuadernos Americanos, 1965.
———. *El positivismo en México: Nacimiento, apogeo y decadencia*. Mexico City: Fondo de Cultura Económica, 1968.
———. *Positivism in Mexico*. Translated by Josephine H. Schulte. Austin: University of Texas Press, 1974.
———. *El positivismo y la realidad mexicana*. Mexico City: Universidad Nacional Autónoma de México, 1985.
———. *The Role of the Americas in History*. Edited by Amy Oliver. Translated by Sonja Karsen. Savage, MD: Rowman & Littlefield, 1992.
———. "Philosophy as Commitment (1952)." Translated by Amy Oliver. In *Mexican Philosophy in the Twentieth Century: Essential Readings*, edited by Carlos Alberto Sánchez and Robert Eli Sanchez Jr., 125–40. New York: Oxford University Press, 2017.

Index

abstraction, low degrees of, 93, 95
abuse and harassment, 122n24
Alamán, Lucas, 99–100
Alcoff, Linda Martín, 15n1
Aldama, Arturo J., 114n2
Althusserian Marxism, 52
American Philosophical Association, 11–12, 18n20, 19n29
Análisis del ser del mexicano (Uranga), 9–12, 82–83, 93, 127n8, 128n14, 128n15, 129nn17–18, 130n18, 134n39. *See also* Uranga, Emilio
analogical hermeneutics, theory of, 52
anarchism, 36, 126n3
Anglo American philosophy/philosophers, 11–12, 16n4, 19n26
anthropology of Mexicans, 91
anticolonial struggle
  for diversity of overlapping identities, 98–99
  against social degradation of identities, 97–98
antiquarianism, 116n21
Anzaldúa, Gloria, 11–12, 86, 131n31
archipelago, metaphor of, 53, 117n29, 118n32
arguing and linking, practices of, 55
argumentation theory, 3

argumentative history, 16n3, 46–47, 49, 116n20, 117n26
argumentative reading, 46–49, 55, 83, 93, 114n2, 117n26
Aristotelianism, differentiated, 96
Aristotle, 28, 96–97, 100 101
arrogant/arrogance, 4, 17n16, 34, 36, 59, 75
  affiliations, 34–35
  colonial humanism, 93
  licensing marginalization, 34
  reason, 2, 4–7, 9, 13–14, 17, 33
Aspe Armella, Virginia, 96–97, 136n58
Avilés Parra, Sergio, 128n12

Bak Geler Corona, David, 107, 139n79
Balbuena, Bernardo de, 79
being (of humans), 84, 85
Being and Time (Heidegger), 83
Beuchot, Mauricio, 14, 52
Birondo, Noell, 15, 16n5, 17n15, 97, 136n59
Black, Derek, 3–4, 13
Black, Don, 4, 14
Black Lives Matter, 3
border-crossing, 12, 15n1, 86–87, 90, 114n2
Boullosa, Carmen, 38, 43, 115n17

INDEX

Brandom, Robert B., 16n3, 124n54
bronze race, 94
Butler, Judith, 103, 138n72, 139n73

Camín, Aguilar, 99–100, 128n12, 137n68
campesino(s), 63, 67. *See also* day laborers
cantankerous (*cascarrabias*), 103
capital, available (as meaning of "resource"), 72
Caso, Antonio, 50, 79, 125n3
Cassam, Quassim, 15n1
Castellanos, Rosario, 41, 53, 84, 115n14
Castro-Gómez, Santiago, 19n26
Catholicism, 13, 89, 127n10
Charleston (South Carolina), 5
Chavez, Cesar, 13
Christian social doctrine, social positivism, 126n3
coexistence, 37, 55
collective identities, 25
colonial reason, 7, 9, 27, 33–34, 71, 76, 79, 86, 89
colonial relations of multinational companies, 330
colonial vices, 2, 8–11, 25–28, 31, 35, 37–38, 41, 44, 46, 48, 50–51, 53, 55–56, 60–61, 79, 91, 93, 98, 116n4, 134n38
colonialism, 2, 13–14, 14n2, 27, 32–33, 35, 70–71, 96–97, 114, 132
communitarianism, 69
Companion to Postcolonial Studies (Schwarz and Ray), 114n2
Contingency and Commitment (Sánchez), 16n13, 18n19, 18n25, 47, 116n22
conversation, 12, 17n16, 41, 56, 71, 100, 104
counter-factual citizens, 138n68
craving for novelty, 8, 25, 37–38, 41, 46, 48, 50–51, 53–54, 56, 60–61, 80, 90, 114n5, 134n38

critical thinking, 74
criticalism, 58
cruelty and barbarism, 64
cultural histories of Mexican and Filipino peoples, 19n28
cultural particularism, 9, 27, 57–59, 63, 67, 69, 71–72, 74, 76, 79, 81, 95, 102, 135n55
cultural resource, 73–75
cultural utility, 73–75, 77
culture of domination, 58
customs of freedom, 106
cynicism, 86, 95

day laborers, 63, 67–71
decolonial theory, 3, 15n1, 70–71, 114n2
Decolonial Voices (Aldama and Quiñonez), 114n2
deconstructionism, 1, 14, 36
definitive readings, 48
dehumanization, 3
demand against something, 73–75
Democracy in America (Tocqueville), 107, 139n78
descriptive readings, 48
de-territorialized colonial power, 32
Díaz, Porfirio, 79, 125n1
dispersed indigenous nationalities, 93
Duke, David, 4, 14

Echevarría, Bolívar, 51, 52
ejército iluminado, El (*The Enlightened Army*) (Toscana), 39–40
El Paso (Texas), 3, 5
Emilio Uranga's Analysis of Mexican Being (Sánchez), 127n8
emotional reeducation, 103
epistemic virtue and vice, 2, 77. *See also* colonial vices
epistemology of ignorance, 2. *See also* ignorance
Essay Concerning Human Understanding (Locke), 62

Estrella González, Alejandro, 117n26, 118n33
European Enlightenment, 62
exclusion
    aggressive, 13, 27, 31, 35, 42, 63
    of day laborers, 63, 67–71
    experiences of, 69
    humiliations to human dignity, 105
    identity politics, 63
    of indigenous people, 63–65, 69–70
    persecution, 35
    politics of, 77, 91
    situations of, 69
    white supremacist, 14
    of women, 45, 63, 65–67
exile, 1, 51, 54, 113n2, 117n28
explanatory history, 46, 49–50, 83, 116n29, 117n26, 124n54, 131n31, 136n55
explanatory reading, 46, 48–49
expressions of identity, 44–45

fetishes, 26, 35, 40, 47, 53, 64, 75
    pure and impure, 7, 26–27, 91, 93, 105
    suicidal, 74
Filipinos, 13
filosofía de lo mexicano (philosophy of 'Mexicanness'), 9, 81, 87–90, 128n14, 128–29n15, 129n18, 136n55
Foucault, Michel, 84
freedom, 14, 65, 70, 78, 85, 103, 115n14, 120n10, 120n12, 139n78
    claims about, 65
    customs of, 106
    dangers of, 32
    habits of, 105, 107
    human concerns, 45
    individual, 65
    as nonexclusion, 67, 104–5
Fuentes, Carlos, 1, 15, 127n10, 130n18

Gadamer, Hans-Georg, 5
Galdo, Juan Carlos, 131n33

Galileo Galilei (Brecht), 115n11
Gaos, José, 51, 80–81, 117n28, 130n18
García Máynez, Eduardo, 52
genealogy, 2–3, 100
genome of human animals, 90
González, Juliana, 52
González Valerio, María Antonia, 118n31
Gracia, Jorge J. E., 58, 119n3
grandeza mexicana, La (Mexican greatness) (de Balbuena), 79
"Great Replacement," 5

Habermas, Jürgen, 17n14, 69, 138n68
habits, 3, 25, 38, 46, 60, 99, 103–5, 120n9
    bad, 55, 100–102
    blind, 138n70
    customary, 105
    and customs, 5, 13, 38, 55, 101–2, 104–6, 108, 139n78
    of freedom, 105, 107
    importance of, 106
    social, 102
Hamilton, Richard Paul, 16n12
Handbook of Patriotism (Sardoč), 17n17
Harvard University, 7
hatred, 3–5, 16n5, 16n12, 110
Hawai'i, 133
Headquarters of Power and Thought, 7–8, 10–11, 29, 34–37, 45–48, 56, 69, 93, 130n18
Heidegger, Martin, 80, 83, 95, 129n17, 134n39
hermeneutical maxim, 25–26
hermeticism, 95
heterodox bloc, 52
heterodox mentalities, 96
Hiperión, El (Hurtado), 127n11
historical differentiation, 33
historical understanding, 1, 3, 12–14, 16n4

historicism, 93, 135–36n55
history/historicity, 84
history of philosophy in Mexico, 50–53
Huerta, Dolores, 13
human rights, 60, 70, 86
Hume, David, 48, 62
Hurtado, Guillermo, 15n2, 53, 79, 80, 113n2, 118n32, 123n32, 125n3, 128–29n15, 129n17
Hyperion group (*El grupo Hiperión*), 9–10, 81–82, 86–87, 91, 95, 125n1, 126n6, 127n11, 133nn37–38, 134n39
hypocrisy, 86, 95

Idea of the Good (Plato), 100
identity and inclusion, politics of, 2, 5, 9, 25
identity and nonexclusion, 27–29
identity politics, 42, 79, 87, 92–93, 95
   maxims of arrogant reason, 77
   prestigious affiliation, 76
   triple exclusion, 63
ideology, 4, 36, 121n23, 126n3
Ideology of the Creole Revolution, The (Simon), 100
ignorance, 2, 4, 14, 16n5, 17n17, 98
imaginary citizens, 137n68
immediate rejections—rejections of the stomach, 103
imperialism, 14n14, 89, 100, 114n2
impure fetishes, 7, 26–27, 53, 91
indigenous people, social exclusion of, 63–65, 69
   experience of exclusion, 70
   "impure" plurality of cultures, 68
   indios, 13
   situations of exclusion, 69
   structures of radical republicanism, 69–70
   struggle or recognition, 70
indignation, concept of, 103–4

inferiority complex, 80, 83–84, 86, 95
injustices, 71
Institute for Philosophical Research at the National Autonomous University of Mexico (UNAM), 5, 12, 19n29, 114n7, 122n25
integrative interaction, 55
intellectuals, 80–81, 88, 123, 123n32, 128, 128n15, 134n38
intercultural understanding, 13
itinerant, self-referential reading, 39, 41, 44, 48, 62, 64, 100, 108–10, 137n67
Itliong, Larry, 13

Kant, Immanuel, 5, 7–8, 17, 19n27, 48, 69, 101, 104, 120–21
Ku Klux Klan, 4, 14

Larsen, Neil, 114n2
Las Casas, Bartolomé de, 10, 96–97
Latin American philosophy, 2–3, 9–11, 13–14, 50, 57–59, 74, 77, 83, 113n1, 116n20, 119nn3–4, 125n58, 135n55
Latin Americanism, 51
Latinx, 12, 18n20
laws and customs, dispute between, 99–103, 105
legitimization/legitimacy, struggle for, 11–12, 96
liberal republicans, 120n12
liberalism, 69, 120n12, 126n3
Lizardi, Fernández de, 62, 80
Lomnitz, Claudio, 104
López Beltran, Carlos, 91, 135n50
López Velarde, Ramon, 86, 130n28

MacIntyre, Alasdair, 16n3
Manila galleons, 13
marches in Mexico City, 115n14
marginalization, 11, 34, 71, 77
Martí, Jose, 41, 75, 84, 115n16, 126n6
Marxism, 51–53, 117, 130

maxim of data, fetishes, and materials, 26, 35, 47, 53, 64, 75, 93, 105
maxim(s), 7–8, 17n18, 25–26, 34–35, 47, 53, 55–56, 64, 75–77, 93, 105–6
Medina, José, 15n1
Mejía, Tomás, 61–62
Melchor, Fernanda, 10, 108, 139n81
Mesoamerican civilization, 114n1
mestizaje, 15, 88–91, 93, 97, 131n31, 135n50, 136n57, 136n59
metaphysics, 50, 52, 60, 97–98, 128n12, 134n40
meta-problem, 26
Mexican anthropology, 45
Mexican economy, 45
Mexican genome, 91, 135n50
Mexican philosophy, 2–3, 14, 15n2, 18n24, 26
    abstract universalism, 57–58
    anxiety for affiliation, 12
    challenges to habits and customs, 59
    criticalism, 58
    cultural particularism (*see* cultural particularism)
    horizontal nomadism, 60–61
    human rights, 60
    interest in studying, 57–58
    map of, 59
    nomadic epistemology, 60
    protective attitudes, 60
    static epistemology, 76
    struggle for legitimacy, 11
    vertical nomadism, 61
Mexican Revolution of 1910, 76, 79, 117n29, 125n3, 126n3
Mexican sociology, 45
Mexicanism, 51
México profundo, 114n1
Mignolo, Walter, 114n2
migrant workers, 13. *See also* campesino(s); day laborers
migration, 1, 4, 26, 41

Mills, Charles W., 18n20
Monsiváis, Carlos, 62, 120n10
Mora, José María Luis, 99–100, 137n68
Moreno, Mario, 80, 128n12, 128n15
multiculturalism, 4, 36, 123n31

National Autonomous University of Mexico (UNAM), 5, 12, 14–15, 16n5, 19n29, 51, 122n25
nationalism, 3–4, 7, 41–42, 131n33, 133n37
nationalist zeal, 25, 50
    complications with nationalism, 42
    cover for crimes, 40–41
    deficiencies of, 38
    delusion, 39–40
    generator of traumas and resentments, 41
    impure fetish, 42, 56
nationalization, 90
native controversy, 96
Necromancer. *See* Ramírez, Ignacio (*El Nigromante* / the Necromancer)
negative bloc, 52
neoconstitutionalism, 36
neoliberalism, 36
nepantla, 12, 86, 92–93, 131n29
Nezahualcóyotl, 64
Nicol, Eduardo, 51
Niños Héroes (child heroes), 39
Nocturno de la democracia mexicana (Nocturne of Mexican democracy) (Aguilar Camín), 99
nomadic thinking, 1–2, 6, 9–10, 15n1, 17n18, 26, 28, 33, 36–37, 47–48, 55, 57, 59, 61–62, 71–72, 74–75, 89, 92, 94, 100, 114n1
nomadism, 1, 12, 26, 38, 61–62, 67, 74, 77, 84, 87, 113n2, 119n4, 124n42
nonexclusion, 9, 25, 27, 29, 67, 69, 77, 99, 102, 104–5, 120n12, 123n35, 139n78
Norway, 5
Nuestra América (Martí), 41, 119, 126n6

Octavio Paz, 81, 115n14, 125n3, 127n7, 130n28, 133n37
ontology of accidentality, 92, 99
ontology of the Mexican, 87, 90–91, 97
Orosco, José-Antonio, 2, 58, 76, 118n1, 119n4
Ortega y Gasset, José, 80, 126n6
oscillation, idea of, 18n19, 91
Oxford University Press, 7

Pappas, Gregory, 2, 70
Paris (France), 7, 34, 53, 79, 134n38
particularism, cultural, 9, 27, 57–59, 63, 67, 69, 71–72, 74, 76, 79, 81, 102, 135n55
patriotism, 7, 17n17, 42–44
Paul III (pope), 96
Pedro Páramo (Rulfo), 100, 137n67
Pensar a México: Entre otros reclamos (Pereda), 14
perceptions of *nobody*, 82
Pereda, Carlos, 1, 14, 15n2, 16n5, 19n29, 114n5, 114n7, 116n19, 117n26, 117n29, 118n38, 129n17, 135n55
Pereda, Nicolás, 16n12
Pereyra, Carlos, 52, 118n32
personal autonomy, 101, 107
Philosophy of Right (Hegel), 101, 139n78
Platonism, 36
plurality of reason, 7, 17n16
polemical analogies, 100
populism, 37
porous reason, 1, 6–7, 13, 17nn16–18, 26, 55–56, 105, 108, 138n70
Portilla, Jorge, 51, 58, 80, 82, 119n2, 130n18
postcolonialism, 114n2
poverty and ignorance, 126n3
prejudice, racial, 16n12, 17n15, 61, 103
principles of universality, 101
professionalization of philosophy, 81
public life, 37, 66, 106, 129n17

Quiñonez, Naomi H., 114n2
quotas, 136n61

race war, 5
racial egalitarianism, 4
racialization of biomedical research, 91
radical republicanism, 9, 27, 69, 99
Ramírez, Ignacio (*El Nigromante* / the Necromancer), 9, 27, 61–62, 72, 77, 87, 119nn6–7, 120n12, 121n22
Ramos, Samuel, 50, 58, 86, 118n32, 125n2, 134n38
Rawls, John, 69, 120n12
recurso, 72–74
refinement, 72, 87, 134n39
republicanism, 9, 27, 50, 69, 99, 120
resentment, 41–42, 65, 86, 88, 95, 103, 110, 138
resources, 2, 13–14, 60, 64, 73–75, 91, 93–94, 102, 105–6, 139n78
revisionist historians, 126n3
Revueltas, José, 10, 27, 35, 81, 131nn32–33, 133n37
Reyes, Alfonso, 76, 125n3
Rising Out of Hatred (Saslow), 3, 16n5
Riva Palacio, Mariano, 65
Robledo, Gómez, 52
Rodríguez Munguía, Jacinto, 128n15
Rorty, Richard, 14
Ruiz Abreu, Álvaro, 87, 131n32, 133n36
  independence from colonial reason, 89
  "Mexican, the," 87–88
  Mexican nationality, 89–90
  on Revueltas, 87
Rulfo, Juan, 10, 130n18

sabotage, acts of, 42, 92
Salazar Bondy, Augusto, 58, 119n4, 119n5
Sánchez, Carlos Alberto, 2, 15n2, 16n17, 17n16, 47, 74, 119n2, 127n8, 135n55, 136

Sanchez, Robert Eli Jr., 2, 73–74, 124n44
Sánchez Benítez, Roberto, 114n5, 117n29
Sánchez Vázquez, Adolfo, 51, 117n28
Santana, Alejandro, 13
Sartre, Jean-Paul, 85
Saslow, Eli, 3–4, 16n5
Schmitt, Carl, 131n31
Sepúlveda, Juan Ginés de, 96
Servando, Fray, 62
Sierra, Justo, 79
Silva, Grant J., 16n5
Simon, Joshua, 100, 137n65
Sittlichkeit, 101, 138n69
slavery, 64, 67, 102
social collaboration, 69, 106–8
social criticism, 84, 86, 89
social habits and customs, 101–2
social identities, 14
social inequality, 64, 76
social positivism, 126n3
social problems in México, 79
socialism, 36, 89, 126n3
Society for Mexican American Philosophy (SMAP), 11, 13, 18n20
Spanish *transterrados*, 51, 117
speech act theory, 36
spirit of association, 107–8
Spirit of the Laws, The (Montesquieu), 106
static thinking, 6, 13, 88
Stormfront, 4
strategy of detours, 43, 49, 57, 61–62, 68, 74–76, 100, 103
strategy of interrupting colonial vices, 46
strategy of transitions, 18n19, 33, 44, 61–62, 65, 68, 70–71, 75–76, 81, 84–86, 97, 124, 135n53
  ascending transition, 8, 34
  descending transition, 8, 84
  example of, 124n55
instances of, 62
in relation to identity politics, 95
structural discrimination, 98
Suárez, Rodolfo, 116n18, 118n32
subaltern fervor, 9–12, 14, 18nn24–25, 36, 37
supply, available, 72
suspicion, 28, 51, 82, 95

tantrum (*rabieta*), 103
Taylor, Charles, 16n3
Temporada de huracanes (Hurricane Season) (Melchor), 108–10, 139n81
Theogony (Hesiod), 81
  abstract universalism (Heaven), 81
  cultural particularism (Earth), 81
Tocqueville, Alexis de, 28, 107, 139n78
Toscana, David, 38–39, 114n6, 115n12
transplantation, 1, 54, 117

United Farm Workers union, 13
universalism, 9, 27, 57–59, 63, 67, 69, 71–72, 74, 76, 81, 95, 102, 119nn4–5, 135n55
Uranga, Emilio, 9–10, 12, 27, 51, 81–87, 91–95, 99, 108, 127n8, 128n12, 129n15, 130n18, 131n31, 134n38, 135n53
US-Mexico border, 3, 12, 86–87, 114n2

Valero Pie, Aurelia, 82–83
Valladolid, Debate of, 96
Vargas, Manuel, 2, 18, 18n26, 73, 77, 106, 135n55
Vasconcelos, José, 50, 79, 125n2, 125–26n3, 126n6
Vaz Ferreira, Carlos, 75
Vázquez Almanza, Paola, 115n15
Velasco, Ambrosio, 69, 116n19, 117nn28–29, 118n32
Vera Cruz, Philip, 13
Vices of the Mind (Cassam), 15n1
Villegas, Abelardo, 83, 129, 136

Villoro, Luis, 9, 15n2, 16n3, 17n16, 27, 52, 67, 70, 72, 77, 81, 114n1, 118n32, 120n12, 122nn25–26, 122n31, 123n32, 127n10
violent readings, theory of, 47–48, 74
Voltaire, 38

Weinberg, Liliana, 11, 62, 120, 119–20n7, 120n9
white nationalism, 3–4
white privilege, 4
white supremacy, 3–4, 5, 13
Williams, Bernard 1, 10, 14, 15n3, 124n54
women, social exclusion of, 45, 63, 65–67

women's autonomy, 101
words, being careful with, 31, 38, 72, 75, 106
World Bank, 7, 34

Xirau, Ramón, 52

Zambrano, María, 51
Zapatista Army of National Liberation (EZLN), 69
Zea, Leopoldo, 16, 51, 52, 58, 118, 124n55, 125n1, 125n3, 130n18, 136n55
zozobra, 16n13, 18n19, 86

www.ingramcontent.com/pod-product-compliance
Lightning Source LLC
Chambersburg PA
CBHW030656230426
43665CB00011B/1114